The Classified Man

THE CLASSIFIED MAN

*Twenty-two Types of Men
(and what to do about them)*

Susanna M. Hoffman, Ph.D.

A PERIGEE BOOK

Perigee Books
are published by
G. P. Putnam's Sons
200 Madison Avenue
New York, NY 10016

Library of Congress Cataloging in Publication Data

Hoffman, Susanna M.
The classified man

1. Men—Psychology. 2. Mate selection.
I. Title.
HQ1090.H63   301. 41'1   79-25249
ISBN 0-399-50544-X
First Perigee Printing, 1981

PRINTED IN THE UNITED STATES OF AMERICA

Acknowledgments

Since I have been watching people and their relationships for a very long time, there is no way for me to thank all the individuals who, wittingly or unwittingly, contributed to this book. I am, however, indebted to each and every one of them. What I can do is thank the people who either helped me with the manuscript or helped me survive while I wrote.

For comments, suggestions, proofing, editing, aiding or asking, "What type am I?", I would like to express my gratitude to Richard Cowan, Sheldon Renan, Ernie Nadel, Milton Stern, J. David Wyles, Tom Vinetz, Brian Robbins, Robert Mandel, William Chambers, George Bowden, Alan Petraske, Paul Ryan, Lee Ambler, Thomas Miller, Paul Podryski and, last but not least, Paul Aratow.

Victoria Wise, Rick Wise, Lisa Rich, Robbie Greenberg, Gail Stempler, Stuart Lake, Joy Adams, Annette Hutchinson, Karin Knowles, Tim Knowles, Nancy Podbielniak and Dennis Sinclair all gave me more hospitality and help than I can ever thank them for and I remain deeply grateful. My colleagues at the University of San Francisco gave me time and assurance. Elaine Markson, Maggie Field and especially my editor, Pat Soliman, gave me still more time, aid and encouragement. To them I owe a special thanks.

No words can quite express how grateful I am to Abe and Florence Hoffman and Levi and Deborah Bendele for every way they have supported me. But above all others, no thanks can quite pay back the debt I owe to Jesse and Gabriella Aratow who never ceased to give me love, joy and comfort while sacrificing the most so that I could write this book.

For
Florence, Deborah, Gabriella, Elaine, Rebekah, Natalie,
Victoria, Lisa, Marida, May, Nancy, Barbara, Gail,
Cielo, Sandy, Margaret, Gerta, Etta, and all the others
too numerous to mention.

Contents

Here's to women, all women,
God's gift, so divine,
Who blossom every month
And bear every nine.
The only little creature,
This side of Hell,
Who can get juice from a nut
Without cracking the shell.

Someone from my past

The Twenty-Two Types of Men

Introduction

How to Use This Book

The Classified Man: Twenty-two Types of Men (and what to do about them) is a book written for women about the various categories of men. Obviously, every man is a complex individual, but like music, books, and art, men fall more or less into certain styles: Some intrigue you, some do not; some please you, and some, most assuredly, do not. At certain times in your life one kind might be just right, but your tastes may change with the years; other types you might like your whole life long. *The Classified Man* helps you to identify these different types of men, through their outer signs, sex signals, money markers, and family aspects. Mostly, it focuses on the way they relate to women. *The Classified Man* offers information to help women sort through the great confusion of male and female interaction.

I suggest, in this guidebook, that you look coolly at the male of the species and categorize. Why? To give you a certain *freedom*. No one can explore every continent; with some foreknowledge of climate and conditions, you are freer to choose which lands you'd like to visit. With an idea of what it is in store with a mate, you are more at liberty to select one who suits your predilections. Also, to give you *confirmation*. You are not the only one to have traveled these roads, encountered these obstacles. If you know that others have been where you have, you gain acumen and consolation and courage.

You could look upon this book as an atlas mapping out relationships. It clearly shows roads that end abruptly, start to wind, or are under construction, and also those roads that have four lanes all the way. You're advised of guideposts to look for, detours to take, dead ends to avoid. With such maps in front of you, you are able not only to pick your destination but also to decide if you *can* get there from where you are or with a particular man.

The types of men described herein are *idealized*. Each portrait presents a synthesized image based on the study of many subjects, and while I fill in all *kinds* of specifics, no one man will fit every detail. You may know, for example, an Instant Barricader whose affairs last months, not weeks. You may meet a Father Knows Best who is generous with money, not tight. Most men overlap, combining aspects of several types—although one type usually predominates.

I have listed related types, in order of relatedness, for each chapter. But there may be different combinations I am not aware of. For that reason, I include in the Aids and Indices at the end of the book a graph on which you can chart the overlappings *you* perceive. Because this is a handbook—and I mean it to be used—I have left space at the end of each chapter for you to make comments about specific men you know. For each type, you can modify the details to describe the traits of people who generally fit the category but differ ever so slightly. I also include a checklist in the Aids and Indices for you to mix and match the traits of your various men. If you check off points for all the men you've had relationships with, your preferences ought to come clear. And I include a positivity scale for each type; most types have both assets and liabilities—the more pluses, the more assets; the more minuses, the more liabilities.

According to age, stage in life, and success (or lack of it!), many men progress from one type to another. For example, Sugar Pie Honeys often become "But I Really Like Women" Manipulators when they get fed up—or else they may turn into Father Knows Best or Loving Polymorphs. With success, a Minimal Misogynist may change into the man Who Would Be Mogul or even the Gender Ascender. On the other hand, some types have little development. Idle Lords don't change with success, because they never have it. Picassos don't mature with age because age freaks them out. For your interest in these potential progressions, I have put them in a chart in the Aids and Indices.

Many people bristle at classification, but in certain ways, it is the most satisfying kind of explanation. You unravel what seems obscure and formless and show a pattern never revealed before; you get a whole new picture of what something *is*. Knowing what something is is essential to knowing how it got that way. After all, there is often nothing you can do about the origins of things; you simply have to live and deal with them the way they are. And classification is never a closed book: New insights and perspectives can lead to the discovery of heretofore unseen types. Since finishing the Twenty-Two Types of Men in this book, I have come upon others that include the Smarter Brother, the "Why Tango When You Already Know How to Waltz?"er, the Jock and Ex-Jock, and the Buccaneer. I hope to describe them later. Perhaps you can find other types, too.

This book results from my insights, which derive not only from being a woman but from being an anthropologist trained to see people reflect their culture's patterns. Perhaps it reflects my age (mid-thirties) and my class (middle). But mostly it stems from my acquaintanceship and research with women and men of all ages and circumstances. It is my argument that there are common types among the men of our times. These types may not be exactly the same as those of generations to come or of those past, but they won't be all that different either. In any case, no matter what your age and social status, the men portrayed here will persist for the next forty years or more; they will be important to the women of this nation. You will meet them as spouses, partners, leaders, followers, friends, and enemies. At the very least, the classification of men should help you decide who to vote for in 1984! Unless by some good fortune a woman runs!

I write from the point of view of a wary but generous-spirited woman who *likes* men. I write not for women who invariably fall into bed at the first moment, but for those for whom sex comes before a full commitment, for whom lovemaking is part of courtship. And ones for whom the act of sex tells part of what a relationship will ultimately be like and how valuable it will be to maintain. I write for women who want one of those things loosely termed a "relationship with a man." This book does not cover anonymous sexual contacts. Although I don't condemn one-night stands, I do think that at some point in their lives at least, most women want more. I discuss men for women who want a transaction, a response, a friendship, a *feeling*. Perhaps I can deal with brief encounters later. But for now I dwell on unions—the short, the long, the likely, and the unlikely.

Except for the section in every chapter called "Where Do You Fit In?" female patterns and types are a topic for another book. Undoubtedly someone could write it. In the meantime, since men are the main topic here, it might appear that they determine each of these relationships with women. Certainly women help create the nature of their alliances—they set tones, provoke reactions, make changes. But many women act as if men *were* the prime movers in their affairs—and this book is often directed to that rather illusionary point of view.

Occasionally *The Classified Man* might imply that the various types of men are conscious of and purposeful about their actions. Not so! While it may be true now and again that a man has full awareness of his actions, I write in this book about *deeply learned* and unconscious behavior.

The Classified Man is *not at all* anti-men; quite the opposite. It is for women who love men (I am one!) but who realize that different male and female personalities exist today. It is for women who believe that men may be different from women, but that they *usually* want what we want—a warm, intimate relationship. So while I mean to be accurate in my descriptions, I never mean to be acrimonious. And although I do not describe in depth the pains and joys men feel in their relationships, I very much empathize with them. My intent is the improvement of relationships for men and women alike.

The idea for *The Classified Man* came to me as I wondered why my many women friends and I were each faced with the absurd situation in which each of us broached similar romantic encounters again and again. Most human learning is vicarious. Learning from others— living, dead, or make-believe—is the keystone of human life. There are books and teachers to tell us how to build a steam engine without having to reinvent it every time we need one. We can find out it is a mistake to invade Russia in the wintertime without having to repeat Napoleon's and Hitler's fiascoes. Why then is every woman compelled to go through the same evolutions and frustrations with men without knowing that others have also done so? Why don't we have the help of an expert adventurer? Some warnings and guidance, corroboration and reassurance?

Now we *do*. An available body of information allows you to make repetition a *choice*, not a trap. It doesn't eliminate the need or desire to experience the options; even with prior knowledge you can still choose to discover and follow the paths on your own. But you don't *have* to do it all. That's what a guidebook is for. The women of my generation had little option but to try all the routes personally. There weren't any guidebooks like this, although sometimes there were wise friends. Now you have this book! *The Classified Man* may or may not help you avoid horrible relationships with men. But with its help, I hope to help you enjoy the men you choose to enjoy—to the fullest.

If you're debating whether or not to try romance, my advice is— YES! It often seems that the only way to control a relationship or to protect yourself is to say no; the party who declines appears to carry the power and the one who accepts appears to be at the mercy of every blow. But instant protection is all you get from a no; you hold sway for the moment, but since you reject an opportunity, you end up holding sway over nothing at all. Yes may seem to lack independence, but it also opens you up to live whatever experience may follow—you may lose control, but you *may* gain something positive. And you can *always* say no later!

Of course there *are* men you definitely don't want to enter a relationship with, whom you should avoid. In this book, I tell you exactly who they are; to them you should say no immediately. But if you aren't sure what you want out of a man or out of love, what a certain relationship might be like, or what you might find out about *yourself*—and if you feel inclined and attracted—why not try him? While loving costs a lot, *not* loving costs a lot more.

1/ The Instant Barricader

Related Types: The Man Who Would Be Mogul
The Romper Roomer

Positivity Scale: + —

Go to the blackboard. Write "Hello. Good-bye." one hundred times. Good. Now you're ready for the Instant Barricader.

Magicians practice sleight of hand. The Instant Barricader practices sleight of relationship. He's a master of disappearance, a king of escape. One day he's around, full of life, and you two seem to have something going. Next day, he's nowhere in sight, and your something isn't going anywhere any more. All that's left is a puff of smoke in your bedroom.

If he seems so available, it's because he *is*. His attachments don't *last* long enough to keep him out of the running, but he's not for the keeping. You can have him on thirty-day loan, then you must return him to circulation.

If an Instant Barricader is exactly what you don't need at the moment, you stand likely to attract one. He heads for women who are temporarily shaky on their pegs, alone and lonely of late, a little too detached in an isolated job or journey. Women who need what he hasn't got to give appeal to him; they give him a built-in reason for getting out. You'll probably meet a dozen Instant Barricaders while recovering from a deep, defunct union with someone else.

Story

I've watched my friend Sally fall many times for the Instant Barricader. One after another, it was always the same song, just a different verse.

Sally came from a small, self-contained, loving family. But for whatever reason, she had never felt very popular or special. Her one long relationship hadn't worked out. She had good friends and all, but she was a bit of a loner. Sally got tired of her small bed, her alienating job, and her solitary dinners. She was anxious to stop being Single Sally.

As a television producer, she was set apart by her work. She met a lot of people at home and on the road who *wanted* something from her—her stamp of approval. When she started to go out with Patrick, one of the footloose men she met, a repetitive refrain seemed to haunt her. Right away the man treated Sally as if she were the greatest discovery of his life. He really *liked* her, was attracted by her, enamored of her. In no time, he moved in. He shelved his razor in her bathroom, hung shirts in her closet, stocked her larder with his favorite canned chili.

Every now and then, he'd mention some drawback. Soon he would have to get back to work. Or—he hadn't quite recovered from some woman in the past. Or—he really wasn't the domestic sort (though he certainly seemed to be). Over at his digs, a strangely large number of women telephoned him. He was very friendly to them all. He talked about their problems and jobs, occasionally took one to dinner. And still Sally's head was spinning. Patrick was warm and affectionate, concerned and considerate. His lovemaking was stupendous, though he took a very long time and didn't always climax.

Then, before you could say Patrick Robinson, he panicked. After all, a woman might make him eat meals at normal hours, borrow his undershirts, or (God forbid) expect to see him on Sunday. A symphony of excuses poured forth. He said he couldn't write if he made love. His future was too tenuous for an involvement. He was busy. He was sick. He had company. His cat had leukemia. A strange black void just ate up all his finances. While building a mighty fence of unbreakable appointments and insoluble worries, he removed himself part by part. Out would go his dandruff shampoo and his bottle of barbeque sauce. He'd brush it off on Sally, saying she was too dependent on him or too desperate for attention.

Patrick Robinson rode off into the sunset before she'd even learned his middle name. But he had left a calling card—with his telephone number—and now she was one of the women who dialed it. He would talk to her from afar like an old friend. When she had a crisis, he would take her to lunch.

That's the Instant Barricader. He appears on the scene as an unexpected *is* and immediately turns into a *was*, in and out the door before you can bake a cake. One part of him wants a woman body and soul, but another part of him is truly terrified. At some time, someone told him that women are an encumbrance, not a joy. And it really sank in. Now, despite all contrary evidence and maybe even despite his desires, he views every fine experience with the female sex as an enticement to disaster.

He has a saving grace: The Instant Barricader is not hard to recognize. He shows himself in many ways; in fact, he almost *always* tells you who he is. The trouble you can get into is not believing him. Then you can end up playing Mother Hubbard to his cupboard, crying when the goodies are no longer there.

How Can You Identify One?

Prepare to meet the Instant Barricader a lot. He holds a very popular spot among the Twenty-two Types. Because he *is* so common, he shows a wider variety of superficial traits than most of the Twenty-two Types of Men. But all Instant Barricaders show certain give-away signals.

The Instant Barricader has a way of pushing out and pulling in at the same time. He has a nervous edge about him. He likes to do just about everything in the opposite way from everyone else, just enough out of sync to grind gears with normality. And he holds back—even in bed.

He has, perhaps, had one early marriage or relationship. One with troubles in it from the start, one to worry over, one in which he played defensive tackle and escaped to the locker room. Fumbled from the word go. Often, this early bond led him to find out just how many women he could meet and bed. It also provides his best out: *He tried permanent pairing.* It didn't *work.* Now he bursts into your life all eager for love. Instantly, however, he starts to tell you all the reasons it could never be. He assembles a veritable gauntlet of impediments.

The Instant Barricader is always just about to go broke. He has always not yet gotten over somebody else. He has always just discovered that he wasn't cut out for marriage: "Some people just aren't, and I'm one of them."

But it's not just with women that he fears he will lose control of his life; he fears it in general. He has trouble letting go; he's possessed by worry of the future, which keeps him from living in the present. He constantly asks, *What's next?* and *Where will it all lead?*

Outer Signs

Take the Instant Barricader's dressing habits. He appears in many different modes, but he always wears a combination of chic and old-fashioned or peculiar. Somehow his hippest clothes come out looking conservative. His shirts are unbuttoned at the top, but not enough. He got a pair of patched and flared jeans, but not until everyone else had moved to stitched, straight-legged French cuts. He wears jogging jackets with dress pants, sneakers with virtually everything. He has cowlicks.

For some reason, Instant Barricaders are highly concerned with their feet. They will only wear doeskin tennies. Or they own an enormous collection of shoes acquired in the pursuit of comfort, but will wear only two pairs of them. The rest were mistakes; the arches wanted to move, but the toes said *no*.

Like his clothes, an Instant Barricader's manners and vocabulary allow him enough trendiness to interact smoothly without his having to give way to the latest craze. He understands, but does not use, the latest slang. He's *sort of* with-it and *sort of* out of it at the same time.

Even his car is a strange combination of flash and reserve, economy and bravado. You might find him driving a gold Volkswagen or the biggest Datsun.

The Instant Barricader uses normal hours when doing business. But in private, he returns to counterclockwise, eating at odd hours or not at all. He gets down to work every day about the time everyone else wants to party. Although it's eleven P.M., he can't come out because he just started working. You call in the morning, and he's taking a nap.

He may drink, or he may almost drink. His favorite cocktail might be a Virgin Mary, or he might hang on the edge with just wine or beer.

He lives just far enough out of the mainstream to be awkward. He likes oddball places and neighborhoods, hiding out where it's just a little hard to get to.

Home is usually an apartment, where he might work as well. If he owns a house, he leases it out and rents a less-encumbered space for his own retreat. His abode is the essence of bachelor style, very male and a bit Spartan. It generally combines tasteful bits with lots of blank space. He has some prints that are almost, but not *quite*, erotic, a big couch, a small collection of favorite records that he plays over and over again. His refrigerator is empty, except, perhaps, for a six-pack of Lite Beer. When he does cook, his specialty is broiled chicken.

Like the Man Who Would Be Mogul, the Instant Barricader tends to be strongly involved in his career. Like the Picasso, his career probably involves some artistry or creativity, and almost certainly autonomy. His labor, especially when he's his own boss, offers a flexible blockade: He can always manage to have unfinished business. He needs to achieve the next goal, through perseverance, to strive for a proper income to support a family. Then only could he risk involvement, he tells himself and you.

The Instant Barricader controls his life extremely well. For each barricade you conquer, another takes its place. He's always keeping track of when to bail out. But under the surface command, he doesn't have all that much control. He instructs his mind to take care of things and hopes his body will follow suit. But it often does not. He's a little too skinny or too fat. He catches colds, a handy way to get out of things. He overreacts to drugs and drinks, or thinks he does. He doesn't exercise with any regularity. His diet is inconsistent.

He shows you, and proves, that he is better off alone, and you without him, regardless of the early magnetism of your affair.

Sex Signals

You have one insoluble problem (and advantage) with the Instant Barricader. He is a very sensual man, a glutton for tactile pleasure. He loves to be stroked, petted, and rubbed, and sucked. He really *likes* sex. He cleverly turns this into another out: He loves sex too much, he says, to confine himself to one woman.

The Instant Barricader is a man in whom you find thrilling and delightful discoveries. He loves to hug and cuddle. He likes having done to him exactly what you like having done to you. You can explore his hidden places and turn all his daring moves back on him, and it works. He loves to go down and be gone down on. He is usually a very good and versatile lover. After all, he's learned from lots of partners.

But it's often in bed that you get the first sign of his inability to give way. The Instant Barricader tends to have trouble climaxing, escpecially at first. Willing or not, he holds back. Even when comfortable, he can take so long to come that the event becomes overly lengthy, something he sometimes rightly and sometimes wrongly considers to his advantage.

To make things easier, he adds the element of fantasy. Often the Instant Barricader indulges in more sexual imagination than sex. Of all the Twenty-two Types of Men, the Instant Barricader spends more time dreaming up lurid escapades than any of the others. Just the sight of a woman on the street can touch off scenes of amorous adventure like a satyric Walter Mitty's. But he doesn't necessarily play out these fantasies just in his head. He brings in a helping hand—his own. He loves to masturbate. When your most constant partner lives at the end of your arm, it helps circumvent permanent pairing.

The Instant Barricader throws himself into mutually satisfying sex with you during that first flurry. But no matter how exciting he may find his sensual experiences with you, at a certain point he begins to fear your blossoming affection. His assumption that you are a living, walking millstone takes control. He decides that you have fallen too hard for him (a serious threat) or, maybe, he for you (a more serious threat); it doesn't matter *what* you intend. He retreats to his castle and pulls up the drawbridge, until he is ready for a new campaign.

He likes women. There is no denying that. He picks them with the care of someone selecting from an assortment of Godiva chocolates, but he goes through them as if they were M & M's. To ensure his freedom, the Instant Barricader picks on slightly desperate and insecure women who want exactly those things that threaten him: a desire for intimacy and a hope for lasting togetherness. While he prefers women with unique jobs and interesting lives, he seems to have an uncanny ability to select isolated wallflowers with style, rather than the thoroughly autonomous; such women are more vulnerable to his short-term interests. He avoids women who don't need what he doesn't have to give, protects himself from ladies whose distancing matches his own, calling them "aloof" and "tough."

Between affairs, he has fits of reclusiveness. He hits Broadway again when a new flirtation appears, for a few days, then beats yet another hasty escape to the citadel. Since he sees all women as wanting to catch him, he flatters himself as the one who got away, but sadly, he gets away with only his own skin and leaves the loot behind. The spells of retreat grow longer as he grows older and more tired of his own pattern. The Instant Barricader has never struck the fine balance between being with people and being alone. He does not live at ease with loneliness but battles with it, keeps it at bay with fits of work, movies, books, and fantasies.

Money Markers

Throughout his comings and goings, he deals with money as he deals with women: He spends it but worries about it. He doesn't want a fortune; he wants a steady supply. The problem is, he's never sure he has enough, and he can't do anything else until he is. Money provides him another obstacle. He spends money easily, even generously. He generally will take you out and prefers to pay. Perhaps it's part of his concept of give and take, since he knows your affair will last only for a short time. Or perhaps he's not shy about spending for his own pleasure.

Family Aspects

While he takes one giant step forward and forty-two steps backward with women, his pattern with his relatives is the opposite—forty-two steps backward and then one leap forward when they need him. He distances himself by space but stays close in correspondence.

He often feels that he had a bad or alienated childhood. He didn't learn how to relate to people because of his strange parents, his physical isolation, or some traumatic event. But although he sees his family as having scarred him, he doesn't harbor blame. He does talk about it a lot, as if for justification.

He thinks he would like children, but he doesn't always get around to having them, which he regrets conveniently late. Or he has children but doesn't live with them, which he *truly* regrets. If he has children, presumably by an early marriage, they alone clamber over his great wall. All gateways are open to them. He is a loving father.

He has male friends among his business contacts and in his career world, but he rarely cultivates close buddies; his main friendships are with females. And he has a lot of them.

Obviously, the Instant Barricader has certain liabilities. Under his seeming independence, he has serious problems with self-esteem. He doesn't take criticism well. It ruffles his feathers and gnaws at his mind. Often he is wildly jealous of other men; he resents their achievements, successes, and especially their abilities with women. Going with an Instant Barricader is short. Your turn lasts one to six weeks. When your affair ends (with your calling him instead of his calling you), it helps his self-esteem. But it doesn't help yours. And he simply can't believe you had no nefarious acquisitive intentions.

But then the Instant Barricader also has his assets, and a lot to give despite himself. He is truly fond of women, a pleasure any woman can appreciate even for a short spell. He is interesting; he sports that kind of quixotic intelligence born of caution (or paranoia). He's fun for a while. And he can ultimately wind up a great telephone pal when you're low.

What Is in Store for You?

Let's say you're at the rodeo, and it's bull-riding time. The ride only lasts eight seconds. It's smooth, it bends, it bumps, it ends. An affair with the Instant Barricader is similar. You're still saying howdy when he's saying adios. Instant Barricaders happen a lot to women who are out there "dating." There are armies of men who play a hard and fast game of "I don't want to get attached." Once you acknowledge the fact that a phalanx of walking walls may await you, you can decide what to do about it.

You can end up feeling like Pavlov's dog. For two weeks, every time you press a button, you get a bone. Then suddenly, an electric shock, and you are deprived. Or you may feel like a photocopy—another one just like the other ones. On the other hand, with some foreknowledge (since he forewarns), you *can* have a nice time, stay detached, and keep on trucking when he detours. Or you can refuse to ride. To choose

among these alternatives, you need to consider what comes at the end
of the line.

Deep down, women frighten him. He can't get over seeing women
as wearing an apron and carrying a fifty-pound rolling pin. He is also
thoroughly unable to handle rejection, so he pulls a presto-chango act
that simply enables him to get out first. He makes you dumped, and he
doesn't get dumped on.

Obviously, when you're still trying to leap hurdles after he's past
the finish line, you can get to wondering. Did your nose turn green?
Does your bathroom have a trick mirror that doesn't reveal your
flaws? You were so great a few days ago. Now you are treated like a
homeless skunk.

To him, you *are* at fault. He doesn't find a multitude of failings in
you, as the Minimal Misogynist does, but just one: The fact that you
want love, he says, means you *need* it. That's bad, he says; being needy
is not good. He forgets that it's human and has no innate badness or
goodness to it, and that in truth it's *he* who can't handle a heady brew,
not necessarily you. Nonetheless, you can come out thinking that a
desire for commitment is some sort of error, somehow unhealthy. You
can wind up eating a plateful of rejection that he ordered.

The Instant Barricader is different from the Romper Roomer. He
does risk involvement with you; the Romper Roomer offers no
emotional output at all. The tiny amount of time the Barricader comes
out of his hiding hole is his saving grace. An affair with him does not
usually end with sour feelings, only resignation. In a way, he
represents a no-blame situation. You can't fault an armadillo for his
scales. You're a fool to kick one and you know it.

Though the affair lasts only a few short weeks, quite likely he will
give you friendship and favors forever, as if your relationship made
you a disarmed sister. His line is always open to you, and his schedule
can almost always make room for you. After it's over, chances are he'll
take you home and then leave. He is almost always a little afraid you
want to start up again. And besides, now that you're a sister, it's a
little abhorrent. Like incest.

What Are the Telltale Signs of Trouble?

Listen for telltale phrases. Any sentence starting "I'm not ready"
constitutes a blinking light. But listen carefully. He's liable to bury the

"I'm not ready" warning in conversations about why Indian ele-
phants have smaller ears. He doesn't want you to pay his early
warnings much heed. He is still chasing you when he tells you who he
is, so he does it in such a way as not to scare you off. But he means it.
Of course, you can scan for his style: the flash combined with reserve,
the going bananas one day only to return to austerity the next, the way
he edges about people, parties, and population centers, the way the
phone rings with calls from lady friends.

Some of the other signals are more subtle. For instance, he thinks
that because he told you, no matter *how* obscurely, you are adequately
forewarned. He assumes you know he's taken out walking papers from
the outset. So when he starts to become unavailable, notice if he's
surprised that you're surprised. These telltale tips should indicate the
presence of an Instant Barricader. Right off, this is a cricitical point
for you. You can decide to go ahead or not, or what controls and
attitudes you want to muster up.

The next critical point arrives when the number of excuses not to
see you equals the number of bricks in the Great Wall of China. His
schedule gets more and more intricate. He has something else
arranged. He has calls to make. Lots of old friends appear with sudden
and pressing demands. No matter how hot the fire, you are becoming
an old flame. It begins to seem as if you see him only when he wants to
see you, not when you want to see him. He pops over to make love and
then leaves right away. When use becomes misuse, it's time to review
who is going to pull the plug.

Then he splits. First go the teabags, then the toothbrush. You call
and his voice gets wary on the phone. You attend the same soirée and
he acts as if you're a virus: He says hello but turns his head and covers
his mouth. He tells you that your romance lasted longer than most of
his, so you ought to feel lucky. This means more than a bend in the
road. This means you are at the end of the line.

What Are the Chances?

Until the Instant Barricader changes, if he changes, all his romantic
attachments end. But his friendships can last a long, long time. It's
true that no one can get through all the protective layers of any other
person. But the Instant Barricader is such a true believer in "An
ounce of prevention is worth a pound of cure" that you can never even

get close to the treatment stage. He stocks every preventative potion and lotion.

You *could* be his youthful early wife. But you will find that he is trying to grow into what he thinks he should be. In the meantime, what he is will sink your marriage.

Some Instant Barricaders change eventually. But they are very late bloomers, if they bloom at all—a decade behind everyone else. You might find an ex-Instant Barricader in the form of a Limited Partner. He's been alone too long, retarded by too many impediments to find other types of permanence possible. He'll only evolve alone. In all probability, you can't ride it out with him. You'll have to meet him once he gets there on his own horse and wagon.

I advise against fighting for a permanent relationship with him. In the first place, he'll probably fly. In the second place, if you manage to hang on awhile, what you get won't be very satisfactory.

Whether or not you should flee from him is another question. That depends on what you think about the other opportunities at hand. With the Instant Barricader you can either: throw him—wheat and chaff—out, or you can gracefully toss the lover part and salvage the pal, though being on a long list of female friends might go against your grain. If you go for the latter alternative, I suggest some time between the romance and the friendship. Depending on how hot your affair was, give him six months or more before you push for a strong new bond. Keep in mind that you will probably have to call him. The calluses on your finger can get insulting unless you just accept them, for his idea of friendship is being called, not caller.

But as always, there is another way to skin a cat, especially if you don't want to get attached. You can take the Instant Barricader for what he is and what he offers. If you know fool's gold when you see it and don't think you hit a mother lode, you can enjoy the glitter while it lasts. When it washes out, you can pick up and pan somewhere else. Enjoy him—then wave good-bye. If you're biding your time and licking old wounds, a passing fancy is better than no fancy at all. An Instant Barricader's flattery and sensuality can most assuredly boost you, especially if he's the one who likes to give the massages, instead of get them. And you don't have to figure out right away if you want him for a long-term buddy; you can probably let it lie until some later date.

But if you can't come out of a short-term affair without feeling hurt and rejected, learn this about yourself and just don't get into it. Go for what is *good* for you; don't repeat things that aren't. Wanting permanent intimacy is not a problem. It isn't a mistake and can't cause a breakup; it's a healthy desire that requires the right environment. It's *not* wanting long-term affairs that causes short ones.

But if you're really in love, really willing and even able to hang in there, remember, the Instant Barricader is like the gingerbread man. He thinks you are the fox. This is not the most restful situation in which to put yourself; there will always be a nervous edge to your life. And you will have to bear in mind the fragility of the situation. He could get claustrophic at any time; you won't know when. As he makes his break, a hysterical reaction won't help; a long, loose rope might. Don't hang him on a short tether.

You'll probably know that having an affair with another man will throw him into a fit of jealousy. Therefore, think carefully.

Some Instant Barricaders attempting to become Limited Partners want to live together and not marry. I don't think I'd settle for it. "No marriage" means he is still holding out for all the old escape hatches. An old Instant Barricader who wants to live alone—with you—isn't ready yet. He stills wants to only half-commit himself. He may want someone at home while maintaining a single profile without you. *Good* Limited Partners, however, acknowledge that they are attached, even if they have separate business lives. They don't carry on a single man's mode in public.

Where Do You Fit In?

Instant Barricaders abound; you are likely to meet more than one in a lifetime. But if you meet too many, it might be time to sit down and examine yourself. There is probably a reason why you link up with persons who fly "Don't Tread On Me" flags. Most likely, you are trying to stay alone but telling yourself you want to get attached. You don't want to stick out by not wanting what other people want, so you contrive a way of pretending you want involvement while ensuring it doesn't happen. One way to handle this is to become a lonely and tragic figure with the dead horse of your last affair always there to beat. It's a good obstacle to a new romance.

Of course, such camouflaged intentions mean you have to get dumped *upon,* rather than dumping on yourself. Lots of women have trouble rejecting men; parents told them long ago they had to do the catching, so it follows they should consider all comers.

Analyze your own behavior and see what it tells you. Then talk to the quieter voices in your head, to find out whether you want to stay detached or get hitched—at least for now. *No* decision is permanent. You may discover you simply don't want to tie yourself down to any one romance, or you may uncover that you *do* want a long-term relationship but have natural fears that thwart you. You can either state openly that you don't want to get involved and give up the rejected role, or you can dismantle your fears. Sally did. She discovered she wanted a husband, but that her own family's claustrophic atmosphere had frightened her. Soon, when a man said, "I don't want to get involved," Sally said, "Well, I do, so see you later."

You may just prefer short-term affairs. And that's perfectly all right. But if you accept that it's all right, then say so; don't think you want forever when you refuse to act like it. If future, family, and farmstead seem too final, but you want some sometime men, indulge in the advantages of the Instant Barricader. Buy the farm later. But also check if you are able to dabble in short romances without regret. Some people can live with here-today-and-gone-tomorrow better than others. Sometimes you can be high enough that no affair brings negative results. Sometimes you can be low enough, they all do.

During such lows, it might be best to go the nun route for a while. Instant Barricaders come into your life, against your will, more often when you run away from sadness. You have to learn about loneliness sooner or later. Since you can't run away from your own feelings, wallow in them alone for a while. Learn to acknowledge when you are shaky and what kind of men that attracts. Certainly do so if you are recovering from an important union, because you *do* influence what ones of the Twenty-two Types of Men are attracted to you. So be prepared.

Last but not least, check one final camouflage. Acting out the maid of constant sorrow is often a way the loner has learned to get attention. That way she can stay isolated and have people say, "Poor thing." Constant affairs with Instant Barricaders are like repetitive colds, a chronic illness. So seek out ways of drawing sympathy that don't involve such wear and tear.

Notes and Particulars

2/ Intimate Type One —The Loving Polymorph

Related Types: Intimate Type Two—
The Oldie But Goodie
Intimate Type Three—
The Limited Partner

Positivity Scale: + + +

After thinking it over, he comes to the conclusion that life is a huge toy store of a very special sort in which you don't just get to look at the games and dolls—you get to live them and *be* them. He emerges from creation's shopping mall not as a single item but as a whole package. He's mate, father, fisherman, businessman, baseball player, teacher, scout leader, bookworm, carpenter, dress designer, and homemaker— a worker and a man of leisure. He's the Loving Polymorph!

Polymorph means *many shapes,* and that's just what the Loving Polymorph has and how he wants to live. He scorns the idea of having a limited identity or performing one exclusive task throughout his life; he prefers to exist as a multiple creature. Whatever combination of roles he ends up assuming, he *is* all of them; he more than playacts or tries on for size. He finds within himself any number of dispositions and feels each one is vital; he gives every facet equal importance and care.

His major desire is to enjoy life, so he heads for pleasure. He aims to adore his lover, relish his work, and delight in his play—or else he'll try another. He's inclined to change and vacillate, especially in his vocation and avocations.

He strives for proportion in his existential goulash. He wants a modicum of success, of romance, and maybe of kids, dogs, volleyball games, and trips up the Ganges. Before he gets overrun with greenbacks, he spends on diversions. He deepens the involvements with those he loves. While he manages to diversify, he also envelops himself.

He tends to become the most concordant of men. He willingly explores and shares the avenues his lady takes as well as his own. If any man can thrive with a woman who lives her life in varied assortment, the Loving Polymorph can. While he sometimes goes for straight-lined career women, sometimes toward domestic sorts, generally he likes the lady who's a bit of a mélange. The Loving Polymorph lady leads life with a very light touch; she displays a brilliant spectrum. She steps through her inner prism and allows herself free range. And she knows that behind all her refractions lies a single beam—herself.

Story

My friend Gabe showed every glint of budding polymorphism. An amazing number of people had dismissed him as having no singular distinction. But every now and then, some lady realized she was talking to a Pied Piper who would lead her on adventures and treat her well. Liza was one. In no time flat, she knew she had met a man remarkably in harmony with himself and yet very adaptable. He would not only share his life but would step right in and join hers.

And she was right. Gabe was the sort who threw himself into every aspect of life with unpretentious abandon. He was always active and yet relaxed; he was purposeful and yet flexible and accepting. Rules about who is supposed to do what didn't faze him. He'd handle whatever was necessary. He was by no means humble but was just so human he didn't have any affectations. He was good to people, good to himself, and just plain lovely company.

Gabe tried business school and hated it. He studied sociology and carpentry and then ended up in public health. Once he thought he wanted to have a store of his own. Despite an indecisiveness with his calling, he never shirked friends or responsibilities; quite the opposite. He figured that concern for other people was the natural way to get the best results. So Gabe was rarely found without someone whom he cared for and who cared about him. And he always had a dog or pet. He kept his own place. He did the laundry, shopping, and mopping. He had open and affectionate relationships with women, and with each one he loved, he sought a rich and full alliance. But that didn't mean that things always worked out.

When Liza met Gabe, he was not without a past. But then, neither was she. Both had loved before, and while those episodes ended in sorrow, neither was afraid to take a chance again. Loving·and risking were part of life to Liza and Gabe.

Liza met Gabe in a most haphazard way: She bumped into him in a used-book store as he was leaning on a rack reading *Captain Marvel* and *Conan*. To cover her embarrassment, Liza asked his advice in getting a comic for her four-year-old son. He asked her to lunch. And she went.

The Orange Julius and corn dog could have been champagne and lobster thermidor and they wouldn't have noticed; they were too busy hitting it off. Liza still claims his lunch choice was in retaliation for knocking into him. He says the Doggie Diner provided the only suitable repast to go with the Bugs Bunny comic they purchased. At any rate, lunch led to supper, supper led to a double feature, and *The Pink Panther* led to bed. They left in the middle. Why watch United Artists when you can go home and be them?

Their sex life, says Liza, was and is still wonderful. Gabe is all warmth and intimacy; he gives himself completely to her pleasure and his own. He melts her like butter, and he adores the times she takes over. He can be silly; he can be hot. He can just hug and not make love.

Liza and Gabe are still together. Slowly but steadily after that first day, they just merged. Gabe introduced Liza to his pals and his whole world. Liza made it clear that she, her kid, her friends, her work, and her funny habits came in a single wrapper. Liza knows that as an occupational therapist, artist, dance teacher, mother, and lover, her life will never be simple. Adding Gabe makes it harder yet. In order to follow his tangents and participate in his ways, she gives up and adjusts some of her own. But she gets something else—he also helps her, shares her burdens, and allows for her crazy notions.

After two years together, they had a child; Liza had wanted another. Since she had just gotten her first gallery show and Gabe had wearied of his work, he quit to manage the home and baby. Three years later, Liza cut back, plunked down all her funds, and they opened Gabe's bookstore.

They know the future will always be quixotic. But they never know which one is Don Quixote and which is Sancho Panza: Clearly one or the other is always preparing to do battle with some windmill while the other assists. They've had some rough times. They went through two retreats into separate space, during which time they shared the children equally. They don't give eternal promises that they'll be together forever, only that they'll try. They prefer not to have affairs, but they know if one happens it would not break them up. Not by itself. After all, their relationship takes a lot of work. But it's worth it to them. They have the gifts of remaining true to themselves while being totally involved.

Women have long found themselves with many diverse duties in their laps, now more than ever before. You find yourself keeping house and managing one as well; we all know that the management is a whole separate chore. You go to work, you quit, you try one kind of job and then maybe another, or you follow one straight through; you toss a splendid spaghetti, you fix a shelf, you throw a five-year-old's birthday party, you volunteer for charity. You drain the dirty Pennzoil, you buy three shares of Polaroid, you knit a "You Too Can Look Like Farrah for Fall" from *McCall's*. And you know you're not only one of the above, but *all* of them. You thrive on going from one role to another. Happiness is switching from funky to fancy at fifty-five miles per hour.

The Loving Polymorph is much the same. He has come upon a philosophy of life, by desire, that many modern women have come upon by necessity. He wants to do it all and be it all, and he's never been so free to try before. When you look for the Loving Polymorph, get ready for the liberated man.

How Can You Identify One?

The Loving Polymorph holds a special key that many men never discover: He can say *no*, but more importantly he can say *yes*. He contradicts the single-identity male syndrome. He breaks out of being just truck driver or judge or any one title. He thinks of himself as the world's greatest lover, soccer instructor, vacuumer, and baby tender also. He cooperates. At a party when someone asks him what he does, he's left at quite a loss. He says, "Well, let's see. I clean, wire, write, doctor, lob, jog, use Aramis, drink J & B, have a great mind, and roast a terrific turkey."

He likes change. He may not know he does, but he seeks it just the same. He balances his act on a ball, not a box. He can't predict his future in absolutes. Sometimes he realizes he must do something else, so his promises are only 99 and $^{44}/_{100}$ percent pure; he'd be a dummy to close down that other point fifty-six and he knows it. The Loving Polymorph comes with no permanent warranties. Balls roll along in life, but occasionally they also bounce. He *does* offer the best of intentions. And the *almost* promises from a Loving Polymorph usually work out better than total promises from a less intimate man.

Since he means his vows but accepts his quirks more than any of the other Twenty-two Types of Men, the Loving Polymorph is honest, blunt, and as real as real can be. He's also a bit loony and impulsive. When he shows up with a fish aquarium bought with your last ten dollars—because he just *had* to raise a koi—you know you just got a vote of confidence. He wants a relationship where he and you can say, do, feel, and share almost anything. And he does it. He's out to like you *permanently*. Better yet, he's not afraid to like himself.

Outer Signs

His look is stubbornly himself. His exercise is on and off; his discipline fights his lazy streak. He lets his body go in some spot, but by no means everywhere. He tends to grow a little thick and shaggy rather than scrawny. He loves desserts.

He sticks to the attire he prefers—mainly comfortable clothes. When he wears what he wants, he makes whatever he has put on look as if he's worn it for years. Even when he has to go before the boss, the devil, or the Secretary General in a brand new tuxedo, which he'd do and enjoy, somehow he manages to mold the material to all his personal creases before the appointed hour.

The ease with which he wears his clothes often covers the fact that his parts overlap here and there. His total arrangement almost always shows a slight mix-up in details. In his switch from dad or pal to man of the world and back, he wears the wrong shoes, a cufflink shirt with chinos, sews on two kinds of buttons, nicks himself using your razor, tries to trim his own hair, or uses his belt as a leash so his Cardin pants hang from toothmarked leather. But his order is only disheveled at the edges and looks like the "I meant to return to it and didn't get to it" kind.

Some Polymorphs keep their cars clean, but never scrupulously so. Many let their cars take total care of themselves and hope for an occasional rain. However he keeps it, his car is more than a car to him; it's a room. If he's going to spend so much time in it, he's going to feel comfortable there! At any one time his auto carries a list, a ticket, half a map, papers, a pack of gum, and an old tennis ball that rolls around the floor. It smells like him. (So do his clothes. But then, a lot of his clothes ride around in his car.) He generally selects a not-too-big, not-too-small kind of car in which he can feel the ride. He cares little about razzledazzle. He goes for buses, Darts, Javelins, Falcons, Rabbits, Hondas, or B.M.W.'s. Even when he possesses wealth, he rarely pays heed to glory and size. Despite the homey atmosphere in his personal vehicle, he often likes to switch and drive yours for a while; he drives whichever one is handy. When you go out together, half the time he'd just as soon you drove anyway. His ego doesn't ride on who steers.

Since people interest the Loving Polymorph more than anything else, he finds himself drawn to people-oriented occupations, often services, and people-occupied places, usually towns. He mixes in with his community. Even when he dwells in rural areas, he knows and is known by his fellows. In the city, he often prefers areas that bear sectional names, neighborhoods that fight freeways, plant trees, and have some sense of politics.

His desire to huddle and participate sometimes leads him to seek even closer quarters than neighborhoods. He might head for apartments and co-ops. When he gets a flat or house, he shies away from the gigantic.

He more than uses his home, he *nests:* His place is cozy, a little zany. He does a lot of living on the floor. His desk, library, and television most likely are alongside his bed. He likes plenty of access to indoors and outdoors; he finds barbeques, sandboxes, and fish ponds appealing. He's intrigued by lots of little rooms, and loves drawers, nooks, and crannies.

The main difference between him when he's mated and when he isn't is that one way all his stuff is mixed up with yours, the other way not. Whether he's with you or alone, the Loving Polymorph abode is never completely fixed up or decorated. With the Loving Polymorph, when friends, family, or funny business come to play, *anything* can wait for another day.

Since he really likes to play with toys (grown-up ones, that is), he tends to acquire things not for status, but because he'd like to try them. Once used, however, the items slip away from his attention and into the garage. Every now and then he puts everything in the trash and goes on to the next stage in his life.

He's a user. His most valued possessions have a "lived in" look. Sometimes you do, too. His volleyball is properly pumped but scuffed from being shot through baskets—he couldn't find his basketball. And if he owned a Gutenberg Bible and Shakespeare Folios, they along with his other books would be on the floor stacked in order of reading. As for his tools—he keeps them in three different places. But which one they're in at the moment is always up for grabs.

If his external space is in disorder, his internal one rarely is. Despite his variations, the Loving Polymorph has an unwavering view of life and of what a good person is. And he lives up to them. Values are important to him; he takes care to keep them. He has a sense of complete mutuality. To him, compromise is a perfectly pragmatic way to live. He knows when giving up and giving in win him the things he wants—love, trust, and respect.

Sex Signals

Since he wants to be so many things, the Loving Polymorph seeks a woman with whom he can feel most free. He looks for an assured maturity that means joy in life, a self-reliance that implies a willingness to flow. The woman he likes has the basic ingredients for flexibility: She's both curious and easily satisfied. He treats a woman as a complete equal, as an across-the-board partner, right from the first moment. He thinks the best companion makes her own decision, but also consults him—and vice versa. He's prepared for and gives a wide range of emotions, but he doesn't go for tricks. He wants you to be you, not just agree with him. He knows whom he's coupled with.

The Loving Polymorph likes nakedness—everything about bodies— as much as he likes honesty. He feels that you look best when you've got no make-up on. He *loves* sex. He's very sensual. He loves his lovemaking rich, down to earth, cuddly, unashamed, not theatrical. He likes lots of foreplay and frequently prefers the bottom position or enters from behind in the double spoon shape. He wants his lady to have enough control that she really gets satisfied. He's nonplussed when you don't feel inclined or he doesn't feel active. Even when he's not making love he looks at your face and touches your skin. He exudes an easy ecstasy; he's warm and radiant. The most difficult part about bedding down with him is getting him not to creep all over your side of the bed.

Money Markers

Money isn't *money* to the Loving Polymorph, it's a Creative Plaything. While you may have plans and goals together, he doesn't think you should *deny* yourselves just to stockpile cash. Dollars are for down sleeping bags, nights out, an old jalopy, or a child! To play with and live with.

Usually his money is your money and yours is his. You give each other support and you split all the work, no matter who brings home the paycheck. Sometimes you may trade off the roles of earner and nomemaker; most of the time you both do both. Occasionally one or both of you may decide to quit and fritter around a bit. It really doesn't matter who makes the bucks and who mops up.

Family Aspects

A Loving Polymorph almost always wants to jump into the generational flow and have children. He may want offspring of his own or he may be perfectly happy with someone else's; he figures children are part of life no matter whom they belong to. He wants to try out his father side as well as be pal, coach, and adviser. He concerns himself wholeheartedly with child raising and comes up with a very Loving Polymorph solution—he treats kids as regular human beings. He listens to and plays with them. He gives his kids lots of time and involvement, taking care of them as much as he can and often as much as you do.

Usually at some point the Loving Polymorph reaches some understanding with his family that frees him truly to like his parents, brothers, and sisters; after that he thinks of them more as friends than relatives. He links himself to other generations as well: His father and mother become pals and confidants. He bypasses rivalry with siblings and aims for teamwork. He discovers there's a common set of interests and a common history with his family—and with yours; that no matter how different they are from him, they have a lot to offer.

But strangely enough, while the Loving Polymorph makes friends with many people, both men and women, he's sort of a loner when it comes to close chums. He gets along with people and finds them the best of playthings, but doesn't especially depend on relationships with buddies. He sees friends for pure pleasure rather than support. Most of his time goes toward his many roles and the intensity with which he leads them, so while he enjoys social occasions and sports, he engages with his fellows less than you would expect.

The Loving Polymorph is unpredictable. Sometimes he takes silly chances; maybe he never gains great heights. He goes against lots of traditional expectations—but meets more contemporary ones. Sometimes he seems to lack drive and direction, dropping things in the middle and never returning to them. He doesn't give you warning to prepare for new brainstorms. You have to be right on top of things with him. He's sort of diffuse and unsettled. And you might be right to worry about where his restlessness might lead.

But he also offers great assets. He sure knows who he is and how to take care of himself. He's one of the best of playmates and companions you could ever get and often comes closer to a woman's point of view than any other man. He certainly tries to. And he's a show you can watch over the years—the Loving Polymorph's serendipity makes for a live version of *That's Entertainment*.

What Is in Store for You?

So you've come to the oracle to ask the age-old riddle: Is there a way to love one and still have fun? A way to love two and still be true? How about a way to love three and have a certain he? Or a way to love four and maybe still more? The answer is—it's not so impossible if they're all rolled into one.

You've got a good chance with the Loving Polymorph. And yet life with him is not always easy. Since the Loving Polymorph is a mixed bag, he may arrive at any time as a mechanic, a chef, a loner, or Casanova. You have to be on your toes and ready to say, "Oh, it's *you!*" He may be one part predictable—maybe one element in his package especially pleases him. Or he may have no traditional traits or predilections at all. In any case, life with him requires that you shed many ideas and categories (if you still have them and he doesn't). That includes preconceived notions about who does what for whom and also about whether life entails working toward ends, staying consistent, or always staying settled in a single town. And you have to be secure in yourself and in a relationship that has few absolute ground rules to hold you together and not many customary habits to fall back upon. The more you can get future-free, role-free, guilt-free, and game-free, the more you can achieve a real relationship with this man.

With the Loving Polymorph, you can expect intimacy on just about every plane. Each twosome varies on how much they collaborate, but in general the Loving Polymorph holds back very little. Most aspects of his life are open, if not to your control, then at least to your awareness and consideration. He lacks closed realms that exclude his mate, unlike the Limited Partner. Nor does he predicate the union on division and domain, as does the Oldie But Goodie. What you have in store is real cooperation; you get independence and yet interdependent support. There's hardly a change from courtship to committed life. He bends to your obligations, endeavors, and hankerings and releases you for your pursuits as much as you do him.

But in some ways you have the subtlest and trickiest of all twosomes. In no other relationship do you so constantly have to calculate the different advantages of surrender and demand as you do with the Loving Polymorph. Since almost every autonomous action on either of your parts entails, if not sacrifice, at least some adjustment, you always have to judge not simply what you want, but whether what you want is worth more than what you have. You also have to size up whether you are due your desire more than your mate is due his. It's true that with the Loving Polymorph you can be many shapes and do many things. But you can't have all you want all of the time and still have a relationship.

Some of the other conditions that come with the Polymorph are also quite strenuous. When two people steadily generate new propositions for their existence, problem-solving becomes a constant process. Almost every day starts with a definition of what has to be done, moves to decision (when, how, and by whom?) and evaluation (will it work for all concerned?), and then goes to implementation. And just because you reach an agreement with a Loving Polymorph once doesn't mean the matter is resolved. Almost every matter you settle reappears on a recurrent cycle.

With a Loving Polymorph you usually proceed ahead in a moderate way; you rarely come into spectacular fame or abundant wealth. Sometimes you do, however, and other times a wealthy man turns into a Polymorph. Usually the Polymorph is simply not that driven, is too diverse to reach ambitious pinnacles. Generally you settle for a certain modesty in your lifestyle. You slide by with some debts and scuffs. You go on trips to motels but not to the Ritz.

The character of the Polymorph has some weak spots that might make him go amiss as you move to mid-life. His balance between compromise and insistence can go haywire, and he can start to exclude you. With his deep-seated mutability, a Loving Polymorph is prone to upheavals and sometimes the desire to shift away from life and wife.

Still, the challenge is terrific. The shape of things to come with him is a parallelogram. You trust life and you trust your mate. If you've discovered that there is no such thing as external security, but that you have security inside yourself, you're in the right place with the Loving Polymorph.

What Are the Telltale Signs of Trouble?

Suddenly the air is clear. You haven't heard a threat (like the Maximal Misogynist's), an excuse (like the Instant Barricader's), heavy panting (like the Romper Roomer's), cloying clucking (like the Sugar Pie Honey's), or a soul-searching cry for succor (like the Intensely Intimate But Crazy's). Instead the man goes off to his labor happily and still calls you up to say hello. He finds it easy to come home to play and leave his work behind.

He and you presumably expect an alliance to grow. The Loving Polymorph couple is usually aware of up and down cycles, love and hate spells, and periods of alternating boredom and interest. Time shifts the perspective in any couple's picture, and sometimes the Loving Polymorph gets out of focus. The first sign of Loving Polymorph trouble is almost always physical. He stops touching and hugging both in public and in private. While he might be angry, most likely he's merely weary. He's not sure what to change next. Usually it's best to give him some distance and time. But if a natural resurgence doesn't soon move him close again, it's time to confer. It may be up to you to offer a plan that will revitalize your alliance.

Occasionally one party or the other starts to desire too much and compromise too little. Then the association takes on an air of dominance and submission: someone starts to win and the other one to lose. If this situation builds too far, you're heading for real problems. The injured party starts to count "turns" and insists on rotation. You take your turn for the sake of the turn itself, not because you need it; then you neglect the real essence of giving and getting. For the Loving Polymorph relationship, keeping tabs instead of meeting needs spells a bad downward spiral.

Some Loving Polymorphs start sliding into the "But I Really Like Women" Manipulator, sometimes even worse—they go toward the Sugar Pie Honey. If your man slyly begins always to get his way or complies overly with you while secretly keeping track of his sacrifices, the intimacy between you just took a dead-end turn. Occasionally a Polymorph turns into an Idle Lord and stops doing anything. Or one gets so enamoured of change either he immediately becomes a Disaster Broker or he distances and reemerges as an Instant Barricader. Obviously, any of these alterations seriously changes the nature of your alliance.

You *can* overcome much with the Loving Polymorph; you can work, wait, call for compromise, or accept. But occasionally one mate decides on a policy that the other simply finds intolerable. You might come to lock horns over lovers, a separation, a move to Uganda, life in the wilds on fruits and berries, or a lack in cooperation. If the changes truly go against your desires, it's better to take a divided road. You can't keep the loving part of polymorphism when you foolishly swallow an unbearable condition. You might stalemate for now and try for concordance later, but since ending a stalemate means one party has to bend, you're usually faced with checkmate sooner or later.

What Are the Chances?

A Loving Polymorph union means *committed intimates*. As mates, you aim to keep on keeping on. So long-term teaming is possible, and in fact, it's highly probable. But while all the relationships with the three Intimate Type Men are rich and full, none of them springs full grown from the sea on a half shell. Nor do they stay rosy without effort. The Loving Polymorph union requires more sustenance than any other.

Two crucial weak spots plague the Loving Polymorph relationship. One is the presumption that what is best for you is best for your mate. The theory is that your fulfillment and your happiness enable your lover and others to derive more from you. And that's true. But there's a hitch: When one of the important points of your fulfillment is the relationship itself, you always have to consider that what is best for you *may* be what your mate wants and not what you desire.

When you eliminate boundaries between roles and responsibilities, sometimes you end up with more fences to mend than ever. With the Loving Polymorph you can experience "upkeep fatigue." Working on relating well requires lots of energy, and people are inclined to get lazy, or they just get tired of paying constant attention. The Loving Polymorph alliance is too intricate to leave alone; to lie back all too often means to lay waste.

However, this is a countermeasure: Work on *yourself*. From there, you can work on how you relate to your mate. The happier you keep yourself, the more centered you are, the better you can live with whatever comes your way and accept change, yet maintain sharing. The more philosophically you lead your life, the less important particulars become.

With the Loving Polymorph, I suggest you sidestep jealousy as much as you can. By that I mean not just the carnal kind—in case of an affair—but the kind that surrounds what you did or didn't get to do. Basically the Loving Polymorph is a monogamous, mutual man; he gives fidelity and openly shares his life. At some point he expects the same in return, as a statement of commitment. Just remember the key to your pairing is your pledge of trust and troth despite peculiar events.

Stay mindful of repression and restrictions. Remember that curiosity and freedom are vital to the Polymorph. Limit your nos and be generous with your yeses. What the hell? Go on and get silly! Drink Chablis straight from the bottle in a rowboat on an off-limits canal. Take up disco dancing. Get a hot tub. Shed your inhibitions and don't resist fun. But stay true to yourself. Your cooperation should by no means mean obedience. If you turn your Polymorph into an unwilling dominant party over a submissive you—or vice versa—you head for a rough spell, if not total ruin.

A parting from a Polymorph is both sad and painful. All too often, separating Polymorphs try to keep close while untying their emotions, so the mourning lasts a long time and so does the disentanglement. If this happens to you, muster all the conviction you have, cut yourself off completely, and reopen channels only after a lengthy period. Usually there is a bond of affection and mutual admiration; in time you can become friends and helpers. But the detachment must come first. If you have to have an ex-lover, at least you have one who cares in the Loving Polymorph.

I must add one last piece of advice. If you're thinking of doing or staying with a Loving Polymorph because the man is *so* good but not because you love him . . . Don't. As a great all-around character and a backer-upper, he can look like the best way to be good to yourself whether you adore him or not. But you don't do yourself a favor in allying yourself with *anyone* for whom you don't have that special spark. Denying yourself love is always a mistake. And it always catches up, in the form of remorse, disappointment, or bitterness, despite what pluses you gain in the meantime. Furthermore, he'll resent your lack of candor and sooner or later he'll retaliate—he may grow selfish, or he may walk out the door.

But if you fall for the Loving Polymorph, I heartily advise that you close your eyes and jump on in for better or worse. If he lacks guarantees and gives imperfect promises, remember he doesn't know what may cause him to change or transport himself to somewhere else; he just knows the possibility lurks inside him as long as he's alive. If he shakes up your expectations and will never be exactly normal, don't forget he will stay where the rewards are good and he'll compromise to keep them flowing.

You could hardly ask more of yourself.

Where Do You Fit In?

The ad hypes that "you've come a long way, baby." Well maybe you have. Certainly you have it in you to do, think, and be all the things you want. And that's a giant step for humankind whatever your sex may be. The resolution to be all you are lies right in your mind. Striving for your full potential goes hand in hand with reaching intimacy. Some people call it self-actualization; some call it being centered, or being your own best friend. Others rightly tag it as having nothing to lose. But whatever you call it, when you're ready to do or be a Loving Polymorph, you have to reach a step that's beyond plain self-knowledge. You have to become full of yourself. It means just *being*, moving beyond myths of how you're supposed to live. That's not to say that you might not then choose to exist as custom dictates, but whatever path you pick, you do so for fulfillment.

Almost every woman I know feels she needs love. And so she searches for it. And almost every woman also questions whether or not she's like other people; not only if she fits in, but if something might be innately *wrong* with her. Some individuals get their feet caught in these mires and never progress. They spend a major part of their lives in a quest for affection and approval. As a result, no matter what they do, they suffer distress. They worry if their dress is wrong, their bearing unseemly, their verbiage derived from Dick and Jane. They're sure others will dislike them if they don't come off just right.

Unfortunately, when you wallow in such a bog, most likely you fritter away all chance for intimacy right when it's in the palm of your hand. The Intimate Type Men, especially the Loving Polymorph, require a personal evolution on your part beyond the need for love and approval. When you discover that wanting love is a strong desire and an easily fulfilled one, then you can take life the way it comes. When you don't care whether you fit in or not, you find situations more curious than threatening. Presto changeo, a great thing happens. You find pleasure however and wherever you are!

Once you've reached this plateau, you derive something even *more* significant, a special secret—that it's challenge itself that keeps you vibrant. You're ready to take on anything new and different. You become the Marco Polo, Columbus, Admiral Byrd, Einstein, and Madame Curie of your own world. You turn your energy from potential to kinetic; you activate yourself. And you know that tackling new problems is as vital to you as food and water.

But watch out for two common pitfalls. If you take actualization to mean you should take on a plethora of activities, you turn energy into just another distance mechanism, and you probably still need outside recognition. The woman who becomes superwoman, super mom, and wonder worker eliminates intimacy and substitutes frenzy. And if you think that having once achieved heights of understanding means you will always stay perfectly balanced, then you fool yourself. Real feelings don't always match up to consciousness. People go up and they also come down. If you deny your feelings you also deny your cycles, and you can go down a long, long way before you come back up.

If you're willing to let your mate both change and vacillate, and also move on to new challenges and fulfillment . . . why not allow yourself? It's good and good for you!

Notes and Particulars

3/ The Minimal Misogynist

Related Types: The Picasso
The Idle Lord

Positivity Scale: + − −

As a child, or even recently, did you pluck the petals on a daisy, chanting, "He loves me; he loves me not," trying to divine your status with a seeming Sir Galahad? Well, there *is* a kind of adult courtship in which both petals tell true. You collect on *both* predictions. But the sequence is crucial: First he loves you, then he loves you not.

This dubious double fortune often falls to women who somehow stand apart. If you are intelligent and stylish, vivacious and admired, watch out! You're the most likely target for the Minimal Misogynist.

The Minimal Misogynist abuses women. But unlike the Maximal Misogynist, the Minimal Misogynist does not beat; he berates with criticism and retracted love. He undermines the capabilities and scars the confidence of the women involved with him.

The Minimal Misogynist is a tidy time bomb. Although he is one of the most devastating to women of all the Twenty-two Types of Men, he is also one of the hardest to recognize from up front. You might say that many of the Twenty-two Types do not really like women, but the Minimal Misogynist perhaps comes closest to that claim. It's not at all a matter of what he *thinks* he feels about women, but of what he eventually *shows*. He treats a woman fabulously at the onset of the affair; his abrupt reversal does not occur until the object of his choice has surrendered herself heart, head, and often hand to a union with him.

As with each of the Twenty-two Types of Men, his choice of women suits his character. Part of his concern is the conquest of something special; part of his makeup is having excellent taste in the things he acquires. In every case, these factors add up to the dollar jackpot or the highest mountain. He likes the Mercedes of ladies. He seeks the independent, the adventurous, the noteworthy, the self-assured.

Story

Involvement with the Minimal Misogynist seems to happen to exactly the kind of woman you would not expect it to happen to. Take, for example, the experience of my friend Clarissa.

To say that Clarissa had zest wouldn't quite describe her. She was bright and alive. She couldn't stop herself from tackling everything she wanted—education, love, travels, and work. Her own nature had made her passage through her early youth rough, but by her late twenties she no longer allowed the facts that she was intelligent, attractive, and emotional to be in contradiction. She rolled it all into a package that was pretty impressive. She was doing well with her career, her social life, and her store of self-knowledge. She cultivated rather than covered her flair. She was writing and teaching, wearing plumes and scarves. Her confidence and attractiveness were magnetic.

When Jon hotly pursued her, he already had what is called a "bad rep"; he had treated previous women in a decidedly callous manner. Knowing this, Clarissa was resistant to him; otherwise, she would not have been an attractive quarry. She thought she had accumulated enough experience and wisdom to be interested only in a man who truly cared for her. She generally could say no to bad pennies.

Jon was *so* caring, however, that, even with her jaundiced eye, Clarissa began to believe the Good Ship Lollipop had arrived. He brought her perfect roses and bottles of rare wines. He cooked fabulous meals and showed her old films. He was very affectionate. He took her prowling through antique stores and brought her to parties. He praised her, never said anything that diminished her; his respect for her seemed to be a given. Clarissa was careful to be her true self with him, to check that he would see her every side and still care. She let her cranky as well as her carefree moods hang out. She kept her distance from him for a goodly while, but he was a match for it all.

When after quite a bit of hesitation, she went to bed with him, all his elegance truly emerged. Jon had taken sex beyond sensuality and turned it into a rarefied and cultivated taste. Everything he did was both exact and exquisite. He sensitized every part of her body. She was so swept away by exquisite technique that she didn't notice she never got held.

From early on, Jon wanted a permanent relationship with Clarissa. She had been unwilling to agree. But when the attentions lasted and the good things continued, Clarissa gave way. She said yes to Jon and she meant it. Jon had won her complete commitment.

It was all downhill from that point. Jon changed radically. Soon Clarissa found herself living in an ever progressive nightmare of criticism and withdrawn affection. Everything about her that had been right before was now wrong. He criticized her work, her looks, her every deed. He never brought her a gift. When she cried, he walked out the door. He used all his money to buy himself belongings and left her to manage the household. She received Jon's consideration only grudgingly; he exacted a price for everything she wanted. For a night out where she wanted to go, he gave her the cold shoulder for a week. He excluded her from his affairs, and to Clarissa the sting of exclusion was far worse than carnal jealousy. She began to lose her self-assurance and to feel constantly beaten down.

She said to me, "The whole second half of our relationship was in twisted perspective. He had put himself out to catch me. Now I had to pay him back in spades. Every day in every way, I had to 'win' him. I cajoled him for a conversation. To get him interested in sex, I performed all the foreplay. He said I wasn't proper in public, so I tried to regain the right to go out with him. I did everything at home, but it was never good enough to receive a piece of praise."

Clarissa was both confused and stymied. She wondered how her original impressions had been so misguided, puzzled over what went wrong. She kept trying to please him, to discover what he wanted, to carry on and wait for the *real* Jon to return. She needed Jon again to confirm that she was special, so she stalled. She knew she should leave him, but somehow she now wanted him as he had wanted her before. She planned to confront him, but the day before the appointed day, Jon, accusing her of countless flaws and misdeeds, walked out on her.

With the Minimal Misogynist, there is practically no indication of how the relationship will go until you are already over the dam. You commit yourself to a seemingly certain set of circumstances only to find them demolished. Such an unforeseen switch can reduce even tough-minded women to gibbering. You almost have to go through the Minimal Misogynist once to learn to recognize him again. Nonetheless, different trees have different leaves. And, while the Minimal Misogynist may hide his ultimate nature in a veil of foliage, he does have characteristic identification signs.

How Can You Identify One?

The Minimal Misogynist likes himself. In fact, inordinately. Not infrequently he is rather a sophisticated, educated, and traveled man. He wants the best for himself; this leads him to a prestigious lifestyle. He may well know good and fine wines, buy himself the best liquor and special tobacco. It is not unlikely that he lives somewhat beyond his means. Getting himself anything he thinks he ought to have extends to realms other than the material. The Minimal Misogynist tends to set high goals for himself in all respects. He chooses a difficult career, desires more than moderate wealth, and prefers glamorous social circles.

He's gregarious. He's charming and gallant. He is as good at socializing as he is at other things. His story of who he is and how it's going is mesmerizing; he has a great line. He's a verbal enchanter, spinning a golden web that's attractive to many, but sticks to very few.

Needless to say, when his pursuit of finer things includes you, he is absolutely magnetic. His constant search for prizes, and his assurance that he will win them, certainly flatter you. On top of that, he seems to adore the image of women. His bait is his love of the feminine flair you yourself love, his hook the fond hope that you will fulfill his quest.

Long before you decipher how much and how well he cares for himself, his charm might be your earliest signal. If you look carefully, he does not seek to scratch the surface to find the needs, moods, and desires under your perfume and silk. He is more concerned with how you initially *evade* him than how you eventually give yourself to him.

Outer Signs

His clothes will probably be expensive. In a store, he walks right toward quality items and is oblivious to anything on the cheaper racks. He demands pure, fine materials—wool, cotton, and silk. He likes scarves for his neck and socks that come up to his knees. He has a conservative streak in his wearing apparel. He thinks the more traditional, reserved styles show more elegance. He usually wears a jacket, often a blazer. The hippest his fashions get is the latest in the continental look for men. Even when he buys more casual clothes, he soon discards them and reverts to run-down old expensive ones. He likes black.

His hair is never too long and never too short. He doesn't seem to pay it much attention, but he must because it never varies more than an inch. He's very aware of his hands. His fingers are long, his skin smooth, his nails long and shiny. His second toe is longer than his big one, and he calls it the mark of an aristocrat.

He does like a fashionable car, one with a touch of class. He picks automobiles that are well known for their performance plus style. The motor is special, so is the trademark and probably the price tag. If he drives an old car, it's the kind that had distinction in its day and is now almost a classic. If he buys a new one, it's among the noteworthy. Since a car is a highly visible belonging, he often has a better vehicle than he does a place to live.

He would prefer to dwell in better-than-just-exclusive neighborhoods—he would like the most sublime location within them. He admires the highest hill, best view, or most unusual house. When he can't own such a palatial palace, he may lease, rent part, house sit, or become a permanent guest in one. Any apartment or house he chooses, he picks for space and taste. He likes delicate fireplaces, alcoves, and arches. He places furniture formally, often stiffly. The air is still, and you feel you're in a museum.

Indeed, his self-arranged environment is full of stuff; in more ways than one, he is a great consumer. You might find nine cameras, two cars, twenty-six silk shirts, and three unused rowing machines, plus gadgets for peeling lemons, opening champagne bottles, and clipping sideburn hairs. It befits a man with high self-esteem to match himself in both quantity and quality. He gets everything he thinks he ought to have, maybe two. On all these things the Minimal Misogynist does not like spots and dents; he wants things classy and kept that way. Interest in his collection of consumer items and admiration of his taste confirm his view of himself.

Public confirmation of his ability is an important and touchy area for this man. Like any person, he wants to be living proof of his own self-image, but the image in his case is a fancy one. If he happens to be good at a particular sport, he will play to the balcony. But unless he can display some special ability, activities such as sports won't interest him. Large crowds are certainly not his style. Fear of heart attacks, excess weight, and ugly flab are his most likely motivations for physical activity. He pedals, runs, pushes, pulls, carries out exercise with the diligence that characterizes his other practices.

Sex Signals

The Minimal Misogynist tends to pick what seems to him and others as the *best* of women. A high achiever, he selects a high achiever among women. He is drawn to ambitious and creative ladies—education, talent, and beauty all rolled up in one bundle; social position and money help, too.

His modus operandi in courtship is the bold announcement that you are special: He extends himself for you; he arranges special occasions and events. He does not say, "Hey, let's watch T.V. together." He takes you sailing in a *tiny* boat. He opens a *very* old bottle of wine. He brings out the linen napkins, unnerves you by wearing his desire for you on his sleeve. He wants to *have* you.

While some types of men regard the sexual conquest of a woman as the final goal, this is not so with the Minimal Misogynist. He finds the surrender of your body useful, even encouraging, but not all that he desires. He wants more: He wants you to pledge yourself. If after some time, sex or no sex, you remain casual, he becomes upset. It is he who introduces the intensity into your affair.

Going to bed with him for the first time is never aggressive. Most likely it is the sensuous, seductive culmination to some fine evening together. It arrives like an elegant dessert—Cherries Jubilee and brandy. He is good in bed. After all, he has cultivated a lot of refined tastes. He appraises you with a connoisseur's delight, treats you like a princess, places accurate kisses just where you want them. He strokes, conducts a guided tour. It lasts a long time.

He is good, but he is not huggy. Sex with him is ornate choreography, an exquisite dance that is not really tender. The intensity of his lovemaking can carry the illusion of intimacy—in the beginning. Often it takes some time for the deficiency of his affection to become apparent. He would have really to *like* you as a woman to be tender in sex. And liking, unfortunately, is his weak point.

Since he pursues only to conquer, and in so doing discovers exactly what he sets out to discover—that his image of woman is not to be perfectly fulfilled—his attitudes change drastically when the victory is accomplished. Once his, you are in some ways more, in some ways less, than he had bargained for. *Yes* is a key word to him. Once the word is uttered by you, the shoulder gets cold. Things differ dramatically. He shuts down your access to his life. He changes the lock on his office door and neglects to replace your key. He outlaws tickling. Suddenly you are too heavy to sit in his lap. He turns his nose up to a serendipitous escapade with you. He turns you down in bed. Slowly it becomes obvious that the cause is not fatigue, but the desire to slight you.

All this is quite characteristic of him; he is truly good at all these little things. Indeed, one of his give-away traits is his ability—all the things a Minimal Misogynist does, he does well. He is expert at romance to start with and, later on, just as expert at rejection.

Money Markers

The Minimal Misogynist's money belongs to *him*. He alone determines what he requires and how elegant his possessions should be. Your earnings, however, belong to *both* of you; they support your mutual household. So after he has indulged himself, you're reduced to eking out your luxuries from the grocery budget.

Quite likely, during the course of your relationship, a great deal of money will be spent—to the Minimal Misogynist, that's what money is for, and the sooner spent the better. The Minimal Misogynist can be very persuasive when it comes to buying things. Desperate and immediate necessities arise all over the place like little mushrooms. Credit cards and juggled debts become a way of life. He resents the sound of brakes on the cash flow and will surely release a torrent of charm or pressure to get your signature on a check.

Family Aspects

Few Minimal Misogynists want children. And they don't look fondly on becoming stepfathers. Children represent too much of an encumbrance on his freedom and money. They require real care. They are messy. They break things. If you do decide to have children, the contract will involve your tending them on a go-it-alone basis. The Minimal Misogynist may come to love his children, but he won't change their diapers. The chances are few that he will bend his plans to babysit. He is a magnanimous father, but not a wrestling-match-in-the-living-room daddy. Having children does not mean that you will give up your salaried job; it means you will gain an unsalaried one.

The Minimal Misogynist's relationship with parents, brothers, and sisters will be marked by estrangements of various degrees. He generally feels he has moved beyond the social level of his kindred and views his bonds to them as personally regressive. He meets his obligations to family only at the bottom line and only after he's taken care of the more important circumstances in his business and social calendar.

Rather than flirt too heavily with public opinion, the Minimal Misogynist finds that his estimation of himself is more easily maintained alone. He tends to have few close friends, men or women, and arranges his relationships so that he is somewhat unapproachable. He creates distance by being the older, the employer, the expert, or merely by being more formal. His acquaintances tend to be from his career field and often only those selected few that have something to offer him. He *tells* who he is and how it's going; he doesn't ask. If someone's vision of friendship with him includes being direct about inadequacies as well as adequacies, he or she has forgotten how narcissistic he is. He views directness not as possibly beneficial but as an attack. It's hard for anyone to be a frank and honest friend to the Minimal Misogynist. After all, he is not your humble sort of fellow; he thinks others are not quite competent to judge him and does not want to keep company with just *any* folk. He may leave friends behind as he sees himself advancing.

The Minimal Misogynist has numerous liabilities. He is selfish, overbearing, and critical, a river of no return. In his elegance there is arrogance. It may be impossible ever to be real with him. He costs a lot. Yet he is always a fascinating man. He has a big and exciting dream of how his life will be, what he will achieve, and how the honey will flow. He has flash, and he looks good—both on his own and with you. His very presence can be a sort of audacious compliment. If you dread sedateness, normality, security, investments, commitments, and boredom, rest assured you will be safely unsafe with the Minimal Misogynist.

What Is in Store for You?

What do you do if you are shown a Lincoln Continental, and only *after* you sign the contract, you discover that you have actually purchased a Volkswagen with no shock absorbers? The first thing is to learn to spot Volkswagens lurking in the trunks of Continentals. Failing that, you can at least try to determine where you are going and what's in store for you. Then you decide whether to bail out or get heavy-duty shock absorbers.

If you resolve that you are dallying with a Minimal Misogynist, there are things to know. For one, the fact that the Minimal Misogynist is a repeater does not bode well; the prospects for permanence are poor. For another, like the foxtrot, a two-step pattern lies predictably in you future. At first, the affair amounts to a veritable treasure trove of support, flattery, and love. For anyone with the least bit of appetite in her soul, such treatment is both a temptation and a delight. But the criticism and withheld affection that appear in stage two are the most important factors; like two bulldozers they gouge away the landscape of your early relations. The early features disappear so effectively, you even wonder if they had been figments of your imagination. Sadly, his preliminary finesse is based on his sensitivity to you as an object, not as a person. Once you are acquired, he is not one to be in tune with you. No more do you receive words of love, affection, and praise. Quite the opposite. You hear more and more about your ever-growing list of inadequacies.

Once a woman has committed herself to a permanent relationship with the Minimal Misogynist, his resentment for the tenderness he extended to "catch" her reveals itself. Withheld love gives him tremendous power over a woman who is trying to be his mate. In these gestures he exposes himself as someone who hates rather than loves, someone who is too angry at women in general to live and let live with one of their representative members. Many women stay with the Minimal Misogynist in the vain hope that the former caresses will soon—or at least *eventually*—return. They search to improve upon whatever he thinks is lacking, in order to reclaim the original conditions. It does seem as if he is saying, "I won you. Now you win me." Once committed, therefore, you may try to win him back. But there's a catch—he's unwinnable, the ultimate "Indian giver." Once having withdrawn the affection and flattery that marked the early maneuvers, he will not return them. Once having started to find fault, he will undoubtedly continue to discover still other black spots in your character.

You can sing songs, do dances, write homilies in his praise, and try every program of self-improvement, but that won't make him blow you kisses from across the room. And criticizing him back only serves to confirm his accusations about you. The end of a relationship with this man rarely develops into friendship, at least not for a long time. You will be sensitive to his ungiven flattery and his overgiven negative commentary. He more than likely will not be able to resist verbally jabbing at you. You might stay attached to him—but through rancor, not affection.

Besides the emotional hazards, some labor problems pop into your life with the Minimal Misogynist, as well—don't forget all those purchases. Someone has to keep them clean. It is in his prospectus for you to play maid to the objects. Despite getting a gadget for every need, the Minimal Misogynist's attitude is not that objects serve you, but that you, not he, serve them. No spots and no dents, remember? You will also have to do all the work and carry on all the burdens of ordinary daily life. Women in these partnerships tend to have to continue their careers, struggle under financial stress, and keep looking good while they become kitchen maids, housekeepers, bookkeepers, mechanics, childcare experts, insurance agents, and party givers. And, while with some of the Twenty-two Types of Men you have relatives coming out of your cupboards all the time, with the Minimal Misogynist, keeping up ties to friends and family will be up to *your* conscience to decide and left to you to manage.

You will have to take care of yourself. You could be in difficult circumstances if you got sick or fired from your job. Considering his standards, he will have trouble putting up with you when you are not of the best quality. If you have children, most likely you will have to hire substantial amounts of childcare to free yourself for work, for rest, and for social events.

What Are the Telltale Signs of Trouble?

Of course, there are signals that indicate that you might have taken on something that was not quite what it seemed. Consider it a sign of rocks on the road if his past partners cry tribulation while you yourself are being treated very well. Especially watch out if the women are much like yourself, as you are hearing about the end stage of his previous affairs while experiencing the beginning of your own. Notice, too, if he enumerates the faults of former women. Chances are things will not go a different course with you. Note if even early on you get chastised for independent decisions that do not concur with his plans. This may be a signal that he is already secretly waiting for you to change yourself in response to how good he thinks he is being to you.

But the major warning is when his behavior abruptly changes. This happens almost certainly at points of commitment in your relationship—starting to live together, getting engaged, married, or pregnant. The first signs are small, but they pile up. Stupendous sex fizzles down to the mundane, then the nonexistent. He stops public displays of affection. Suddenly, at a party, he treats you like a spore from outer space. He says he is always telling you the right way to live and you stubbornly do it your own, *wrong* way just to annoy him. He threatens you because of your overuse of oregano and underuse of Mop & Glo. He won't help you because *you* made the mess. He uses you as the butt of jokes in company. He implies that, despite running five shops, four offices, three cars, and two households, you can't add one plus one. The start of stage two is the critical point for you to consider dropping him.

But when the Minimal Misogynist moves on to new goals in his own life, it is *he* who may leave *you*. He doesn't especially like the things he acquires to walk out on him; he's a keeper. Every time you are about to call it quits, a Minimal Misogynist finds a way to reattach you. Most often he behaves more as he did at first for a spell. Offering bits of the old time, he fakes you out, until *he* is ready to go.

What Are the Chances?

Despite what you do, most affairs with the Minimal Misogynist break up. Either he walks out or you decide to cut your losses.

Unfortunately, within the Minimal Misogynist there is little potential for change. Fortified by his high opinion of himself, he rarely finds he needs to rearrange. And since he loves himself so inordinately, your opinion of his virtues and failings will never match his own. He simply has not got the kinds of chinks in his armor that make alteration possible. He hasn't got a personal philosophy of change. His friends aren't close enough to tell him, and you are liable to be the last candidate on the list of influential "others." Considering the balance sheet, I advise avoiding this type of man. I also advise fleeing from one already in your life.

Once you are pledged to him, the Minimal Misogynist is a heads-he-wins-tails-you-lose situation. It's up to you, the possibilities you see and the advantages you gain in a relationship, but somes kinds of men are more undermining than others and the Minimal Misogynist is one of them. It's a bit more than most women can (or should) handle to be above constant attack and to overcome loveless atmospheres. Why ask for so much difficulty when other situations offer more for less?

Calling it quits makes sense for another reason—liking yourself. If you *were* outstanding, you will find it hard to tolerate yourself for hanging on. You will save yourself energy and self-esteem if you get out early. Remember that the fault-finding and cold-shouldering grow like Hydra's heads. Self-confidence is vulnerable, even for a dynamo of a woman. So it's sensible to cut your losses and save what assurance remains.

There is, however, another possibility to consider other than outright shunning. Perhaps the trick with the Minimal Misogynist is never to say yes. In that light, you can contemplate collecting on stage one and saying "so long" before stage two. Take what he offers, then run. I personally believe that without giving yourself to a relationship you can't get much from it. But if you were not looking for anything serious to begin with, this suggestion has definite possibilities.

If you do want to stay with a Minimal Misogynist for whatever reason, there are some skills for survival. Keep in mind that it was your class, style, and strength that attracted him in the first place. If he has any weak spot, that's it. Minimal Misogynists rise up and pay attention to elegance. Keep your style and handle tough times with all the class you can muster. He cannot be handed intimate knowledge of you with the assurance that he won't abuse it. Make and keep other friends outside the relationship. Better yet, don't stop being your own best friend. To avoid the criticism, cultivate your own opinions of yourself and stick to them. If you are vulnerable in any area of self-evaluation, techniques to help deal with criticism are available: Learn them.

You can end up with lots of fears from a Minimal Misogynist: Are you or will you ever be special again? Attractive, adventurous, financially solvent? One strong foil against such fears exists. Remember, *he* is not the one to quash your doubts. As I said before, many women are held by an invisible string of hope that the Minimal Misogynist will once more flatter and reassure them. But he is *not* the one to go to. Asking a criticizer for a faultless checkup is backwards strategy. When you need confirmation that you are still you, find someone *else* who thinks you're great.

If your relationship goes all the way to breakup, just knowing that's par for the course for the Minimal Misogynist will help fortify you against self-doubt. He did think he was madly attracted to you in the beginning and even that he loved you. It's a great memory.

Where Do You Fit In?

Admittedly, Minimal Misogynists are attractive men. They are out of the ordinary, ambitious, energetic. They have an air of excitement. But if you find yourself consistently attracted to this type—going through both stages, and ending up worse for wear—some insight into yourself might be gleaned from it all. Minimal Misogynists are less likely to appeal to you if you don't form opinions of yourself from the opinions others have of you. That includes even the views of your most intimate companion and mate. Entertain the possibility that you might not be accepting yourself sufficiently as the ultimate judge of your own qualities. Do you still need to be told that you're neat and classy? Most women in our society were raised to seek approval of themselves from the men around them. But learning self-reliance makes for far sounder footing.

Many very independent women have dependent urges hidden within them to which Minimal Misogynists appeal. Perhaps you maintain the old fantasy of being carried away or taken care of: Some loving companion will make it all easier for you, even though you have chosen a complicated life.

Minimal Misogynists, in the courtship stage, fall right in line with those fond, secret hopes. They seem as if they *want* your sassiness and still will romance you. Perhaps also you might feel that without *needing* a man, there will be no way to connect with one, and so you actually fear being independent. In truth, clearing up those last remnants of dependence frees you from endlessly riding the roller coaster of your partner's good or bad opinion or the illusion that some Minimal Misogynist will really take care of you.

Do you feel you have to be flawless to be worthy; extraordinary to be loved? Did you seek a classy man possibly to obtain prestigious outside opinion, just as he did with you, or perhaps because you needed a challenge or match? Take stock of what you want out of life and love right now. If it's any or all of the above, do it with a Minimal Misogynist. If not, *don't.*

Notes and Particulars

4/ The "But I Really Like Women" Manipulator

Related Types: The Sugar Pie Honey
The Father Knows Best

Positivity Scale: + + −

Concealed in a haze of sunshine, speaking in a code of direct honesty, listening through an attentive filter, is the undercover man—the "But I Really Like Women" Manipulator. So used is he to his coat of true blue, even he thinks he's playing one-to-one with you.

But his intentions are hidden, so well that he doesn't even know he's got them. *You* know he does, however, because somehow your plans always turn into puffs of thin air. No matter what your way is, it never happens; no matter how often he has no preference, he always gets it. Little do you know that when he gives you the wheel, he snaps on automatic pilot. Happily you steer away, never knowing you're following the course of his preprogrammed navigation.

The "But I Really Like Women" Manipulator never thought much of himself when he was growing up. Dates, popularity, and sex were a long time coming. Jealously eyeing the jocks and class valedictorians, he learned to cultivate women, to find out how to be their friend and, more importantly, to make them friendly to *him*. He has refined subtle manipulation into high art. On the surface he is cooperative, well intentioned, kind, supportive, and fair. Underneath he is adamant about having his own way.

He goes for women. Almost any women. But he likes earnest ones a little more than the others, because the more practical, straightforward and discussion-prone you are, the easier for him. And if you have the simple goal of just loving a nice guy with whom you feel pretty equal and can be best friends, he hits the jackpot. But he can mold himself to almost any variation: tall, short, lively, sedate, career minded, domestic, snappish, or even tempered.

Story

I've collected many, many stories about the "But I Really Like Women" Manipulator. I'll tell you about Jill. She may seem an unlikely victim to you, but believe me, she's pretty typical.

Jill was a normal, sensible, capable woman who suddenly turned into a sputtering maniac. No one could see any reason for her metamorphosis. *Imagine* packing up and walking out on a nice man like David! The incidents mentioned certainly seemed trivial. She was just having a fit. Maybe it was her thyroid or pituitary? Had she seen a doctor lately?

David claimed total befuddlement. One day all was fine. The next day Jill started screaming and stalked out. (Of course there had been warnings; he just hadn't heeded them.)

Jill grew up as what used to be called a tomboy—in other words, healthy, independent, and full of strength. She went from tricycle to bicycle to car with glee. She loved making things, doing things, and using all her capabilities. When the idea of women's equal rights came along, it suited her nature. Without being political or fashionable, she set about finding a union that contained both love and symmetry.

She had met David long before and considered him just a friend. Then one day she took a whole new look at him. He adored women, espoused equality, and wanted a long-term partnership and maybe, later, a family. Jill, with all her common sense, decided David was a good bet. A long, cautious courtship ensued. Finally she moved in with him. But even that was no impulse. Being Jill, she wanted a good tryout before final commitment.

David was caring and devoted. He shared the household chores; he shared the business matters. They openly discussed all plans and finances. They never quarreled—they "hashed things out." Jill decided they had compatibility on almost every level. "A good working relationship," she called it. Besides, she really grew to love him, so the tryout became permanent.

But what Jill didn't see was that while talking about cooperative responsibility, David never let go of any of his; he merely transformed Jill into a secret pet. He let her talk about and decide all she wanted; meanwhile he did *everything* as *he* thought best.

For example, it was Jill's assignment to pick their insurance. She made numerous inquiries, then made her decision. When she told David, he announced that just that morning he had purchased all the necessary policies. It seems he had independently called the various companies and reached his own conclusions.

David would ask Jill to choose the evening's entertainment. He didn't care, he said. He'd like whatever she did. After Jill happily picked a play, they'd end up at the movies—bad American comedy, not even foreign drama! Jill would survey the pantry and make a grocery list. David would go to the store (it was his turn) but come back with everything different from what she asked for. When Jill went to purchase the car she wanted (a sports model), David said "wouldn't you rather" so many times she found herself buying another—a hatchback wagon. She wanted a Lamaze birth, but as soon as things began to get difficult, he had her put under. How could she complain, when the baby emerged healthy?

But if anything vexed her the most, it was sex. David had a problem with maintenance—he just came too fast. In fact, instantly. Being modern and open, they not only discussed it, they worked on it. But despite Jill's foreplay, afterplay, tricks, and bizarre devices, which did bring some satisfaction, David remained unchanged.

It was David's persistent sexual standstill that gave Jill the first insight into what was happening. When she realized that no matter what she did or said to David she never got through to him, she saw something remarkable. By getting in and out quickly, David could keep total command over himself. She realized that their sex life merely exaggerated everything else in their relationship. Deep down, David never delegated anything to anyone else's command. All her work, in bed and otherwise, was futile.

She began to view David as a sneaky opponent. She tried to fight, but she couldn't argue with him. He always listened, then he'd ask her to explain and reconstruct. In so doing, he trapped her into the old pattern: He skirted around her with agreement and went on as before. Then she tried to pin down how she always lost. Still, decisions slipped through her fingers so insidiously, before she could say, "Hey," it was too late.

One day she found herself alone at home. They were going

somewhere that night she didn't want to go. She had agreed to "just this once" once again. The house was full of furniture she couldn't stand. Suddenly, it all became intolerable. As he came home and said, "Hi, honey," something snapped. She pulled down a suitcase, threw in some clothes, grabbed the baby, and said, "It's all yours. I've had enough."

He's a hard one to spot, the old "But I Really Like Women" Manipulator. After all, manipulators are as manipulation is: indirect, inarticulate, and undercover. If things keep happening (or not happening) to you as if by magic, you have your first clue. The second one is equally indirect: If you're fuming and blathering, feeling like you're frittering your life away, you've probably got a Manipulator near. Nobody makes you madder than a "But I Really Like Women" Manipulator.

How Can You Identify One?

When it comes to prevalence, the adult "But I Really Like Women" Manipulator is way up there. Almost every man has a little of him in there somewhere. But whether a man has a little or a lot, the manipulation boils down to one thing: *liking* women does not mean *trusting* them. While he seemingly accepts a female person as on a par with himself, secretly he's sure he's superior.

He was raised a boy, after all. And unconsciously he assumes males—or at least this male—are just a touch smarter, better, and more capable than females. Often he grew up alone or with a brother, with no sister to tell him off. Besides, like anybody else, he wants what's best for and what pleases him. So when he combines his belief in his higher native ability with his hidden self-indulgent streak, he comes out with a shiny key to a smooth existence: He relies only on himself. He knows, however, that his singular self-reliance strikes others as decidedly antisocial. Smugly confident persons appear too self-contained for friendship. And repelling others, especially ladies, definitely acts against his best interest. So he curbs his egocentricity and covers it, then he pulls it out at the last minute.

He seeks the company of women to make his life more comfortable;

he's not so sure with men. When he believes he has the deciding factor, he simply feels safer.

Outer Signs

He dresses for comfort; he's not a high-style man. He likes to look like the boy next door, your brother, and/or a milk drinker—somebody who's sincerely unpretentious. Look for him in cozy clothes, ever so slightly wrinkled, washed in Tide (by himself). He wears the same shoes (brown) till they look like Kentucky Fried Chicken legs.

He doesn't smell perfumey, but he doesn't smell sweaty either. He wafts . . . *humanity.* A very huggable odor. If he's tall, he tries to look shorter (more your size). If he's short, he jokes about it, as if he's sublimely synchronized for females.

He likes his car, and he keeps it quite a while. He's a long-time clinger. He prefers use and familiarity. His steering wheel has smooth spots; he holds it from the back side with the palm of his hand (it gives him the feeling he's heftier). There's an old blanket to wrap cold shoulders or a pillow that never leaves the vehicle. He drives a normal car. Part of his approach is never to be surprising. Look for him in a Toyota, Dodge, Ford, or Datsun.

Often he's a do-it-yourselfer. His surroundings might show bits of carpentry or photography. The basement or garage become work-rooms or darkrooms containing fix-it benches. Other than that, he's not much of a decorator. He surrounds himself with items made or picked by people he knows, rather than anything store-bought. The objects he hangs on the wall are always in odd places; he needs help in the arrangement department. It takes him ten years to change anything.

His home or apartment is not in an especially nice or convenient area; it's maybe ten blocks farther out, up, or down than it should be. It's not that he's hanging back; it's because he just got tired of looking. Once situated, he hangs onto his spot. He's not much of a one for leaving.

He's outwardly amiable. His conversation always contains a lot of questions. His walk is never too driven-looking, and he makes frequent stops. He always gives you three choices of where to go and what to do there. Sometimes you wonder if his personality resulted from Parent Effectiveness Training.

All in all, he treats himself quite well, except for one major failing—he's unable to furnish himself with honesty. Unconsciously or not, he connives, contrives, and even lies. He double-talks. His thinking wheels scheme so busily, he pays an awful price: He doesn't *dare* let in diverting stimuli, including love. He can't recognize what's really going on around him. And he doesn't hear what you tell him.

Sex Signals

It's not unlikely that he finally mates with someone who *grows* to love him rather than falling head over heels for him. That's his secret hope. Using his friendliness, his ease and harmony, and all those questions, he can talk to (and win) almost any woman. His desire to befriend women and his insightful thinking lead him to become almost everything he says he is and almost everything you could want. He seems concerned with inner qualities as much as beauty. He grows so close, he knows and appreciates your mind. He can be a very appealing man when his "But I Really Like Women" part comes out.

But his fear of giving himself to anyone else shows up abruptly during sexual intimacy. He just can't hand over that much of himself. He does it quick as a rabbit. He gives you all kinds of leeway—until he gets inside you.

As reluctant as he is to let go of his body, he's the opposite with his mind. He loves to talk about sex and sexual problems. To make up for his fear of things in depth, he focuses on surfaces: He learns intricate, exotic practices to compensate for his jumping-the-gun tendencies.

He usually keeps his promise: He's a faithful spouse. He generally won't take or give humiliation or hand out criticism.

Money Markers

He's not tight with money, but he is exacting. Neither parsimonious nor a spendthrift, he simply examines every expenditure. In order to make a purchase, he starts an inquisition: He checks brands and prices, asks every possible inquiry, fiddles with every model, gets at least seven opinions, and reads *Consumer Reports*. He uses his money eventually, but he can't spend spontaneously.

He doesn't care if you don't make the money he does. He prefers to contribute all, or at least more. Even-steven finances threaten his assumption that he's the more qualified. Whatever funds he has he generally applies to both of you. But whenever you buy anything, he goes along. Having his funds doesn't imply you can use them freely.

Family Aspects

He wants to have a family. But if he frustrates you, he nearly *suffocates* children. In his adoration, he goes overboard. With them as with you, he pretends to be fair, but he always keeps the final decision. He finagles them until they get quite snippy; they have to ward him off *some* way. He has his fingers in their every pie until they yell, 'Stop it." He *means* well, as usual. But he has a hard time giving anyone independence. Unlike The Father Knows Best, however, he pretends he does, even to his kids.

He's close and kind to his parents. So kind, in fact, he's never gone through an open rebellion. He didn't have to; he learned how to be furtive. Usually they think of him as sweet, compliant, and good. He's liable to be their "best son." In turn he thinks of them as benign. In their eyes there's no way you can come up to him. You're never "good enough" for him.

He maintains a "blood is thicker than water"—i.e, blind— approach to his brothers. They assist one another anywhere, anytime, if one calls upon the other. If he has a sister, he's very protective toward her. After all, he "knows better" than she does. He has a pal or two from childhood, often a similarly unpopular type. He picks up other close male friends, one every five or ten years. Each, amazingly, resembles him in one way or another—in inertia or broken love affairs. He has long-term women friends who have always been platonic.

The "But I Really Like Women" Manipulator has heaps of potential. His riches are like an oil well's: They can gush or flow and last a long time. But you have to crack through lots of layers— deception, chicanery, and self-ignorance—to get to them. And even then you have problems: You have to pump what he's hiding to the surface.

What Is in Store for You?

In almost every story there's a hero and a heavy: One character is scurrilous, the other draws your sympathy. Then the cunning author twists the plot, to make it more entertaining. The bad guy shines through with a streak of angelic while the good guy looks evil. The "But I Really Like Women" Manipulator throws you a monkey wrench. Like Bugs Bunny with Porky Pig, he's the one who acts rascally, but *you* wind up looking like the imp. In the end you *are* one. The "But I Really Like Women" Manipulator makes your decision appear caprice, your desires appear as mere whims, and your fashion as fancy. When there's nothing about you that's taken seriously, you get your essence plucked away. And then you've really got problems; the most difficult thing in the world to get over is being taken lightly.

All too often with the "But I Really Like Women" Manipulator, when you can't fight back you simply join in. You have no gravity, so you might as well float. After all, nothing happens the way it's supposed to. And everything you do turns to meaningless thumb-twiddling. So you just disconnect: You get giddy or, worse, you get paranoid.

Perhaps you make a few stabs at defending your sanity and declaring your anger. But the "But I Really Like Women" Manipulator in all his furtive glory can throw cold water on hot ashes so fast, your rage turns into whining. He says, "Are you sure . . . ?" and "Don't you think . . . ?" He washes over your assertion with semi-sweet phrases that he knows you have little on-the-spot defense against, because those phrases are just the sugarcoated sort that women sometimes use to make men think *they* made the decision! The fact that you inevitably appear either a meanie or a fusspot starts to keep you silent. You don't yell very often when you discover the outside observers blame you. And since he discusses around you when you try to explain, you begin to think you have no *reason* to complain. So you store up your ammo until it's bazooka size. Or else your unheard cries come out as perpetual nagging.

Over the long haul, if this process isn't halted, what happens becomes far from comical. If you can't grab onto what's gone amiss and get back your self-assertiveness, you simply slip into acting as if you've received a frontal lobotomy. You carry on as if your thoughts were totally disassociated from meaning and your gestures thoroughly unrelated to any goal. Often you waver in and out of depression and go into senility before your time.

Or if you're lucky, some peculiar insight brings all the vexation to a culmination. If you act on inexact instincts and don't know why, usually you attempt some sort of unfocused self-help channel. You see counselors, join women's groups, or take some sort of personal action. You don't know why you've started, but soon you begin to understand. Then you attempt to correct your situation—or you leave your man.

If an especially strong perception bursts on you in a flash, sometimes immediate slash-and-burn tactics result: You launch bizarre retaliation. Perhaps you run away, torpedo your domicile, and smash your existing life.

When you break up with a "But I Really Like Women" Manipulator or regain your self-direction while still remaining paired, another strange phase often comes along: You discover the joy of being as utterly non-sensible as you were previously made to feel. Suddenly, out of the blue, you live up to the wacko image that was never you before. You act out your version of living free, much to his dismay. You wear bracelets and bangles. You take on a string of short-term intimates. You put the children into alternative schools. You move to the country and live in a van. There's nothing as thrilling as a "look Ma, no hands" reentry into life.

Sometimes you normalize again. Sometimes your new abnormality becomes the new you. But you learn a big lesson—the power of the absurd and the strength of leaving rules behind. Even if you stay with him now, he'll have to dwell with your new self. And so will anyone new, if you go on alone.

What Are the Telltale Signs of Trouble?

With the "But I Really Like Women" Manipulator, trouble doesn't burst upon the scene. It gathers. Like little puffy clouds, one almost inconsequential annoyance after another rolls by, only to accumulate into a mighty storm. It's a major warning. When every vexation is a minor one, remember that sometimes little things need big attention.

You reach a critical point as soon as you discover that you've been meandering. You go from assignment to assignment, chore to chore, task to task, none of which accomplish anything at all. If it occurs to you that the only reason a man would fill your days with trivia is to keep all the decisions for himself, you're on the right track.

The first sign of an impending ending is when you think you have no reason to be angry with your man, but you're *really* angry anyway. If you snap at him, he'll say, "What did I do?" and you'll be damned if you know. Sooner or later you'll blow up at him whether you have a reason or not. But by then you'll do it in some irreparable way.

Still, better to be angry and better to end your relationship than to feel like the nuts and bolts that hold your brain together have come unscrewed. If you feel floaty, useless, or like a pet puppy, don't flip off your switches. Blow the whistle instead.

What Are the Chances?

This may sound crazy, but when it comes to the "But I Really Like Women" Manipulator, I say—fight before fleeing.

It depends on how fed up you are and how deep your affection is. If you're up to the gills and no longer feeling any fondness, then it's best to head for the nearest exit. But if you've still got a glimmer of patience and love, then hang on a little longer. There's no way to find out if he's a hopeless case unless you try to reclaim him. You may or may not have success. If your efforts fail, you can always walk out later!

Consider what you have in hand to start with. He's already supportive, loving, and good—up to a point. Chances are he is as he is and does as he does *unconsciously*. And though that doesn't make him blameless, it does give you a chance. If he prefers to stay in the dark and keep his underhand power, consider it his loss and responsibility. But if he wants to see the light, you have a big, big start—namely, his saving grace, that he really does like women.

The thing to do is call him on it. He starts out thinking and claiming he likes women, so he can hardly say no when you show him he's not following through. Since he says he considers you an equal, all you have to do is catch him every time he overrides you. He really doesn't see that he believes himself superior until you point it out. When you do it again and again, you'll eradicate his doubt. Most "But I Really

Like Women" Manipulators mean well. When caught betraying their standards, they lose face with themselves. So unravel his actions to see if he really *does* like women before thinking that maybe he doesn't.

Calling him on his superiority complex entails two quite different problems. The first one is yours: You have to become both quick and blunt. You can't stop decisions from slipping through your fingers if you're not on top of them. Looking back and remembering how it happened is already too late. You have to know what you want and see that you get it. It takes work to stay on the button, but you have to do it.

The second is his: He has to give up tried-and-true methods of winning and start to abide by you. And that takes *incredible* effort. He has a lot staked on his old system, and he'll find the new one threatening. He may or may not be able to change. He may always have a problem with trust, and you may always have to struggle against his manipulative ways.

Even with success, you'll have another dilemma—not going overboard. You have to recognize when things have reached a balance so you can stop pushing and trust him again. Half the power is all you should ask; remember to leave him his share. You can easily overdemand your own way once you've started, but that's just another way to ruin a relationship.

There are bound to be backsliding, false starts, and hopeless moments. I suggest a good strong commitment. Lots of time is needed, so is vision. Without thinking you still have a rainbow together, why try?

If you are currently with a "But I Really Like Women" Manipulator or expect to meet one (don't laugh, it's highly likely!), keep in mind a simple equation that will help in your decision to fight or flee. Before making the effort to save or establish a good union, size up how much you like him as opposed to how much you love him. Believe me, they're different. If the like equals or tops the love, the odds are in your favor. But if you don't like him all that much, you're better off to cut the cord. Try to stay fond of him and friendly, but don't let him hang around your door—or bed. The "But I Really Like Women" Manipulator tends to switch roles once rejected. He, not you, becomes the soulful pet. If you left because he wouldn't change or you wanted something else, avoid this situation. You'd be surprised how easily the wind can blow him in again. You'll begin again. And end again.

Where Do You Fit In?

How does the "But I Really Like Women" Manipulator get away with it? you may well ask yourself. Well, he does it with the help of another party—you.

Consider the possibility that you've got a foot in two worlds. On the one hand you're strong-minded and know your worth; on the other you're still a bit of a willow, resulting from how you grew up. A manipulator can't work without an edge. How you fit in is by giving that edge to him. He can gain a foothold on domination only if, when push comes to shove, you act like a *lady*.

It's not that I'm against ladies. Quite the contrary. I'm warning against learned, so-called *"ladylike" behavior*. That's what gets you in trouble.

When you lose by default, the fault is still yours. It means you didn't show up, you backed out, or you tossed the game. Unfortunately, women all too commonly do just that. Women learn how to give up and give in, while growing up. It's one of the best things to learn how to stop. But first, you have to become aware of the habit. Consider that you may still be following that old, buried pattern, no matter how liberated your outward philosophy.

For example, you may be too flexible, because "a woman is always gracious." Or you're too ready to give up your convictions—especially when they come up against a man's. You may hold a belief that men are or *should* be more right. You might acquiesce when you don't feel like it, because it's "feminine" to give in and it earns you brownie points.

Sure, you might still want to achieve your ends "nicely," that is, without fights or hostility. But if you always back off in the end in order to please, you can bet that the "But I Really Like Women" Manipulator knows it. He can bargain that you will bend before you'll open fire.

You also need to check your language for feminine cover phrases. If his lines are persuasive, most likely yours are submissive. Women, from early on, learn language that gives men the final decision; we have a style of speech and phrasing that men don't share. Males use direct statements to show their command, like "Get me this" and

"We're going now." We women learn little linguistic ways to win approval and make sure we're not alone, like, "I like this, don't you?" as opposed to "I want this one," or "Don't you think it's time to leave?" instead of "Let's go!" But when you speak this way, you hand over the vote. You mean for him to agree with you but give him the chance to oppose. When women make delicate decisions, they often make soft requests for confirmation. When you say, "Aren't you," "would you," and "could you," you look feminine and open to discussion. But when someone uses your rhetorical queries to disagree instead of concur, it can make you very angry. And you can't fight back because, after all, you asked!

The best way to save yourself is to stop using such futile ploys. Say what you mean directly and forget the need for consensus. As your speech and gestures become less ambiguous, you become more assertive, and being assertive, no matter what some say, is in *no* way unfeminine. There are a hundred ways to combine femininity, softness, and romance with being clear about your desires and meaningful in your actions. When you coordinate your speech, motions, and preferences, you gain spectacular freedom. Once there, you can be any kind of lady you want. The choice is yours.

Notes and Particulars

5/ The Doe Stalker

Related Types: The Picasso
The Father Knows Best
The Disaster Broker
The Man Who Would Be Mogul

Positivity Scale: + − −

Here comes your local Lone Ranger. A little removed from the others, he's riding his stallion down a slightly different trail. He's hard to miss. He's distinct and he's definitely male.

A female doppelgänger means too much cussedness to the masked hero. No, when it comes to a sidekick, he wants something special— someone who concurs with him and never gives him trouble. Someone who makes it look as if his gun shoots silver bullets. You guessed it, kimosabe. The lady he wants is a little Tonto.

The Doe Stalker picks young women—twenty-two is about his limit; or else passive women from cultures other than his—he sees them as lusty or exotic. But what he's not admitting is the desire to remain top hand.

Many fruitful unions can occur between older men and younger women or people of diverse societies. Age has no rules; background doesn't either. The Doe Stalker, however, seeks a relationship where age and cultural criteria decidedly *matter*. He assumes that with a little deer or less savant woman, he can get sex, care, and company for practically no strife.

He's great for infatuation, and he knows it. He's got all the aspects of fantasy romance turned real—almost. He's masculine, independent, a formidable guide. He drinks, he dances, he calls you "babe." He's older, wiser, has powers and resources you haven't. Besides, he plays on being a first sexual turn-on. Or a further step for a not-so-naïve woman. If he wasn't sexy to start with, he becomes so by the time he stalks doe. Sex is part of what he sells, what he wants to be sure of.

You're supposed to take his lifestyle spit with spittoon, to learn that jealousy is a no-no—since one young thing is *rarely* all he ultimately desires. What he never stops to realize is that the little doe he harnesses will grow up to buck him.

Story

I know many Doe Stalkers. Most men at least flirt with the idea. Of those that activate the notion, some start early, some late.

Jake picked up and packaged Pam. She was just eighteen and looked even younger. Like twelve. It seemed she would wear bangs forever. Gavin spotted and soon settled with Penny, who was round and firm and Japanese. Jake and Gavin were old bucks compared to those bambini; they thought Pam and Penny would stay demure and docile. But instead the ladies grew from fawns right into mastodon.

Pam's and Penny's relationships ran remarkably the same way. In the beginning, both women were overwhelmed. The men had real presence and fine lines: Both Jake and Gavin implied they could unlock Pam's and Penny's womanhoods. Pam and Penny fell, hook, line, and sinker. They found personal guides to worldly ways. To have an affair with such a manly man, not at all a boy, seemed more than alluring, it seemed irresistible.

Pam and Penny experienced a blast off of sex and sensuality, a ticket to the garden of delights. First Jake and Gavin thrilled their ladies with new erotica. Then they taught them that all bedroom activity, no matter how wild, was just a daily diet. They insisted that sexuality was so plain and earthy that even their dalliance with other women was too normal to call for jealousy, although they didn't feel so later when it happened to them. Pam and Penny thought all they had to do was follow their men. But when follow began to mean swallow, something else evolved.

Penny happily settled in with Gavin. But that didn't mean Gavin meant to settle down. He was in and out of town and in and out of other ladies' chambers, while Penny potted petunias. He brought more and more rowdy men over and chased more and more women as the months went by.

Jake drifted steadily toward the ideal of *Deliverance*. He wanted a life in which high society and city slickers couldn't disrupt him, in which Pam could be his happy Pocahontas. If Pam was to stick to Jake, she had to stick in the sticks. She had no chance to form her own cosmos. All she had was hanging on to his.

Behind Pam's and Penny's compliant demeanors, change began to happen, growth not in inches but in will. Like slowly rising water hindered by mighty dams, their new inclinations didn't burst out at first; they seeped through the cracks. The more Pam and Penny felt devoid of power, the more they discovered age-old female ways. They began to wage the battle of the sexes in guerrilla warfare.

At first Jake and Gavin didn't know the homestead had turned hostile. But somehow things just stopped working out their way. Then their women's resolve openly erupted. Jake's and Gavin's welcome mats covered mine fields. Bombs burst whenever they crossed the threshold. They could do no right.

In truth, Jake and Gavin had made only one mistake. But it was a big one. They forgot to foresee that "superior" versus "inferior" all too easily turns into oppressor versus oppressed. With Penny and Pam, age and cultural difference took on the colors of revolution. Their simple Doe Stalkers took on the roles of slavemaster and tyrant. Like time bombs on the shelf, Pam and Penny ticked off until they grew up and blew up. Pam threw her man out. Penny pushed hers into town, into the ground, then left. Each had seen the enemy—and he was *man*. The women were sexually radicalized and weren't about to defuse. Not for a long, long time.

Sometimes the Doe Stalker's a little crazy, sometimes evil, sometimes soulful, sometimes power packed. But he's always awesome, always sensual. Trouble is, the Doe Stalker isn't after the ones who have his number. He bedazzles the ones who don't. Learning to spot him doesn't always change the fact that you fall for him, but it does help you take the experience with a grain of salt.

How Can You Identify One?

The Doe Stalker plays a trump game with only one face card: He holds the mystery of the unknown male, the Jack of Spades or the Knave of Hearts. He suspects it's not too high, so he doesn't pull it on obvious queens or aces. Rather, he drops it on little deuces and treys.

Then he bluffs even himself. He puts his tastes down to desire instead of the desire for dominance. As a result, he usually takes a loss.

The Doe Stalker, like the Marlboro Man, is just a paper poster. He looks long and craggy, but he has no dimensions—he can't get thick with a woman of equal age, rank, and moxie. Whenever he walks into the great saloon of life to order a mate, he says, "Make mine sarsaparilla." That he can handle. But the heavier stuff? He's not so sure. It could be he's a loner because it's easier, because there's no one in the way. But one thing is for certain: When it comes to resistance, he's an all around side-stepper. Cities cow him. The rat race horrifies him. Being out of money and having secrets known terrify him. *Women* scare him. He covers it all pretty well. But he's fidgety.

Outer Signs

He cultivates a recluse image. Cowboy suits some; you can do a *lot* with hats, belts, and boots. Others go for the offbeat editor image, the eccentric writer, or the skittish star, rock or otherwise. Somehow or other, the Doe Stalker makes himself into a unique character. He has a definite but distinct maleness. He tends to be skinny and restless. Often he has a southern or western drawl he never quite loses. He's a little macho in style and looks, but not in talk. He doesn't *need* a line about male superiority. Quite the opposite; it just falls in place naturally for him.

He finds a profession where he can work more or less alone, or one where it's lonely at the top. But it has to have one added aspect. It has to attract groupies. He *loves* them. He has something they haven't, and they come to him.

He almost always looks older than he is. Even his dress reads "well aged." It may be his poncho, his wild grey hair, his old worn jeans. Somehow, old styles, old clothes, or old looks (which he accentuates, consciously or not) match his lankiness.

His act gets old as well; he's a repeater. As his relationships end, he wants to try again. After the last bitter taste, he goes for an even less resisting girl-child. The disparity in his coupling grows even larger with time: He gains in age against your youth, gains in power against your weakness.

He smokes. Or has smoked. Or *seems* like he should smoke. He drinks beer, tequila, or bourbon. Practically no sport interests him, except for individual sports. He may do martial arts or admire a good rodeo, but no teamwork for him. He has secrets. He doesn't like to be talked about, mostly because he carries on differently in the different aspects of his life and he wants no mixing. His behavior in bars differs from that at home; his sweet talk to women contrasts with his Businessman Billy-Goat Gruff. So he hides. And often he lies.

He prefers his transportation almost bizarre, definitely not your usual sort. When everyone else has a European car, he has a Jeep with Charlie Pride singing on the tape deck. Or an enormous station wagon (ranch-style). When the others go American, he has a battered old sloop-backed Saab. Or an ancient, unrestored Packard. Whatever he drives, it's a Lonermobile.

He likes folksy, ethnic stuff, items with roots. Blankets and quilts. Menorahs and mezuzahs. He finds comfort in the texture and flavor of a poor or distinct people, even if they aren't his people.

His home is usually somewhere removed; the Doe Stalker has trouble with cities, so he lives across the bridge, or at the very edge or out of town altogether. Sometimes he bounces between an urban and rural existence like a Ping-Pong ball. Almost every occupation compels him into the city, but much of his thinking focuses on finding a way to survive in the hills.

He doesn't really want to be a modern man. That's why he treats himself to fantasy and to situations that don't threaten his illusion. If he can't really live in another age, at least he can hedge around contemporary times, steel buildings, and enfranchised women. His nymph-chasing is more old-fashioned than you think—rather like a warlord's prerogative.

But the strain is hard on him; he doesn't always handle it well. He may have bouts when he overuses drugs or drink. He follows up with stringent periods off all chemical influence. He may be unpredictably taciturn, tactless, or prone to temper. He may offend people enough to gain some real adversaries.

Sex Signals

Women of his age and stage of life don't exactly admire him. Some become restrained friends to whom he consistently defends a man's point of view. But then, such female acquaintances must always contend with the smart of rejection, for he doesn't choose to tarry with them. Rather, he heads for the feather bed of the young, the docile, and the less knowledgeable. It's not just that he wants his woman dependent—he's into putty, not only passive but elastic.

Like the spider in the parlor, he usually has a web, an *advantage* that draws women to him. You find the Doe Stalker, for example, when you come as a student (he's a teacher), with material (he's an agent), as an admirer (he's a politician or performer), as a model (he's an artist). He invites you to meet the crew, to attend a party, to join the group. Then he suggests a drink or some such. He offers no frills or goodies, just a one-thing-leads-to-another approach. To his home and his bed. Eventually you become the woman he brings along.

He tackles you pretty quickly once alone. After all, he lusted for you from the minute you walked in the door. His penchant for young women, black women, white women, Asian women, sweet women comes across with a lot of eroticism. He's hot to trot. You're soon on his couch, floor, or office chair—even the carseat. And then to his big brass bed.

There he likes to take you and render you senseless. He likes to know a lot more than you. He's certainly not standoffish about showing his *Kama Sutra*. He's tour guide, you're tourist; he shows you the back roads. But he wants to *make* you have thrills instead of letting you have them.

At first he definitely gives more than he gets. But he uses sex for position in more ways than one—he hopes for a later recoup. He leads you to learn and like what *he* wants to do.

When he wants you in his playpen for keeps, he can be very good to you. In his own way, that is—when he's around. He does get attached to having you there—with your adhering to his ways and whims, of course. But he wants permanence without contention. He thinks silence means no fight, so he become a ready victim for manipulation. He even ends up giving in. He doesn't want to start from scratch and retrain someone again.

But usually he's also a chaser on the side. A very few Doe Stalkers are content with the baby at home; the majority are prone to poaching. Infidelity is almost a game for him. Most Doe Stalkers' women eventually do some of the same back. Bringing information about your affairs home is one way to backstab. And when you first have assignations, he's utterly dismayed. He's even more dumbfounded when you threaten total breakup. He pretends he'll change. But an ounce of persuasion is worth a pound of alteration to a Doe Stalker.

Money Markers

The Doe Stalker almost inevitably ends up footing the bills for your mutual keep. And for his other adventures, too. Little does don't usually have the earning power or income that he has. But even when they do, he handles the household budget. One thing a doe can do is withhold her own money. But he's never too sure how he feels about this arrangement: As part of his image he can't make too much fuss about supporting his woman, but he's not an easy giver, he's a silently grudging one. Beyond household expenses, he can be a bit tight with money. There's a limit to the flow. Clothes and paraphernalia come out of your own pocket.

He prefers to spend money on his stability. He likes to be unusual but not down and out. Running out of money strikes close to his panic level, so he never cuts totally free from the employment that binds him. He doesn't take too many monetary chances. He keeps his pennies if he can; they go toward his home, his bank account, and to pay for any children from past unions.

Family Aspects

When the subject of having babies comes up, the Doe Stalker says no. But that doesn't mean he won't get anyone pregnant; in fact, he often does. That's how he acquires progeny. He's ambivalent about children. He thinks they will slow him down and catch on to his number, but he wants descendants. So somehow he just slips up and has some. Once an accident is fact, he can face it.

Then, since he follows his masculine image, he becomes a strong father. Very male, reliant, protective. Especially when his daughter gets to the age he finds attractive, usually about five years younger than his present companion.

Most Doe Stalkers maintain good ties with their families. They don't break with parents, brothers, and sisters, no matter how much aggravation there is. The family is a unit, a little corporation. He likes the way it carries on in time, so he stays in touch.

And friends are very important to him—men friends, especially *similar* men friends. Sometimes he gets real raunchy with them. He may have them over a lot. He uses one vocabulary with men, another with women. When he's with his pals and a woman joins, the men become bullring competitors: They try to out-male each other for the female audience.

The Doe Stalker has great assets along with his liabilities. He imparts speedy lessons in life; he fulfills all those dreams of white knights and supermen, at least for a little while. He's an indulgence in fantasy. He can be a great first fling. But he doesn't have the flexibility toward your development that real love demands, and that's his failing.

What Is in Store for You?

Once you know the Doe Stalker's script, you can guess the end. In the final scene, after the Doe Stalker thinks it's all settled and going his way, some little Indian says to him, "What do you mean 'we,' white man?" It might be you.

The Doe Stalker's scheme always backfires one way or another. When he picks women with another ethnic background, he lets himself in for her society's ways. Each ethnic group has tactics only natives know, use, and expect. He doesn't understand them. When he chooses a young girl, he can hardly end up as anything but an obstruction to her growth.

If he didn't meet change with resistance, perhaps his pairing would last. But since he *does* resist, to a Doe Stalker's woman, evolution becomes revolution. Whenever you stretch your wings, he seems to be standing around with poultry shears. Breaking with him is almost like separation from your parents. You probably went from one to the other, or overlapped, so freedom from him symbolizes breach with them all.

What starts as the chamber of love winds up as a hotbed of devious aggression. Once you've seen King Kong's soft underbelly, you can oh-so-secretly attack from the passive position. Fussing begins. Nagging trickles in. You forget errands. You somehow arrive late, then later. You start rubbing salt in wounds and picking bones.

Maybe, just maybe, you follow him one night. Or you find a few phone numbers and call them. You appear where he is expected, but you are not. Some night on a dark street (not yours), you sabotage his steel-belted radials.

You start to do the same kinds of things he does. You lay down new rules. It's your house, too, by George. The boys and beer are out. You start leaving evidence of your sexual encounters. Inch by inch the big breakup comes; usually it's volatile by now. A friend, some emerging repugnance, or some book tells you that his carryings on are just plain unacceptable. Roles switch. He becomes innocent. "I don't know why she turned so vile on me," he wails. Which makes you even more angry. You think he knows how much he molded you. He hadn't seen it and is amazed. But not enough to learn.

Unfortunately, the aftermath of the Doe Stalker entails a lot of black bile and anger. An overlord overturned rarely receives your sweet forgiveness. And when you don't come back, he gets very mad and very hurt. Each of you feels an anger that often lasts for years.

What Are the Telltale Signs of Trouble?

The Doe Stalker's warning signs depend a lot on his and your physiques and circumstances.

I'm sorry to say that if you're young, sheltered, or nymphlike (small-bodied, small-breasted, with a woman-child air) or from certain cultural backgrounds, you'll have to be extra wary of the Doe Stalker. That's just the way it is. It's smart to recognize those to whom you'd be especially tasty. You don't have to get angry—just don't make it your *problem* and don't get exploited.

The next step is to learn the Doe Stalker's trail signs. Since you might lack an experienced eye, scout for these markers: When his age, skin color, facial features, mop of curls, or *something* is definitely different, it means be wary. Certainly if he says anything about opposites attracting, don't just nod in agreement. Consider taking another path.

A masculine, loner image should flash like a hunter's red vest. Note his approach. You go to him with some mission in mind, but somehow business turns to pleasure; he's one up on you.

Next he takes you as a tag-along. If you not only follow, but feel furry, remember there's an unequal status between him who holds the leash and her who follows it.

Reputation is one of your biggest warnings. He had to start somewhere. And it probably wasn't with you. Follow the clues. Ask about past relationships.

Once involved with the Doe Stalker, sooner or later you start to think about splitting his pen. Perhaps you've been doing things his way because you didn't have a way of your own. One day you realize that you had no say in the rules. Maybe what's going down begins to come up—his other women or the nights he spends away. If things no longer seem equitable or tolerable, you've reached your first critical turn; you're about to find out if he's going to like you full-fledged. If you're seething with resentment, it's time either to introduce plain speaking as your household language or to break camp. If you're about to exact revenge, it's better just to backpack away.

What Are the Chances?

If the Doe Stalker is stalking you, should you (a) run from him, (b) flirt with him only to flee from him, or (c) fight for him? Considering how much you'll change and how little he will, I'd say go for (a) or (b).

In the first place, if you really *are* very young, run far away from the Doe Stalker, for you can experience serious injury in very fragile areas. I personally think men who chase teen or younger tail ought to go to jail. And I've heard every justification about "modern teenagers and their sophistication." I find both the excuses and the excusers repugnant.

But for you of age, you on your own, consider how you want your Venus to climb off her half shell. With Adonis or Lazarus? There exist any number of ways to grow into maturity, independence, and self assertion. The Doe Stalker simply is not the greatest of them. He prolongs the child in you in some ways and causes you to skip your youth in others. He postpones your individualization and renders you younger than you should be at a later date, and yet at first he deprives you of experiencing emerging adulthood as you would with a mate your own age. You take on a bogus age to match his.

He *is* one way to grow up, and he often looks like a good one. Certainly he imparts enormous experience. He's sensual, assured; he propels you. But remember, there's a catch to solutions (b) and (c). Due to inexperience, immaturity, and lack of awareness, most women who take up with him are unconscious of what they are doing. Even what looks like a one-night frolic can affect you adversely. You might go through a blind passage in which you can't see yourself. Only once outside and looking behind you do the events that transpired become clear.

If love leads you and you get involved, try to do him for the right reasons. Be sure that you have a sense of yourself and little desire to wind up a victim. Don't dally one day longer than the first day you feel abused. When you discover he wanted only a passive or childlike quality, try to have your feet firmly on the ground. Look at it rationally—you can't stay a nymphet forever. And you shouldn't, either: Maintaining your baby face into advancing age or remaining submissive to your detriment can lead you into massive insecurity and a huge life crisis. Recognize that change will come and get ready for it.

One final thing: If you've been with a long-term mate (probably you hitched up young) who turns into a Doe Stalker, consider a quick, blunt walk-out. Worries about inexperience, a sheltered existence, children, and so on can detain you for years, but the situation rarely improves. Jaded sophistication leads nowhere. Let the satyr go stag and get into the thicket with someone else.

Where Do You Fit In?

It's hard, but it's possible—you *can* be a baby doe more than one time over. When you do the Doe Stalker once or more, you might want to wonder why.

Could be you nurture a touch of toddlerhood that's tough to eradicate. You want someone to do it for you. You hover between walking on your own and wanting to get picked up. You want someone to make your decisions, break your trail, raise you, praise

you. Someone to take your chances and make your mistakes—then get
the blame for the blunders.

But in real life no one can make the breaks for you or suffer the
consequences. Even the Doe Stalker dishes out a brand of growth and
a type of growing pain. Maybe he can protect you from *you*. But who is
going to protect you from *him?*

Men are not heroes, or gods, or gauchos. Perhaps you expect a man
to be superhuman, to notice your every anger, hurt, or dislike; you
think he should see without being shown, hear without being told. But
no one else can look through your eyes, and no one can read your mind.
Particularly if you docilely pretend nothing is going on.

Men are just like regular people. Sometimes they're sensitive,
sometimes not. Sometimes they're super and sometimes they're lesser.
Sometimes they do right and sometimes they do wrong. So you might
as well go for one who admits it right from the start.

Still if you did one Doe Stalker in naïveté and found he didn't suit,
don't blame yourself or him, but consider one thing. Living alone into
and through your twenties has definite advantages. Everyone needs
time, space, and an empty place in order to find herself. You only
learn to know yourself by living with *you*. The sooner you start, the
faster you get there. It's hard, but there's nothing in the world like it.
There's no other way to get over the "alone is lonely" syndrome. To
discover that alone is *not* lonely is a good lesson to get under your belt
early.

Notes and Particulars

6/ The Gay Man Type One—Intimacy Except For . . .

Related Types: The Instant Barricader
Intimate Type One—The Loving
Polymorph
The Gay Man Type Two—You
Won't Meet One Anyway . . .

Positivity Scale: + + − −

Oh, the wheels are ever turning. What was out is now in. What was pariah is now persona. What was outcast is now typecast. He's gay. And he's everywhere.

So many men now dare to be homosexual, they've achieved the respectability of becoming ho hum. They may think they're unusual, but as eccentricities go, theirs are mighty conventional. Still, gay men are still men, and they're often good ones.

Accepting that you'll never be his number one chum, why not make the best of him? The Gay Man offers plenty of the best. When he likes women, he's a great pal. Perhaps being oppressed sensitized him. His childhood probably wasn't all easy, nor is his current life. His psyche propels him to another wavelength. At any rate, he's often closer than a heterosexual to the middle of that strange emotional spectrum between men and women. That means better contact for you, and less misconception. He is miles ahead on empathy and three fathoms deeper on sympathy. He makes an easy, warm, and intimate friend. A companion when you are alone. An enthusiast when you want to talk about opera, a gourmet when you want to try new food, a peaceful presence when you want to sit around silently. Sometimes he is more like you than you are. And he has one other advantage—he knows what it's like to deal with men. But, as for a paramour: He doesn't come up to requisite snuff. So there's one key to a relationship with your local gay—look for a friend, cultivate not a mate.

Story

I have known some women so taken with the companionship of Gay Man Type Ones that they overplayed their hands. They accentuated the negative, eliminated the positive, and came out with nothing in between. For example, take Vivian.

Vivian met Chris while visiting Paris. Talk about a born companion! They instantly formed a club, the membership limited to two. Together they toured the city, thrived on the joy of their fraternity. But with a certain limit: Chris was homosexual, Vivian was not. Nonetheless, when Vivian returned to San Francisco, Chris soon followed.

Vivian was a native San Franciscan. She grew up the only child of a well-established family; her impresario father ran his clan as he ran his business. Vivian never felt she quite came up to her father's fierce expectations. Without her knowing it, he scared her off. As an adult, she leaned toward men of a totally different nature.

Chris was not the first gay man Vivian had found attractive. As a teenager, she got a crush on a young man in her father's office. When he confessed just exactly *how* he "roomed" with his roommate, she covered her shock (and disappointment) with a sophisticated approach—she attempted to rise above prejudice about people's sexual preference. In no time at all, she discovered a lot more homosexual men than she ever knew existed. In fact, she seemed to attract them. She lived among the wealthy and stylish, had lots of social connections to the art and theater world, where gay men flourish. She forever attended openings, parties, and events with a clique of similar celebrants. And she was great at witty repartee.

But sexually, she was thoroughly straight arrow, or so she thought. Behind those opera glasses lurked one conventional lady. Still, despite auspicious beginnings, no men pursued her. In response, she developed protection, covered her anguish with good one-liners, a worldly flair, and a phalanx of pals of both sexes, the males largely preferring other males. She may have wanted, but managed not to need, a lover of her own.

Chris was her most constant squire. He was always available (at least after noon and until midnight). He willingly ran about town as her escort and confidant. He knew her and her friends so well, they could gossip like jaybirds or say nothing at all. They shared continuing sagas of his latest fiasco at the baths or her latest mad artist who never called. They hugged a lot, held hands, and even slept in the same bed—upon occasion.

One day, Vivian decided to bridge the one remaining gap to Chris. He had openly hinted at having intercourse before, but only when Vivian was safely involved in a solidly heterosexual infatuation. Chris encouraged sensuality and enjoyed a Romeo role, so Vivian took up the idea of sex for real.

Chris was taken aback. After all, she *knew* he only slept with men. He liked cruising and discos! And while he often complained, he actually cherished his late-hours life with ships-in-the-night encounters. Vivian was just a safe, sisterly traveler, a friend, never a potential lover. He just liked to add a dash of flirtation and thought she understood.

Vivian felt rejected, dismayed, and foolish. Chris drew back, insulted and threatened. Their friendship foundered. Each had breached a tacit agreement—Chris when he had proposed a playful idea he never really intended to carry through, Vivian when she had tried to alter a condition she pretended hadn't mattered.

A cold, awkward separation resulted. Suddenly left without her main man, Vivian saw the light: For a constant companion, she had chosen a man with whom the ultimate intimacy was never forthcoming. She had spent all her time with people who couldn't meet all her needs. She had smoothly avoided the hard times of a full-blown male-and-female relationship. Vivian decided to coordinate her actions and desires. If she didn't want a total male-and-female union, she was O.K. the way she was. If she did, she would have to try to find it. Either was acceptable. She came to grips with the fact that she was a very sexual person. She started to travel alone. Suddenly, opportunities blossomed. She no longer put men off with her gay bodyguard.

Meanwhile, Chris did some honest thinking, too. He learned to accept his own homosexuality without heterosexual titillations. Vivian and Chris reestablished their fine friendship. But as back-pocket pals and not social shields.

Obviously, nonhappenings as well as happenings indicate when Gay Man Type Ones are on the scene. You have the choice of making friends or not; first, you have to know if whether or not a person is gay is any skin off your nose. If not, it's go, the best of both worlds, for you can have the cake of homosexual friends and the eats of heterosexual ones too.

How Can You Identify One?

Spotting the Gay Man Type One—Intimacy Except For . . . isn't *too* hard. Just use geography, topography, and choreography. You see, birds of a feather stick together, often wear the same plumage, share the same habits, and frequent the same bars. If anyone has denominators in common, he has. That's what "homo" means.

The Gay Man Type One is often a mockingbird. His dress is standardized, his circulation circumscribed, and his circumference often circumcised. It's a better mating game when all show identifiable tail feathers. And the size and shape of that tail hold a lot of significance.

He even has one key characteristic: He's preoccupied with his personal life. Romance and encounters take up much of his time, most of his energy, most of his happiness as well. It's not that he doesn't have other interests. But private life is primary; the rest he remainders or at best gives second rating on his scale of attention.

His life often wears him thin—a trait he considers *essential*. He tends towards dissipation, smokes and drinks too much. He's low on energy, gets sick a lot. He's a bit of a fickle fowl. Since he follows the path of individual, subjective experience, his quest defies pinning down, his quarry varies. He samples and moves on, relishes diverse places and things, mostly people. He nestles down only to fly the coop again.

Outer Signs

At the moment you can usually find the Gay Man Type One flying in one of two formations. One subspecies leans toward continental coloration—he's a caged canary, tied to the city. You find him wearing tight French-cut pants (with aubergine bikini shorts beneath). His shirts are sheer and silky with *very* narrow collars, cut to hug his body down to the ribs. He saunters about in soft cordovan loafers without socks, sports a bracelet or necklace. His hair is scissor cut and fluffs about the ears. "A friend of a friend" styles it. At least once in his life, he tries altering his hair color. But his skintone knows all and tells all. The continental type moves in fast circles. He's into what's hip, who's in *Who's Who*. He's a social climber, a people collector, and a name dropper. He knows the pecking order of fame and class in any particular territory, sometimes in French and Italian. He cruises world capitals if he can.

The other Gay Man Type One lives more woodpeckeresque. Country casual. Button-fly denim Levi's with white jockey shorts—or nothing—beneath. Pendleton plaid flannel shirts he alternates with corduroy or T-shirts bearing the names of restaurants like Kiss My Cookies or The Cat Got Your Tongue. His boots, square-toed cowboy or with hooks for lacing. His hair is *very* short and trimmed like a hedge. This subspecies is more prone to stay home than the continental: He takes a lot of naps. He'd rather receive visitors than go out. He's a little softer, cuddlier, less high flying.

Both types are very affectionate, and both are very, very tidy. One style or the other, the Gay Man Type One lovingly fills his nest with bits and pieces, bric-a-brac, and heirlooms till it looks like an aviary display case. He's domestic. Even when he's renting a room, he decorates it. And can he cook! He brings home exotic things from afar to delight his fancy. He wants his place light and airy. He likes high ceilings and lots of Boston ferns and philodendrons. As he possesses a green thumb that works like magic, his houseplants exude utter happiness. The Gay Man Type One often shares his house, has a roommate or a separate room for roommates, one-night and other-wise. He might live in someone else's place as a housemate or house-sitter. The Gay Man Type One usually likes company.

However he shares his space, he lives in his ecozone: Where the town turns gay, that's where he's gathered. His section is almost rundown, almost old, and almost historical—Deteriorated Ritzy. But gay men give the neighborhood a special renaissance. They cause a mushrooming of cafés and activity—starting from brunch on, but not breakfast. In such places, you'll find the crowd rather homogeneous.

While nest is important, wheels are not. The Gay Man Type One doesn't much care what kind of car he has as long as it gets around, though he tends to like little ones. He doesn't get attached to his cars; he acquires them from friends and passes them on to others. He doesn't even keep them especially clean. Cars seem like so much trouble, he'd rather walk or take the bus. Or better yet, get someone to pick him up—someone cute, hopefully.

He loves restaurants, art galleries, and concerts. He likes the baths, but he doesn't always go to the gym. For exercise, he prefers to chin himself on a bar in the doorway or do ten minutes of yoga stretches, not to jog. And tennis is not usually his favorite kind of ball. Still, he's obsessed with weight, tries to stay boyishly thin as long as possible. When that thirties "fill-in" begins, he's anguished, and suddenly, the diet begins. But a not too consistent one, and rarely one excluding liquid libation of the spirit persuasion. Any temptation, and he's all too eager to roll off the wagon. In fact, what's truly erratic about the Gay Man Type One is his self-care: He can be stringent, he can go on binges; he can work hard and still go out all night; he can do nothing and still get weary. In seconds, he can swing from immobility to peak activity. He can overdo and overdose, undereat and underachieve. He gets hepatitis and multiple colds (plus other communicable diseases). But none of this makes him lead a more regular life; it just leads him to try mysticism, health foods, hot toddies, or to grow a little more fussy.

Sex Signals

He prefers women along the same lines as his choice of theater: He likes those who have an interesting act that gives him stories to tell. He leans toward the lively, the witty, the jaded, the crazy; always toward a lady marked by elegance or oddity, depth or brassiness. Usually, if he hits it off, he does so instantly, then loves you for life. By the second meeting, his relationship with a lady friend becomes a movable feast of fun, food, companionship and commiseration, symphony and sympathy. It seems he's known you for a thousand years.

You'll treat each other like kindred spirits, a little like blood kin—kissing cousins. The friendship is charged with a certain sexuality: You both act as if incest would be interesting but never quite broach the subject. There's an invisible line, approached and avoided, between you. While physical affections abound, gestures stop short of carnality. You can bill and coo together, but you can never lay an egg. You can flirt and flatter but can't probe or penetrate. If you ever cross the line and the touch becomes too much, a shock wave usually repels one party or the other.

Money Markers

It's easy to see how the Gay Man Type One spends his money—for personal indulgence. And that's how he pursues his education, too—to make life more pleasurable. Some Gay Men Type One live on inheritances, aid, or unemployment. Some have moderate to fabulous incomes from jobs in education, industry, entertainment, fashion, real estate, graphics, or publishing. Certain members rule the art world; some live off others. But wherever he gets it, money usually runs through the Gay Man Type One's hands faster than he ever expects. He so incessantly spends on little luxuries, he finds himself short for the big, though he usually manages to hustle up the cash for them somehow. He spends for his senses, his entertainment, and his friends. Funds flow so rapidly in his community, it's hard to tell who's buying and who's selling. Never has a group of people been more ready to utilize each other's money. If you can get an income without much labor or from freelance esoterics, you're a much admired member of the clan.

With women, he and you give and take hospitality with no tabs kept. Every now and then, you split the bill, or each shows up with part of the fare; when he's flush, he pays for you. Still, if you have the money and feel the spirit, he uses your capital easily when in your company, but usually not when you're apart.

Family Aspects

The ties that hold him to his family are strange and strong. Sometimes his parents and siblings know his romantic preference; sometimes they don't. In either case, he's extremely protective of them. He even safeguards the way he makes them face the truth about him. He considers himself enough of an outlaw in his choice of mates, so he's usually willing to be a good boy for others. He idolizes his sister, tolerates his brother, thinks of his father as sweet, his mother as complex. He forgives them, even if they don't always quite forgive him.

He usually loves children. He's more than happy to play uncle to any babies around. He'll even live in homes with children, especially with single mothers. Still, he's glad the children are *yours*. He'll seek them out, keep them company, relieve you of them, but he's happy when they're gone. He has the qualities that make a wonderful teacher, which he often is. He'd never hurt a hair of a child's head.

He's an ideal man in many ways, except for that one drawback—no sex with you. And it can be a big one. Whatever's the secret of sexual intimacy, most women prefer it over one hundred other kinds.

He does have most of the assets of a fantastic friend: He's there when it counts; he knows you and what you're thinking and feeling; even when he doesn't sympathize, he listens. He is, after all, interested in people. But often, he'd rather be with someone else. He's looking for love, too, and not with you.

What Is in Store for You?

The real issue with a Gay Man Type One is not what's in store for you, it's what's *not* in store. In short, a relationship with the Gay Man Type One is a bit like a Steady-State Universe—beginning, middle, and end about the same. No big bang at the start. No violent finale at the end. At most, an exhaustion of energy. When you take male and female and remove the tension, the wire goes from tight to slack. Compared to heterosexual types of men (the ones that serve up all the courses, from soup to nuts, for you), the Gay Man Who Likes Women is a veritable Rolaid and perhaps should be used as such. He spells r-e-l-i-e-f; he soothes. But he's no final remedy; removing symptoms rarely cures. What you probably need is some of him and some of someone else. For the very best of prescriptions take a Gay Man Type One and a heterosexual union as well.

A good Gay Man Type One relationship provides a deep friendship in which both lead very separate lives. Once you establish a link, the only alteration comes from what your other involvements bring. The long-term Gay Man Type One pairing generally lacks distinct stages; it bears a lethargic drift. But while quantity of company diminishes, the quality remains the same. And yet special problems set in with a

Gay Man Type One after a while. It's hard to think up something *new* to do. When you feel like soul mates right from the beginning (added to the knowledge of where things will never lead), it's sometimes easier to shut down than add stimulation. Since you do things *with* and not *to* one another, you can slide into doing nothing or spending a lot of time thinking up what to do. One says, "What do you want to do?"; the other answers, "I don't know. What do you want to do?"—until it's your ritual. Or you collapse on old standbys—like eating, drinking, going to old movies or the same old gatherings.

Strangely, even the old reliance bears a one-sided nature. More often than not, you two use your acquaintance to cheer each other up, not to grow maudlin. There seems to be a rule against acting agonized in unison. But while good cheer can be comforting, it can also cover up avoiding the issues. Be wary of excessive dependence on your gay friend. As much as you love him, he *can* impede your progress and you his. Sooner or later, due to your romances or his, your new curiosities or his, you might drift apart, but not forever: Call out his name, and he'll be there. You've got a friend.

What Are the Telltale Signs of Trouble?

No matter which way you're coming, the Gay Man Type One gives you ready warning. In certain places, it's become the practice to consider any well-groomed man gay until he proves otherwise. You don't need binoculars to tell the Gay Man Type One by dress and habits. You can certainly decipher his coming-and-going patterns— usually with a number of the same gender. He frequents places where the female half of the population is scarcely represented, spends an inordinate amount of time with his "roommate" and male buddies. Sometimes they wear each other's clothing; they seem all to wear the same size.

And of course, there's another way to peg him; you could call it the "gestures in absentia" method. Usually there's little doubt when a man desires women sexually: You can hear, see, and feel him telling and asking. With the Gay Man Type One, the onslaught never happens. He's close, but not *too* close. His kisses are self-conscious. If you touch him by surprise, he jumps back.

Sometimes the identification problems don't exist—He tells you before you guess. Haut moderne gay men often detail not only that they're homosexual but when and how and why it happened. When you're out together his eyes move around the same half of the crowd that yours do—the half that's got pants on and shaves. Only you eyeball from top down, and he goes from bottom up, lingering at a certain point halfway up.

Though misreading him may bring disappointment or exasperation, the real warnings you need to heed are not what the relationship is, but how you are using it. Beware crossing that line where both he and you can need each other too much. Keep uses and abuses straight from the beginning. The Gay Man Type One is very aware of energy drain; he's a little selfish and fearful of attachments even in his love affairs, so when a woman soaks up time, he tends to run and hide. And if he's leading you to think options are open when they really aren't, he's setting you up for fall person. He may be proving to himself once more that he's gay, or he may need a cover story. I'd call him on it.

And note still other points. Sometimes, the continental Gay Man Type One might be seeking you out for social position or money. You should be wary of him. All friendship has some use involved. Some kinds may be all right by you, some may not. And it's equally problematic when you use him. You may desperately need entrée, frivolity, or someone to hang on. And his closeness leads you to lean his way. If you're keeping company to the detriment of a more satisfactory relationship, you're working for your own self-defeat.

What Are the Chances?

Very occasionally a Gay Man Type One turns heterosexual, but only *very* occasionally. Currently the opposite switch seems more common. By and large, when it comes to sex, people have a favorite flavor and they stick to it. That's not to say that homosexuals haven't tried the opposite sex, or heterosexuals haven't tried out their own, or that some people aren't just plain bisexual. But most individuals show a strong inclination one way or the other.

If you have a man who has affairs with men, you'd better decide if his gyrations are within your emotional scope. You can bury agitation and feign approval, but if you find yourself saying about your relationship "It's O.K." as opposed to "It's great," cancel your endorsement and close your account. Everybody deserves the whole works—sex, love, and attention. And sexual rejection is the worst kind.

When a man is solely gay and you are solely straight, I advise that you need neither fight nor flee; just keep your fingers out of the ointment. Look for a best friend, not a lover. Rather than refuse the relationship, use it, but use it properly. The Gay Man Type One is an elective, not a requirement. He's best as an enhancement to your other essentials. His material is delicate, so don't abuse it. Apply yourself carefully; hang loose to hold the most. Let your gay friend lead his own life. You get the best of it if you don't ask for too much time, attention, or sexual interaction. Prize your intimacy with him; don't overburden his natural sympathy. If you unload problems too much, he'll need to cut free.

Some women flee from gay men or pay them little heed, feeling homosexual men divert them from their own potential coupling. Some working women prefer gay men because love affairs cause too much interference on the job or because they want companions but not sex. Some mated women find gay men the best males to befriend. Each of these reasons is fine, if it suits your needs. Probably no other relationship with a man offers such flexibility in matching what you need from it, except for carnal coupling.

If you seek a heterosexual mate and haven't got one, keeping to a low quota of Gay Man Type Ones is simply pragmatic, but don't totally dismiss homosexuals. Killing off one kind of male/female pairing doesn't promote the growth of others. Shunning any variety of friend can take away from your own scope and potential: You *can* play all possibilities if you keep the forms in balance.

Where Do You Fit In?

So what happened? You look around and discover that you've culled more than two or three or four homosexual friends. You've signed on a regular bevy! Or maybe you've surrounded yourself with just one who's so intense he *seems* like a swarm. In the meantime, your nest is empty.

Sometimes the Gay Man Type One can become an albatross. In his company, you parody male/female harmonies, but never sing the Song of Solomon. You're due to examine yourself if for one reason or another you're avoiding a serious link-up with a man. Perhaps you're an Instant Barricader yourself. Behind an abundance of Gay Men Type One in your life may lie fear of sex, fear of tyranny, or fear of another broken heart. Sure, it's entirely possible for you to discover that you simply don't *like* sex, that you want autonomy to the point that any permanent romance would equal forfeit, or that you find one experience with love more than enough forever. That's fine. But if the cause is indeed fear, perhaps you might want to consider conquering it and taking new steps.

If you want to like sex and can't, many avenues for help exist. If you open up to some expertise, you'll find others have worked through similar problems. Sex *can* often seem like an ordeal by fire; you worry so much if the ice maiden will ever come that facing even the possibility of bed becomes torture. What you may not know is that sexual confidence takes *years* to gain, a fact that most sexual propaganda neglects to state. You have a right to give yourself plenty of time and seek out the right situations, no matter how many turn-downs it takes.

The compromises involved in permanent relationships seem like surrender to many. Indeed, many men are petty despots towards their mates, but a union doesn't *have* to be that way. To assume so is flagrant overgeneralization. Usually when you see any alliance with a man as slavery, the real tyrant is in your head. He's twisted from some male figure in your past, or he stems from a family where the men were always dominant and the women submissive. Rather than live a life haunted by old ghosts, try to be here and now and construct something different. Purge the boogeyman within to find a better man outside.

If you had a broken love experience in the past, realize that, especially with present odds, a broken relationship may be a lost battle, but it's certainly not the whole war. It's nice to have wanted one man to love forever, but very few people achieve that any more. And maybe some of the ones who do shouldn't have—complacency can kill empathy. Rather than hide, muster your courage and try, try again.

If a chaste life holds little reward for you, don't be a dodo: Remember a cock in the hand is worth two in the baths. And you *may* become one of the fortunate ladies who can enjoy *men*—both gay and straight!

Notes and Particulars

7/ The Intensely Intimate (But Crazy)

Related Types: The Disaster Broker
The Courtier
The Amoral Passion Monger

Positivity Scale: + + − −

He's a reverie. He's a nightmare. All for guess who? *You.* You know you've been had from the first look into his eyes. Or rather, his first charge into yours.

When you return from a night out with the Intensely Intimate (But Crazy) you feel feverish, exhausted, as if you've been through the heavy soil cycle in a Maytag. And it's *great.* He's so . . . there. He notices the changes in your eyes and moods, keeps tracks of your strong points and your weak spots, your appetites and dislikes. He wants to soak them up. Watch them. Appreciate them. He has a marvelous vocabulary of affectionate gestures. He calls you by a pet name, concentrates on what you say, joins in when you tease. He's silly with you, wise to you. He seems as if he has perfect insight. He turns you inside out.

But here's the rub: He's intense in other parts of his life too, fused into his own mind. He walks the line between genius and craziness. So everything he does is both idiosyncratic and extreme. Done without relief. To the hilt. He plunges as deeply into thoughts, music, oceans, crime, or drugs as into you. Either he wants to be with you incessantly or else he leads a crazy double life. When he's with you, he's obsessive, you're obsessed; he is so with you. But when he's gone, he's *so* gone. You *know* he has another woman, is leading a life of crime, is in the underground, or something equally grave.

He tends to choose intense women, too: either distractingly cerebral, vivacious, or explosive, but deep. Or he gathers turbulently dependent women who are despondent, perhaps attempt suicide, or have other crises. It's not unlikely he has one of each sort. The Intensely Intimate (But Crazy) almost always has another woman. He wants another soul to explore (temporarily). Or he wants another full-time bond, as involving as yours, in which to struggle.

Often his women are opposites: one blonde, one dark; one frantically energetic, one hardly moving; one vital and verbal, one ponderous and petulant. Extremes fit him. He's black and white, on or off. He wears no shades of grey.

Story

Everything my friend Caroline does she does to perfection, though she claims to be riddled with indecision. A visible passion marks her life. Perhaps that's why she has a penchant for the Intensely Intimate (But Crazy). He meets her standard of how grand a love affair should be.

From the start, she always has a glimmer that such a furious fusion will be a disaster. Then she forgets and plunges into the emotional whirlpool the Intensely Intimate (But Crazy) creates. She fell head over heels for one man in particular—Kevin. Their involvement lasted for years.

Kevin zapped Caroline from the first minute they met. He wasn't especially handsome, tall, suave, or anything else that would normally call attention. He was simply *electric;* his first look seemed to go right through her. And Caroline's nerve endings leaped to attention.

Soon they knew each other so thoroughly the world seemed to contain only the two of them. They had names, phrases, and gestures only they used, games only they played. They read each other's minds. They were braille to each other's fingertips. Life became steps in a private dance. They'd break into one another's houses and leave notes. Gifts that appeared bizarre to anyone else had secret innuendos for them. Their love became narcotic for Caroline. No one but Kevin seemed to exist. After a time she could hardly function without him.

Yet he was *gone* a lot. They never really lived together. He always had some place of his own to go to. He said he wasn't prepared for total involvement. He had to have his independence; he'd call when he wanted, be there when he wanted, and she'd have to wait.

His own place was a one-room hovel where he burrowed, his clothes heaped in piles, his bed always without sheets. Books and music lay scattered around.

One day, another woman called. She too went with Kevin, she said. And Caroline should know they were very, *very* involved. Kevin confessed. But the other affair didn't hold the same significance, he said. The other woman needed him, he said, and he couldn't leave as he feared what she would do. Deep down, Caroline knew he liked the triangle. Other women popped up, without warning. Kevin would lie, yet somehow his escapades always became known. Unwittingly, women came to the door looking for him. One was pregnant, one had venereal disease.

Then one day a different kind of call: vice squad men and gunmen were both after Kevin. He fled. He was only trying to make money, he said. But since he loved only intense situations, his deals had been dangerous and his partners unscrupulous.

Enough was enough. Caroline knew she had to grasp control of her existence. She was thinking about Kevin night and day. She lived constantly through *him,* not herself. He exhausted her without promising any returns. She began to pick up her pieces. She went away.

Kevin lingered in her mind a long time. She missed the rapt tête-à-têtes, longed for the engrossment, but she had a very stable streak. She liked the freshness of a simple life, didn't want to be crazy. And slowly, her passion for Kevin died.

Indeed, the Intensely Intimate (But Crazy) makes a better recollection than a daily diet. Some women figure him out fast and lock their doors. But to others, he's that "once-in-a-lifetime experience."

How Can You Identify One?

Think of the Intensely Intimate (But Crazy) as a pole vaulter in the sexual Olympics. He leaps before you look. He's there inside your skin before you know it, and he's headed for your inner sanctum.

When you piece together all the parts of his behavior, you wind up with something not unlike a spontaneous combustion engine. He spends energy. He consumes every ounce he gets. Even his skin looks as if he's drained his vitality away. His hair has no spunk left to do anything but lie there. In some ways, the Intensely Intimate (But Crazy) is reminiscent of a creature from a faraway planet with a dying sun who comes seeking thriving environments and to absorb new humanoids.

He doesn't prepare for the future or dwell in the past. He's *now*. Whatever he does he *does* with an active verb: He penetrates. He expends. He dances. He wears things out: people, places, clothes, machines, precepts, and you.

He treads close to the Disaster Broker. But he doesn't invite crisis. Rather, crisis beckons to *him*. He's prone to his own demise. If the police don't arrest him, his thoughts do. If death doesn't claim him, dissipation does. If he doesn't end up at a mental hospital, he lives in fear that he will.

Outer Signs

An air of exhaustion hangs about the Intensely Intimate. He has bad breathing habits. He exhales more than he inhales. He probably smokes. His head, sometimes his whole body, leans forward with an air of preoccupation. He forgets to eat and frazzles himself down to the bone. He walks a tightrope. He looks as if energy leaks right out of his pores. He strains his eyes, which grow dark circles. He rubs his eyesockets with his fingers and fists. He needs glasses and uses eyedrops. He looks a little shiny and transparent, even when just out of the shower.

He's not a careful dresser. His style is camouflage, to blend in anywhere, without dashikis and leather pants. He prefers you in the same sort of clothes—simplicity, jeans, jumpers. He likes the brilliants of soul, not silk. Why draw attention to your private tea party?

He's a user. He can render a coat elbowless in no time, reduce jeans to ravels in a fortnight, scuff his brown Oxford shoes instantly. His heels wear as thin as a crêpe; his soles flap. His shirttails fall haphazardly about.

You don't love him for his sense of dress, nor for his looks. If he's good-looking, he doesn't notice. And if you do, he denies it. His style lies in the elegance of his nearness. You seem to be the only object of art that he desires.

One thing is for sure. He has a place of his own, although he's rarely in it. He's idiosyncratic, a loner. He's not the roommate sort. He only wants togetherness of a furious kind. His sheets don't match, if he has any. His books are scattered, and he throws all their jackets away. His place isn't meant for comfort. The bed doesn't quite fit in the alcove. He has little or no furniture. The part of town he burrows in doesn't much matter to him, but he likes depressed and scruffy areas best.

His car hardly matters either. He purchases almost any kind as long as it's secondhand, then uses it till it falls apart. It's always battered. Terry towels cover great holes in the upholstery. The tires could be used for the "One of These Things Is Not Like the Others" game on *Sesame Street*. One door is a different color, too.

Obviously the Intensely Intimate (But Crazy) doesn't treat himself very well. That is, if you judge by exteriors. He treats his inner self a bit better, following his passions with a vengeance. He's like a child whose parents have bought a candy store. He can't learn to feed on treats slowly. He'll risk malnutrition rather than lead a meat-and-potatoes life.

Sex Signals

As for women, he picks bittersweet chocolate types with something heady about them. An extreme flavor is necessary to sate his palate. Once he likes a woman's spice, he wants to devour it. What intrigues him are women who mirror him, women who are, somehow, overly *keen*. Looks, elegance, and flair seem to have little to do with it. But once he spots you, he hovers around. No longer do you breathe oxygen, you inhale his presence. No longer do you exist isolated within the shell of your skin. There is somebody in there with you.

Sex is one part of you he *must* know. He is the ultimate in intimacy. Lovemaking with him takes a long time. It moves from rug to bathtub to bed, a feast of places, of twists and turns, of straight in and to the depths. He looks into your eyes. He wants to hold your head, wants your ears and mouth, wants to share *thoughts*. Sex becomes a song you continuously sing to each other. When the two of you are together, you always smell as if sex has just occurred, everything about you moist and warm. He leaves phallic, funny gifts you learn to open alone. The woman he loves would leave Eden willingly.

He may not mean to victimize his women, but he does. He certainly dominates the relationship. You are the fatted calf, he the devouring lion.

Money Markers

Money is the Intensely Intimate (But Crazy)'s foible. He doesn't seem to know how to get it. Or how to hold onto it. Or exactly *how* he spends it. Perhaps it's a fuel for his madness. He almost always manages to use or lose every penny. Mostly, he doesn't *care* about money.

You almost always have more money than he does. But he hesitates to spend yours. He wants to spend you, not your cash. And yet he resents being broke. He refuses to solve monetary problems by normal means, but hatches schemes. He'll try to free-lance a wild idea, take a crazy job, or make a fetish of a nonmaterial life.

Family Aspects

The Intensely Intimate (But Crazy) man is often angry with his family or pities them, but he can't break with them. He tends to be the oldest child and has never figured out his mother's love and what to do about her. He's secretive. His parents don't know how he lives. He knows he differs from them, and he thinks he differs from his brothers and sisters as well. But still he idolizes his siblings, not understanding how he achieved such a different character from theirs. He's an alien invader, perhaps a genetic mishap or a secret adoption, and no one will tell him the truth. He puts himself through visits with his family that he considers unbearable.

He doesn't really want children; they terrify him. But often, during his passionate involvements, one is conceived. By accident. An embryo catches him between the devil and his deep blue guilt. The odds on your terminating a pregnancy are fifty-fifty. If by some incredible chance he becomes a father, he's an intense and close one.

An Intensely Intimate (But Crazy) selects pals as odd as himself, mostly men, some women, as long as they burn equally brightly. His companions run from priests to criminals, geniuses to gamblers, but they're solid friends. They need one another. They may be separate from his love affairs and they may not.

*   *   *

The Intensely Intimate (But Crazy) is an angel and a monster. A delight and a disaster. Those not involved with him consider him a crazy, a loser, or at best, peculiar. But those involved with him dote on him; they can't do anything else but be his playmate. He takes them into time-warps. There's no avoiding him when he's around, no reading of detective stories, no T.V.

What Is in Store for You?

Have you ever heard of Space Mountain? It's the ride of a lifetime at Disneyland—a roller coaster that runs in the dark. The Intensely Intimate (But Crazy) is similar to Space Mountain. The ride entails thrilling climbs, devastating dips, bloodcurdling curves. You never know where you are; all is a breathtaking rush. Then, somewhere in the middle, hides a big loop back. After that, more swoops, rattles, bangs, and crashes, still speedy, but lower down.

Suddenly, it's over. It always seems abrupt, even though you know the end is coming. And somehow, you wind up pretty close to where you started.

Part of the thrill is that edge of potential calamity. Might a car careen off the tracks? An occasional person get bashed or broken? Might you fly right out into thin air? Getting off is really hard. Staying on is really unhealthy.

But there is one major difference between Space Mountain and the Intensely Intimate (But Crazy)—Disneyland advises those with weak hearts not to chance it, but the world does not so clearly forewarn you about the Intensely Intimate (But Crazy). The real trick isn't spotting him. It's getting away on two firm feet. You can hardly tell you've started with him until one foot's already gone.

The uphill climb, the curves and descents are the first stage. Every new feeling is sheer delight. Then there's the U-turn. Despite the passion, the relationship with the Intensely Intimate (But Crazy) gets older. Stage two comes along. You mark time by his departures and arrivals. And you settle near the all-important phone. You drag it into the bathroom and leave the shower door open to make sure you hear it. You take it off the hook when you're out so he'll think you're chatting and try again. You install a very loud doorbell and look out the window a lot. He dominates your existence whether you share a home or not.

He gets amused and sad when you're not home. He acts as if *you're* the one cutting *him* out. He pretends he's your second choice. You soon feel that you're stabbing your true love in the back. Rather than risk that, you tie yourself back onto the marionette sticks. You're a lifeless doll until he pulls the strings. And you know that you are *always* less important than the fevered pitch he seeks, his involvements apart from you that you *know* threaten your survival as a pair.

In the second stage, he becomes critical of you. If you don't live up to his expectations, he gets petty. If you make a mistake in perceiving his motives, he snaps. God forbid you should ask him directly what he's doing. You're supposed to understand all, so you pretend you do.

Despite the intensity of your relationship, a great deal between you goes unspoken. It turns out that your special language, your gestures, and looks are very inefficient. Neither of you really knows how the other is feeling, much less what the other is thinking.

The utter joy ebbs away to agony. His other passions chain you; his desertions devastate you, make you jealous. The ride becomes one of negative emotion, more dips than pinnacles. The problem is how to stop a tailspin into unhappiness. The true hazard of the Intensely Intimate (But Crazy) is an overstretched relationship. When the two of you become utterly dependent upon one another, you pass the point of healthy breakup. All too quickly, "suicide" becomes part of the vocabulary, and "nervous breakdowns." Your family or a doctor steps in to terminate the affair; you can't. With the Intensely Intimate (But Crazy), the fuel does burn out. So do you. Six months—or twenty years—later.

What Are the Telltale Signs of Trouble?

You can't see without looking. And with the Intensely Intimate (But Crazy), who wants to see? Funny flaws exist from the beginning, but not many people want to notice them. The warning signals of an impending Intensely Intimate (But Crazy) crisis are the ones everyone always tells you about, and you always wish weren't true.

But they are. Intimacy that's too good to be real ought to make you stop and take heed, especially when it happens fast. No matter how much you want to believe it can happen, real intimacy takes time. Sharing yourself, as opposed to losing yourself, is a delicate procedure that evolves step by step.

To have a good relationship, you also have to stay down to earth. When little games you two invent separate you from others, it's hard to notice, but it's an inkling that things are amiss. A playmate is pleasant, but if it's carried too far, you're out of this world and into one of your own.

If you find yourself hungering for only one kind of company, consider yourself addicted and ask, "What happens when he's not here?" You've become overloaded on him. No matter what, that's an unhealthy sign. You aren't *fused,* you've become each other's circuit breaker. No him, no lights. You've let love become a drug instead of life's best additive.

If you're not yourself without him, you fit the definition of clinically depressed. Rather than become a couch case, consider calling a moving van before you get worse. Sooner or later, your own sense of survival will make or break the habit. The deeper the addiction, the harder the withdrawal.

What Are the Chances?

It's sad to be sage, but cheap thrills do cost more in the long run. The Intensely Intimate (But Crazy) comes ready-made. But he has his price. He just bills you later, in monthly payments that can go on and on and on.

If the one you know is in his heyday now, chances of your reaping a harvest many years hence are minimal. Some Intensely Intimate (But Crazy) men do indeed change: They weather their own storms, mellow their intensity, and become some other type—often, the Loving Polymorph. But they do it alone. Only their own upheavals cause them to change. And the loss of a partner is one of the upheavals.

In other words, the best Intensely Intimate (But Crazy) is an ex-Intensely Intimate (But Crazy)—a man, usually over forty, who was once such a zealot, but who has deintensified himself and become a positive person. By then, in order to steady himself, he has usually whittled balancing beams for himself. Oh, yes, he might still fall off the tightrope occasionally; you might have to add ballast. But he has usually learned the right proportions—still intimate, but not so consuming.

On the other hand, an older, unreformed Intensely Intimate (But Crazy) still means troubled waters; he's almost like an Amoral Passion Monger. Beware and steer clear.

Certainly you need some sense of when you've feasted long enough. He's like devil's food cake. One piece is sweet. But if you eat and eat and eat, the odds are both you and your recollection of the food will suffer. He makes it all too easy to play tit for tat—the "I can be as crazy as you" approach. Maybe you don't want to use it, but some women succeed in holding him by guile, playing "poor me," having breakdowns, constant colds, agoraphobia, and other such self-defeating manias. Who needs them? Not you. His vividness makes other experiences pale. And who needs that, either? There's a lot to be said for pastel affairs.

Since I seem to be saying "He's great" and "He's terrible," what do you do? If you're a heavy romantic who falls in love with the dream of love, don't do this man. Remember the warning: not for women with weak hearts. But, if wild rides don't fluster you in the least, go ahead and enjoy it. Just memorize your name and address before you leave.

If staying on with an Intensely Intimate (But Crazy) should somehow become important to you, here are some things to work for: *Hang loose.* It's hard, but healthy. *Stay detached* from his comings and goings. When your existence starts to get dictated by his appearance, rub yourself down with Cling Free. Don't cut yourself off from good times with other people. He's not the only person who can give mouth-to-mouth resuscitation when you're drowning. Don't play victim. And watch your emotional scale. If unhappiness outweighs joy on a constant basis, reconsider your relationship—it might be time to lighten the load.

Where Do You Fit In?

More than any of the other Twenty-two Types of Men, the Intensely Intimate (But Crazy) tends to pick women similar to himself. If you lean toward the type and you've keeled over all too often, what does it mean?

Perhaps you expect the impossible dream. But *expected* can be a million painful miles from *getting* when the dream is anything but real. Not every aspect of love is stupendous. Somebody still has to take out the garbage.

To ease your personal wear and tear, sit down and decide which outfit you want to wear in life. They come coordinated, no mix and match allowed. For the passionate set, continued search and short-term—but boy! are *they* loud. For the stable set, long-term and make do with what you've got—but they come in prosaic colors trimmed with routine. Either choice is O.K., but be advised that one set clashes with the other. You don't get loud and long-term, search and stability.

Admit it or not, but if you constantly keep company with turbulence, it most likely means that you too like crisis. Count the upheaval level in your life. Maybe day-to-day existence frightens you. If routine looks like death to you, it may be dying, not men, you have to come to grips with. The Intensely Intimate (But Crazy) can provide a good escape from depression for a while. But if you're low when he's not there, the problem isn't him. It's you. You can't look for someone else to serve as the be-all and end-all for yourself. It's asking a lot of another person to provide your reason to live. If you do, consider yourself a loverholic—and seek help. Relationships don't thrive on addiction.

And, conversely, you might need to pick dependent men. The Intensely Intimate (But Crazy) may call the shots, but he desperately needs somebody to love. He needs to recharge, and he can't do it alone. Sure, it feels good to know you're needed, and it's thrilling when he comes back. But you can get so caught up in his gratifications that you forget to order somebody who loves you for *your* sake, not his.

No one ever forgets what it was like to be with intensely intimate men, but remember—even ambrosia should be sipped, not gulped.

Notes and Particulars

8/ The Gender Ascender

Related Types: The Idle Lord
The Maximal Misogynist
The Doe Stalker
The Picasso

Positivity Scale: − −

Once upon a time all creatures made babies by splitting in two and cloning themselves. Then, one fateful day, somebody invented sex. Two of them, to be exact. Ever since, there's been trouble. And a lot of merrymaking, too.

Now, although it looks as if the female was the basic form and the male the afterthought, some members of the masculine variety got it into their heads that they were better than the original—the ladies. There is *very* little evidence, other than what they've written themselves, to support such an assumption. Still, myriad descendants of these upstart specimens meander around in the guise of the Gender Ascender.

It's the Gender Ascender's *mind* that's the problem. He believes men are creation's highest creatures. That they are and were meant to be superior to women, that woman must remain inferior to man.

Of course, a lot of men think their sex is preferable. They feel they are endowed with facilities sadly lacking in the opposite gender. Due to these specialties, they wouldn't want to switch. Not even in reincarnation. Many women feel similarly—that the female got the better end of the deal, that theirs is the sex par excellence with benefits unparalleled. And they wouldn't trade for the whole wide world. So both sides end up figuring, O.K., our sex is preeminent, maybe transcendent. Certainly men and women are different, but in most ways, we're roughly equivalent.

113

The Gender Ascender subscribes strongly and totally to male supremacy. He feels that men not only have precious paraphernalia, but that they inherit privileges as well, that they own a singular hold on intelligence, ability, and rank. And they have an exclusive right to mastery over the opposite sex. Men are free and able to do what they want, and women simply aren't.

Man, the logic goes, *must* have sex. The Gender Ascender chases almost *anything* feminine to see what he can get. He believes that women come in two classes, the "loose" and the "touch me not." Yet his classes overlap; he always tests you to see where you fit in and find out just how badly he can make a lady behave. And when he pairs up permanently, he wants his woman to arrive almost holy, never look sideways at another man, but bust all her buttons in the sack with him.

Story

In my travels I've met many Gender Ascenders and have known numerous women who lived with them and had stories to tell. Of all the tales, Glynna's is the proverbial. Her man Dean wasn't just a partial, minimal Gender Ascender. Dean was a regular catalogue of the qualities.

Glynna grew up in a small city where long-standing, commonly-agreed-on ideas influenced everyone's lives. Her hometown taught that while boys "sow wild oats," girls "gather reputations." Men were natural family heads and decision makers. Women, at tops, were second lieutenants with leverage; they lacked the mental capacity and physical stability to lead. Everyone also canted that, once married, a couple should live and love as a pair and be true to one another.

Glynna unquestioningly looked forward to a traditional marriage. And she stayed "good" to win it. She was sure her and her man's domains would differ—hers to be home, his labor. He would take general precedence as the most important member, but all else between them would be equal. Both would become instantly and permanently loyal. Together they would operate like a system of checks and balances, Oldie But Goodie style. A young and starry-eyed Glynna eloped with her high-school sweetheart Dean when he returned from the service.

But Dean's view of marital bliss diverged from Glynna's. According to him, couples weren't concatenate, they followed the lord and master's dictates. Whether single or married, males had prerogatives. The only thing that changed with the wedding cake was how Glynna could behave; she could no longer do anything of which he didn't approve. She belonged to him and did what a woman should—kept the domicile, followed his commandments, served and serviced him and only him. She didn't wander around without him; when he wasn't there, she stayed home. He could do what he liked.

On their wedding night, Dean drank so much he passed out before she undressed. Then, in the wee hours of the morning, he grabbed her—and that was that. The next night, he didn't come home till three. Despite her anger, he insisted not only that they make love but that she do things to him she never knew were possible.

As time went on, she told herself they had a wild sex life. But she couldn't deny that if there wasn't force, there was always an element of *coercion* in their sex. Dean insisted that Glynna would like whatever he did—or *learn* to like it. She often pretended more delight than she really felt. She had little say when they did it except for occasional "headaches." Since she never knew when or what he expected next, she was always a little anxious.

At first, in bed and otherwise, she did what pleased Dean. To do so seemed the rule for women; she had no other footsteps to follow. But while she willingly gave up her independence, a lot of her personal freedom slipped away with it. Dean dictated how she was to wear her hair and dress. He tore up all her pants. He wanted her tone of voice sweet, her manner compliant, and her hospitality ever ready. She couldn't work, so she had little or no money for herself. He gave her a minimal allowance on which to run the house, buy food, and cover all her "extras."

As they slipped past the honeymoon era, Dean began to stay away more and more. Hunting and fishing trips grew more frequent. So did nights with the boys. Sometimes he didn't show up for dinner and occasionally was out all night. He'd have powder on his collar, and his socks would be inside out. People started cooing and consoling her and wouldn't tell her why.

Then, when Glynna got pregnant, Dean hardly came home at all. On the night of the big event, he couldn't even be found. A neighbor took her to the hospital, and her sister held her hand. When Dean finally arrived, he seemed to like his day-old daughter. Still, he told

Glynna, "The next one better be a boy." And though he bragged about his child, he wouldn't pick her up. Glynna had three more daughters before she bore a son; she kept trying for Dean, who wouldn't give up. He never helped with the home and children and came and went as he pleased.

Finally, at long last, his affairs, his temper, his domineering, and his absences got too humiliating. She locked him out. He followed her like a possessed hound dog—watching for another male—until she let him back. But after three weeks of good behavior, a new joint bank account and a two-day vacation, the old pattern reappeared.

Right now, Glynna has told herself and Dean she'll give him one last chance. She has said that before. She doesn't expect him suddenly to transform, but she does expect him to alter certain conditions she will no longer tolerate. She claims she doesn't mind most of the restrictions but does mind the belittlement. He still chases every woman he can. And she has cooking, church, and children, but no cash.

She's not sure she could be anything but a traditional wife. She still thinks the man of the house should hold a dominant place. Dean does provide for her and the family and is fatherly in his own limited way. But she doesn't mean to be ill treated or deprived of respect again.

During one separation, she really began to enjoy her single state. She got to drive and go out to lunch. She even camped with the kids on her own. She began to realize that giving up the idea of a one and only man might not be so bad. She isn't kidding about the last chance. Nor is she holding her breath.

The Gender Ascender comes in all degrees, from slight to gigantic. Surprisingly he is quite easy to discern, though his case might seem moderate and end up big. But what he is often seems to concur with your conscious or unconscious expectations of what men should be, so you find it hard to object to his ways. But presuming that being of different sexes may entail having different conducts is not the same as living with flagrant, unfair disparities. The Gender Ascender doesn't hold his assumptions just for discussion. He's a literal man who practices what he preaches. After a union with him, his opinions end up your personal habits and not necessarily congenial conditions. Since you may or may not find what you bit off chewable, better stop to analyze those assumptions first.

How Can You Identify One?

The Gender Ascender thinks everything—from can openers to honor to women—exists in limited quantities. His worth and esteem, therefore, depend upon getting as much of everything as he can (certainly more than his rivals); protecting what he has from others; presuming that everything anyone else has means so much less for him; hence, taking theirs away when they're not looking.

With that view, homes become castles. Women become pearls. His own—wives, daughters, and sisters—should stay around his neck; the rest are for diving after. Prestige becomes outdoing and outowning other males. He becomes a conquering warlord. He adds to his territory and guards his valuables; he likes guns. And he's a very jealous man.

Outer Signs

Being, looking, and acting like a man are of utmost importance to him. There's nothing froufrou about him; he's bold and he's heavy. He shops in men's stores, at men's departments, or by mail at Sears. Anything tagged as "unisex" he avoids. He only dares to go to the second-floor ladies wear to purchase a gift to lure a woman; even then he asks the salesclerk to pick one for him.

He wears his pants a little low on his hips and anchors them with a big, thick belt. He likes large patterns and prefers blue, black, and red. His suit material is twill or plaid. His jackets aren't blousy or fitted; they're long, straight to the hip, and often Western. He wears his leather coat the most—it's black or dark brown with one row of round buttons down the front.

He prefers flashy cars—the newer and larger the better. Often he owns *two* station wagons (each one with wood panels). He has a hankering for pickups, trailers, and campers; all of them fit his idea of pleasure. And all of them give him his kind of ride—hard, bumpy, and rough.

Before he pairs up, the Gender Ascender cares little about how he lives. Concern about décor just isn't his style. Often he lives where mothers and sisters can do the upkeep he won't. When he does have a bachelor abode, he leases a furnished place or else gets the trappings from Abbey Rents. He picks big square rooms, an enormous rectangular coffee table, carpets, and conveniences. He wants his hideaway not so much near work as near the after-hours action. He dwells downtown, near the campus or the music and tavern section of town. He rarely cleans his place. He always eats out. He sends all his clothes, towels, and sheets, of which he owns one set, in stripes, to the laundry. And if he forgets to pick them up, which he often does, he sleeps on the bare mattress and wipes his face with yesterday's shirt.

Once coupled, he likes to live in quite the opposite manner. He wants an isolated tower away from the bustling metropolis, if he can afford it. Whatever he picks he treats like a castle and says is "good enough," especially if you don't think so. He prefers a modern house. Since he wants a good amount of turf about, he idolizes corner lots—the fewer neighbors surrounding the better. Of course you'll be the one who's there while he goes into his man's world daily. You'll find it's easy to get to schools, churches, and shopping, but hard to reach town for lunch.

He loves appliances; he defines them as making your life better. The purchase of new gadgets comes high up on his list. Your kitchen will probably have three ovens—upper, lower, and microwave. He installs dishwashers, freezers, and an enormous refrigerator that pours cold water and crushes ice. He puts in washers, driers, compacters, and acres of Formica counters. He doesn't know much about small knicknacks, but he's aware of all the big, expensive, and obvious ones.

He wants the living room to shine like an old-fashioned parlor. It's rarely to be entered and never messed up, so it holds your best furniture. Here you entertain guests—when he's present. The family has its own, run-down room.

He eats a lot. He drinks a lot, too. He loves red meat. Especially steaks. He has a barbeque on the patio. He alone is in charge of the fire. He insists that you put on enormous meals and keep the freezer stocked with food. He tends to get portly as he gets older. He doesn't like it, but he's very bad at dieting. No matter what you do, he eats on the sly. How could *you* know what's good for him better than he does?

He's usually a sociable fellow, though some Gender Ascenders are quiet and severe. Certainly he's lively around men, whose company he prefers. Often when he's out just with you, he talks more to the restaurant owner, head waiter, or bartender. He exaggerates. He likes to be on the go. He gets agitated if he's not at some active spot every other night or so.

He has information about all those things that men should know about. If he doesn't play sports, he watches them and knows all the current statistics. If he doesn't do business, he knows about it and knows all the stock reports. If he doesn't fish and hunt, he used to. If he doesn't take a car apart, he "hasn't got the time." Or else he's waiting for his son to grow old enough.

He may treat himself well in terms of luxury, but he always treats himself well in terms of allowables—he does anything he wants to and blows up at any attempted limitation. In fact, the only emotion he readily tends to show is rage. He so armor-plates his psyche with muscle and fat that when a feeling does come through, it's usually explosive.

Authority means he gets to make a lot of rules and restrictions that all apply to you. He gets mad, rowdy, and even violent when you neglect to do things he told you to do, particularly if he's been drinking. He has a big vocabulary of curse words and profane phrases that he uses mostly around his buddies. But when he gets angry, anything and everything pours out in front of anyone's ears.

Sex Signals

He chases after any member of the female gender, except *perhaps* the *present* mates of his *best* pals. He's a howler, a chaser, and a prowler: Nurses, secretaries, and waitresses aren't safe around him. He doesn't approve of women higher-ups, but he'll still give them a bit of a sexual come-on. Distinctions such as married, single, innocent, or wise don't faze him, but he usually goes after the very young only if they know what they're doing and can satisfy him.

He'll only settle with a woman who proves she'll remain his private property. That doesn't mean you have to be a virgin till you go down the aisle. But he has to court you, meet refusal, and give commitments before you succumb to his charm. And there should have been no more than one other before him, a man he despises in retrospect. Your resistance assures him you won't give away what is "rightfully" his, although he's never absolutely sure of you.

His version of courtship is to take you with him where he goes. He also calls a lot on the phone and shows up at the door unexpectedly.

He's persistent and relentless until you're won. Once that's done, he installs you at home and proceeds to take you with him less and less.

There's never a moment that his attention isn't sexual. Part of his definition of masculinity is his closeness to a hard-on. His presence is heavy, musky, odorous. His eyes roam your topography. So do his hands, at any opportunity. He makes the first move without hesitation—also the second, third, etc. You're constantly in the position of "fending off" or "letting happen."

He's not a relaxing companion. He treats you like a gopher, himself like a tiger. Bedding down with him is not usually a sensitive or languorous experience. He's too much like a starving man released at a banquet, even when he has feasted on another feminine morsel only a few hours before. He sees himself as the doer and you as the receiver in any sexual action. He tells you what to do and what position to move to next; since he interprets independent gestures on your part as aimed for his pleasure and not your own, he tends to interrupt you just when you like it. He thinks good sex means length of time and speed of rhythm. He varies some, but in actuality he's rather limited. If the proper body parts don't reach standard contact somewhere along the line, he gets unnerved. Occasionally he has a problem with impotence. When he does, he involves you in a mutual campaign to help him overcome it. Pretending it doesn't matter just won't do. And if all else fails, he'll wait until you're asleep, get an erection, and wake you to prove himself.

Money Markers

Sometimes he's a steady earner; sometimes he's a drifter who changes jobs and locations, with you following along. But however he works, he considers all wages his to give out. He dispenses dollars like paper towels: They should be used only when needed, and they should go a long way. You and the house run on what he doles out when the mood hits him. He pays the bills himself. Often he travels around by car on Saturday and settles accounts in cash.

Now and then he does secret things with money. He always considers his expenses none of your business and lies about many things: He may invest without telling you, purchase things without consultation, despite stringent finances. He spends on drinks, bets, sports, guns, and pals as the fancy strikes him.

He doesn't like you to work or have money of your own. If absolute necessity drives you to seek an added salary, he may see that you lose more jobs than you hold. Certainly he demands that your occupational position be below his own and that your job take place where few men abound. Your boss equals one other man too many. He'll drive you to work and return on the dot of quitting time—or five minutes early. He expects your earnings turned over to his control.

Family Aspects

The usual Gender Ascender wants about four children but only with his wife. With "other" women, some use condoms; others have vasectomies after they've sired their kids to keep themselves out of trouble. All your children reflect on his virility, but having boys is better. It takes a whole flock of daughters to give him the same bravado as one boy. He isn't quite sure what to do with girls except spoil them, buy stuffed animals, and watch over them like a hawk. With boys he's rough, strict, and he pushes sports over school subjects. He likes all his kids to call him "sir."

He *respects* his parents. However, it's *your* job to serve them in his stead. He expects you to take second place and an underling role around his mother and father and sometimes even his brothers and sisters. He supports them against you. He never settles a certain animosity with his brothers and your sisters. Unless he can win their undying admiration, he stays very distant from *your* kin. He even posits himself against them and divides your loyalties.

If he's close to anyone it's his male friends. He and his pals seem unable to admit how much they care for one another in any way other than to seek each other's company. To call it love isn't "manly," but love it is. Often his chums come clear from his preschool days. Others are from later times. But all in all, they're just like him.

He makes a statement that separates the men he trusts from those he regards dimly: "I'd trust him with my wife." If a man's not his friend, he's an enemy. As friendly as he appears to *all* men, he lets his hair down only if he's sure he's safe. He tends to socialize with a very limited circle.

He rarely forms true friendships with women. Occasionally a Gender Ascender has a woman pal he sees on and off, sort of mistress-fashion, over many years. She alone becomes a friend and adviser and gets treated like one of the boys, but she's never brought home. Generally the Gender Ascender would have even *you* shun women friends. He'll accept ones from your childhood but view new ones as a threat. He prefers you to keep company with the consorts of his buddies. So, often, you tend to spend all your time with the same six or eight people—for years and years and *years*.

He does have some sort of allure. His male confidence is highly persuasive. He emanates something that's somehow . . . comforting. He can give you the feeling that he'll take care of you, that all compliance will be worth the price. He makes you think only *he* can turn you on, that he's hot and without him you're not. He gives you the assurance he can handle anything from a hurricane to a broken toaster. He himself may not be safe, but at least he protects you from those who are worse.

But his liabilities double, then triple, then quadruple over time. The fact that he's a jealous tyrant and invades your freedom seems natural to him, never a drawback. He grows even more resistant to new ideas or changes. New notions make him pull back farther and get even worse.

The predators from whom he protects you are usually invented. It's the Gender Ascender who makes you a victim; he just calls it guardianship.

Before going on I have to tell you about the Gender Ascender with a twist. No, thank God, it's not a cocktail. It's a modern-day, old-fashioned man. He's a double-standard man whose ascendancy is threatened. In response he decides that if women want equality they're going to get it with a vengeance. He knows all the latest liberated social mores and uses them as weapons against the women involved with him. He not only demands that you pay half the restaurant tab (that's fair, though taking turns has more grace), he insists you pay the cover charge at the club *he* chooses and knows is beyond your range. Then, when you refuse, he leaves you at the entrance and goes in himself. He wants his ex-wife (especially one who's left him) to pay him alimony. He asks for child payments on the months he has the children or counts how many meals he provides and deducts the price.

He fights for custody every time you get a boyfriend. He serves you with restraining orders every time you turn around.

Though he seems in almost all ways different from the regular Gender Ascender, the essential element remains: He believes in separation as much as or more than the old version did. Under the guise of splitting things down the middle, he forsakes all reciprocity. While he may look up-to-date, underneath he's the same old thing. Now, back to the regular Gender Ascender.

What Is in Store for You?

One thing is sure as shooting. Sooner or later, he'll say he's going to make you feel like a natural woman. That's a signal to stop and reconnoiter. "Natural" might be fine for a forest primeval, but how does it do on twentieth-century cement? There's another trouble. What exactly *is* "natural"? Anybody who tries to tell you what nature is and isn't is actually preaching personal opinion. Nature boy isn't telling you how it *is*, because nobody knows for sure—he's telling you how *he* wants it. He can fool you. You can even fool yourself. You might agree with him and never find cause to change your mind, or you might find what seemed sweet and natural ends up artificial and smacks of saccharin. So you'd better check out how his world turns.

You may start with a Gender Ascender thinking that your natural coupling is as simple as Tarzan and Jane. (Strange that their only child was Boy, not Girl, isn't it?) But the Gender Ascender believes that disparate things are meant to stay that way, like oil and water or apples and oranges. Mating doesn't mean blending to him. Two separate elements—your genitals—attach for certain purposes, but the dividing line remains. And that dividing line is unbreachable. To the Gender Ascender, a double standard not only refers to who gets to hustle and who doesn't, it also stipulates who gets to use what space, what time, what things, what clothes, what words, and what etiquette. It even states who gets to stand behind the altar and talk to God and who has to sit on a bench and listen to the sermon. So with the Gender Ascender, you lead very separate lives that overlap *very* infrequently.

To him, women need limits and restrictions, while men get all the permission. You live with the implication that you are by nature recalcitrant and hard to discipline. Only incorrigibly mischievous creatures deserve so many no-nos. Instead of being an innately good person who might occasionally do wrong, you are, to him, basically bad stuff who must try to do good. You're walking, talking trouble. You're ever so slightly tainted.

You don't exactly have stages ahead of you; you have a permanent condition that comes with the category *woman* and starts as soon as you're his. When you can't make a mistake without its reflecting on your character, shame and fear soon enter the picture. You become your own constant rebuttal; whatever you want to do, you stop yourself. You police yourself, and you lie a lot.

With him, as a woman you have to move in tight circumferences: You go from home to the store and trek back again, plus church, school, and a job if necessary, but you have no unknown whereabouts. You reappear at home by six and never wander after dark. You can bake, boil, or fry your food, but you can never trap it in the wild. You can drink wine or add soda to your whiskey, but you must restrict yourself to two. And you can say "heck," "darn," and "shoot" but have to censor anything stronger.

Even in the house your reign extends only so far. He's the dictator; you follow orders. What power you get comes with age, his debility, or death, grown sons and married. daughters. Meanwhile you get the kitchen, the wagonful of kids, and the work that goes with it. He doesn't cross over to do your work.

He holds forth over the living room and sits at the head of the dining table. You can wear your halter in the back yard only, but he can wear trunks in the front. He owns all the major machines; you own all the linens. All the items the double standard attributes to females become your personal burden. You come to accept that you're mindless, less capable, and confused, that you can cause a lot of trouble.

Every time you approach his world, you threaten your own self-worth. Therefore you have no choice but to stay away and grow ever more distant. That's the only way you're sure you're doing the "right" thing. A relationship with a Gender Ascender eventually bars almost every avenue to intimacy.

Many women who at first want closeness with a Gender Ascender eventually give up trying. A continuous built-in put-down has a way of making your skin grow thicker. And living in separate worlds tends to produce a deaf, dumb, and blind attitude toward the disjoined bedfellow. The women become more and more uninterested in their mates' existences. The link that holds the partnership together becomes progressively more figurative, until even sex disappears. The women devote themselves to home and family and simply submerge themselves. Their lives become their reward and their futures get lived through their children.

What Are the Telltale Signs of Trouble?

You don't need a radio to receive the Gender Ascender's frequency. He comes on loud and clear, from far and near. Tune in and take note of vocabulary. A Gender Ascender has a hundred terms for females; none refers to them as human. He never says "woman" and hardly ever "lady." To describe persons of feminine gender, he chooses words for small animals, vegetables, inanimate objects, and morsels of food: "chick," "bird," "fox," "doll," "tomato," and "piece," to name a few. He also uses a number of pejoratives: he calls certain women "cunts," "twats," "slits," and "whores." The females among his friends and family he calls "girls." "Woman" is just too grown up, and grown up is too close to equal. He expresses his interest in mammary equipment with terms like "knockers," "bazooms," and so on.

Gender Ascenders think sex will cure rebellion, depression, sadness, anger, and bursitis of the hip. It's a black day when a man says, "All you need is a good fuck" to cure a mood he objects to. If he identifies himself as a member of the men's 4-F club (whose motto is "Find 'em, feed 'em, fuck 'em, and forget 'em") consider the fact that he may well plow you over and plant his seed elsewhere as well. If he mauls you, then says its not nice to stop him after *you've* gone so far, put him away. And if you hear that other old standard, "Keep 'em barefoot and pregnant," it may be prophecy, not joke. Put your shoes on and get walking.

He has notions that your body's not quite wholesome. He blames things on your period, which he calls "the rag" or "the curse." If you do anything different from normal, he asks you if you've got "it." Either he won't sleep with you those days or else he says it's "better" then—for him. He thinks you have to clean up before and after sex, but that he doesn't because he's as pure as Ivory Snow.

He opines that women can't drive, add, plan, build, make, or do anything, that they're natural companions of Clorox and smell best in Cascade. He doesn't necessarily say it right out; rather he blasphemes lady drivers, lawyers, doctors, executives, and everyone he calls "women's libbers." He sees no need to squire you once he's got you; you're *supposed* to stay home. This is the critical point. It's time to remember we're living in the 1980's—and change your living conditions.

What Are the Chances?

You can keep a coalition with the Gender Ascender from now until forever if you so desire. But the conditions give cause for pause. What you can't do is change him. Remember the ice cube in hell? Or the sun rising in the west? Altering this man is just about as possible.

The Gender Ascender holds his convictions as self-evident, and he holds himself as proof. He doesn't even listen to contradiction seriously. He just bellows, teases, or ignores you back into place. Or he shows you his biceps, asks if you can match it, and then says, "See, *there*'s the evidence."

If he changes at all, he's inclined to get worse. The Maximal Misogynist lies but a step away from the Gender Ascender. Yours may not include violence in his bag of tricks, but for any man who believes he has the right to keep a woman in line, that means is always a little too close for comfort.

Personally, I advise that you evade any Gender Ascender who comes within your range. I also suggest saying "So long" to one you've got around, sad as it may be to do so. He is *not* (now hear this!) the Oldie But Goodie. There's nothing wrong with different realms or with the man as chief if that's your expectation and desire. But there is a built-in problem with a man who disrespects all womankind. And ill winds come your way when a man takes liberties that debase his mate. Men should be pleased to be male. But supremacists belong in another time and place—maybe they never belonged at all.

You're the one with all the reasons to alter a Gender Ascender relationship. Forever with him is a long, long time. Dissolving a Gender Ascender connection, once cemented, can be quite hard. He often sees your breakup as a reflection on his reputation. Besides, he has both his cake and his cookies while remaining hooked up. Chances are, you have a lot at stake as well: home, children, financial security and your own upbringing. You may even come from an ethnic background where one man is all you're supposed to get.

In such a situation you may want to try for some adjustments, declare your toleration limit and outline what's due for your self-respect before making a break. You may achieve some discretion and even improved treatment from him when you draw the line.

I suggest *against* baiting the Gender Ascender as a means of teaching him a lesson. To taunt the Gender Ascender with exactly what he can't stand is like playing with fire. Don't slide over to another male, tease him with hints of adultery, or dishonor him for the world to know. And make sure your brother and father are on your side before you use them as a back-up force. They may subscribe to male dominance, too.

If you determine to end your relationship once and for all, muster your courage and do it cleanly, clearly, and legally. If you truly want out (and not just an explosive reaction) use documents, distance, and doors. And *you* do the doing. Applying tactics that will make him leave you is simply too dangerous.

You *can* stay and try to make the best of it. But before you go "total woman," make sure it's right for you. Don't be intimidated into echoing his standards if they aren't *your* standards. Trust isn't built on restrictions; it's based on faith and it goes two ways.

Where Do You Fit In?

Almost inevitably a woman who falls for a Gender Ascender once does so again, if perchance she goes another round. Such a penchant cries for revelations.

The Gender Ascender doesn't exist in isolation; he's always two for tea. When you consent to his domination, it means you concur with his dogma as well. If you find your unwitting compliance leads to baneful circumstance, better examine your dormant assumptions before you do the Gender Ascender again.

Do you hear yourself say such things about the feminine condition as "It's our lot"? Do you hide your Tampax and pretend you don't have sex (while he goes around boasting about it)? Do you think a woman has to accept any advance from any man? That's either the old "a woman has to take what she can get 'cause they're the pickers and we're the picked" theory, or else you respond to all men as bosses. Do you feel that if a woman does not stay a virgin (or at least highly discreet) till she makes a permanent alliance, her union will always bear an invisible scar, but that a man's past never carries a taint; in fact, that men "improve with experience" and you wouldn't want them otherwise? Or what about the idea that men can always find other women, but a woman, once used, cannot? So, once you mate, hold on for all you've got or else head for the junkyard?

To find that you may unknowingly agree to ideas of female inferiority—and there are more than those listed above—is not such a terrible condemnation of yourself as it seems. After all, the Gender Ascender learned the double standard; so might you have. I say *learned,* not possessed innately. Women do belong to the same culture as men. They absorb the same lessons and pass them on. Did your mother say sex with all men was bad, then tell you your marriage would be made in heaven? It's just as hard for us to undo such unfounded assumptions as it is for men. Except for one factor: We're on the bum end of what turns out to be belief instead of fact. And since we make ourselves suffer for such assumptions, it pays us to find out what is real and what is not.

The double standard implies that your femininity causes men to behave as they do. Just by being female you tempt every male. His arousal is all your fault. But the chromosome that bears gender doesn't contain character flaws; no man's behavior derives solely from your heady presence. His actions belong to him; likewise, when you do the seducing, you really can't claim your flesh was weak. *You're* responsible for what you do, for the grief and pleasure you derive.

Many woman, especially the traditional kind who lean toward the Gender Ascender, want to live out a vision in which they love one he-man who loves them back for life. But you must weigh that fantasy against the cost of its reality. When you haven't got love and life is not so good, what's the point in living out a dream instead of a romance?

When your relationship with one man doesn't work out (and with many of us it doesn't anymore) the fault isn't necessarily your intrinsic character or your behavior. It didn't work out because it didn't, and that's that! Saying adios may not be what you wanted. But you've still got what you've got—yourself and the chance to love again!

Notes and Particulars

9/ The Courtier

Related Types: Intimate Type One—
The Loving Polymorph
The Idle Lord

Positivity Scale: + + −

Once it was just a dream carried on between *The Days of Our Lives* and dinner. Or 3 P.M. break and 5 o'clock quitting. You're queenly; you catch some young man's fancy; he eyes you in your ripened glory and comes courting. Previously, it stopped there, with an accept-flattery-but-hands-off policy. Now the idea is no longer a fantasy lacking carnal knowledge. The Courtier isn't new under the sun; he's coming out from behind the clouds. Hallelujah!

There are plenty of reasons for a younger man to seek an older woman. Or a man with less to attach to a woman with more. You see, the Courtier is not necessarily younger in years. He comes in two styles. In one, age and experience count: He is younger and has less, you are older and have more. In the other, status and money figure: He has neither, you have both. But in either case, the primary item to remember is this: When it comes to the Courtier, some are good guys, some are not.

Sometimes the Courtier means to remain only temporarily, but he's fond and adoring while he's there, and that's OK. Other times he just wants to conquer what you have—or see if he can; it's a test of his ability. If he just wants to use up your supplies, he loses interest, walks off, returns nothing, and can even grow cruel. Sometimes the Courtier wants to settle down and harvest—for the long-run benefits. In this case, he can be shrewd while pretending to care—not so good. Or he can just plain love you and love to stay because part of what you have is you.

Whatever the minor variations, his theme remains: NOW. He wants the ripe fruit, not that due to ripen. Whether the affair is to be short- or long-term, your problem is discarding the pretenders and getting the prince, so you benefit as well. Quite obviously, he goes for a certain sort of woman—older, wealthier; more famous, successful, or simply more skilled than he. He finds women with depth of experience the only ones who intrigue and magnetize him, sexually and otherwise.

Story

Take the story of a woman I met and grew to admire a great deal, Lois. At the age of forty-seven, Lois had been married for twenty-one years and divorced for six. The breakup of her marriage had come as a complete shock to her. Then, six years after she picked up the pieces, she started to date and learned to love again. At first, she had thought she would travel into old age alone and empty. But she had finally passed the panic. She had known that, someday, *something* would work out. But how that something surprised her!

Like most women caught in similar situations, she found very few men of her age and station available. She found herself slowly lowering the age of men she considered as proper suitors. She began to see one man of thirty-nine and ended up wondering who was the loser—he was down and out and obviously used his charms while she took him in. He bedded her a month or two and disappeared.

While still quavering from that experience and determined not to repeat it, she met Alex. Alex was soft and slow, open and lovely. He wanted to live every day as if it were forever, wanted everything there was to have right now or never. And he was only twenty-seven.

Throughout her marriage, Lois had worked part-time as her husband's assistant. She had dealt with many people and had her hand in a lot of happenings; she was active and involved even though all she did officially was raise her children.

Lois missed nothing. She thought about life, devoured every experience, and had a lot of wisdom. People loved her; her friends were long standing. She didn't have much money, but internally she was a very rich woman. And Alex knew it. At first, Lois was uneasy about Alex. She denied any future hope to the affair, claiming he was just a lark. She feared he wasn't bright enough to discuss things with her, that she would find herself stuck with a burden and lose a few more years.

Alex never pretended he was different from what he was. He couldn't guarantee he would stay with Lois forever. He never said he wouldn't enjoy her possessions or connections, didn't feel diminished by taking advantage of something that was none of his own doing. He did find Lois enthralling, with much more to offer in thoughts and insight than his previous young lovers. He knew he wanted to be with her. And for that privilege he was happy to offer anything he could muster. A rarity, he was uncluttered by ambition, unperturbed by guilt, kind, considerate, helpful, even joyous. Sexually, he was warm, huggy, and ever-ready. Lois found herself physically awakened in a way she had thought she could be only within a steady union, but had never achieved in her marriage. What she did know from all her previous practice she taught Alex.

As they grew together, they expected the hard part to come from her children. But strangely enough, after a few upheavals, because Lois and Alex were bluntly honest, the children came to the conclusion that what was good for their mother was also good for them. Divorce had strengthened them; they had the capacity to appreciate something novel. When their father objected, they lined up against him until he became a "family friend."

Lois used her experience to open her own insurance firm. Alex both assists her and dabbles in real estate. They share cooking, go camping. He gardens, she relaxes. They have a lot to talk about. It's hard at this point to figure out who's the main adviser. Their ties are loose in some ways, tight in others. They have a solid friendship. There is some jealousy on both parts and some fighting, even an occasional separation. They live for the moment—Alex introduced that. They spend, travel, take what comes. Sometimes, Lois fears the future, but she's decided to deal with later later. But lucky Lois has found the grace to let life ride without reservations and nagging worry. If Alex exploits her, she's willing. Why? Because she likes it.

More than the other Twenty-two Types of Men, Courtiers require picking and choosing on your part. Before you dismiss them, it's time to consider that perhaps fewer years or lower position don't put a man at less advantage. For years, older men have considered younger women as personal enhancements; maybe it's time to turn the tables. Especially if we can avoid the hustle of Doe Stalking and do it with a little love and style.

How Can You Identify One?

Day in and day out, the television asks, "Why wait?" It never says, "Take baby-steps in life's game of Mother-May-I?" No way. Those commercials trumpet that there's no need to grow it, make it, bake it yourself—whatever you want is already manufactured. And while the idea refers to products, it easily translates to people. Why else would so many folk wander aimlessly in and out of singles' bars looking for *the one right* person? It's obvious, of course: Lately, people expect other people to come packaged like pizzas and perfume.

The Courtier buys the line. When an item says "partial assembly required," he's off in another direction. The latest model of modern man, he's ready for anything ready. Pop Tarts and Big Tate. He may have grown up that way, or may be a recent convert; it depends partly on his age. At any rate, the Courtier's not patient, even when he's sweet and abetting. He takes his turn now, no matter where his place in line is. When it seems he's dedicated to Number Two (you), in most ways he's still looking out for Number One. You are part of how he takes care of himself. And, usually, he's part of how you take care of yourself.

So consider the Courtier a user: Don't expect him to save money on his clothes, hold off on his sports car, or stash the best liquor for some distant occasion. Don't even freeze last night's dessert. Remember that saying, "Make hay while the sun shines"? It was written for him. He doesn't see life as Mount Everest—no struggles for him. He's here and now. Rarely is he with you to boost himself to the next state. Mostly he just wants to enjoy whatever is available. Usually, he's quite willing to reciprocate for his pleasures. If you have achievements to make, he may support you in your climb. Some Courtiers would like career success along with their ladies. Others, usually speedy ones, become front men—they promote or manage for you. Earthier ones prefer to calm you and keep you cozy. If you have no outer-world pressure, but pass your days at home, a Courtier might still keep your house together.

Outer Signs

Through and through, the Courtier likes quality, which is flattering for you. His mode of dress may be in style or quite individual, but each piece is hand-picked, particular. And he appreciates beautiful gifts of your choosing. He tends to fancy specialty items, not just regular attire—he's disposed to scarves and jewelry, Borsalinos and cravats. He likes to look a little unusual. He claims distinction outwardly, even if in nothing else.

He takes pride in his car though, strangely, he selects either a Mercedes or its opposite—a V.W. bus. Brands in-between lack allure for him. As far as the Courtier's concerned, material goods are toys, and vehicles are some of the best ones. It's as if they came from Tonka—they exist for fun. He has, or has had, a motorcycle. And, once in his life at least, he'd like to ride in a limousine.

Houses are less easy to have fun with, at least when he's on his own, so when the Courtier lives by himself he looks as if he's on the move. He simply prefers to live *à deux*. His place is always bare, except for his favorite playthings, not quite in order or even in boxes. He selects places that resemble motel rooms and evoke entrance foyers. (The better to get out fast.) He cares about nice furnishings, comfort, and aesthetics, but part of that means having another human being to create the atmosphere, so he moves in with you.

Sex Signals

He's more than civil, he's downright polite; sometimes, he's urbane. He's amiable. Oily-tongued Courtiers are passé. He can be direct and honest, but usually he's also good-humored and soft-spoken. Odds are high that he's nice looking. No matter what his origins, he seems to have good breeding. And when it comes to feeling, he definitely *likes* more than he *loves*—to like is to enjoy, to love is often to suffer. He finds himself pleasurable as much as or more than you do. Despite what others might think, he is not a passive fellow, at least in private. He speaks his mind. He stipulates living conditions but compromises to get them. Since he's a creature of the moment, he lives in active verbs: consumes, imbibes, carries on as he wants to. He treats himself like a lover as much as he does you, but he gives you precedence over himself because you gratify him. He thinks of women as a connoisseur thinks of wine: He doesn't want the raw new press; he savors full bouquet, nose, fine head (in any number of ways). Sometimes, he cares about the size and shape of the bottle; sometimes he doesn't. What's more important to him is your decision that he's worth it.

To approach you, he places himself in your attention, often enough so that you know it's persistence. He waits for you to break through the polite conversation and make a high sign; in true Courtier fashion, he's attendant. You make the first advance or let it happen. Soon, you both understand that you're advancing in some unspoken process. He's more and more available as your company until you move from public to private pairing. Then you work out your relationship until you're ready to go public as an item.

Sex comes immediately or sometimes not at all. Occasional women want permanent escorts without physical relations; some Courtiers are gay. If he is sexually inclined, he's ever so subtly persistent: He stands close, picks up and fondles a strand of your hair until you ask, "Why not?" If you're hungering to try his body right away, he wants you to; if you're not sure, he waits. It's amazing how far nonaggressiveness gets him. He's hard to shoo away because he's never abrasive. Usually, he's a very sexual and enthusiastic, if youthful, lover. He's not into educational programs; he likes the fact that you both know what you're doing. Novices are not his number and nothing virginal appeals. So you indulge in a mutual refinement of old techniques instead of new ones. What he lacks in quality he makes up for in quantity. You're in a sexual peak, and he's up and coming—and coming. It can be a perfect combination, for two people who like to use themselves.

How he treats you once you're a twosome changes little from courtship. You become one another's major interest. Differences sink to the bottom; the courtesy goes on. The Courtier relationship is one of the most delicate—it can't tolerate much abuse—and both parties seem to know this. Its maintenance depends on formal consideration: Respect reigns, along with regard and obligations.

Money Markers

Though some Courtiers earn money, generally the major amount comes from your handbag. If you don't provide cash, you probably supply property. He doesn't care where the money comes from; it exists to use, and he's good at it. If you like to spend for pleasure, too, it's all the n rrier. An older Courtier, or one who ponders aging, might want an account in his name alone. As your agent or helper, he might ask for (and deserve) a salary. It's not unlike a Courtier to keep some money separate for independent purposes while generally living on yours. Occasionally it bothers the Courtier if he has little or no income, but more so if he has no creations, so he attempts separate endeavors. But his projects have an uncanny tendency to not happen or to simply become follies.

Family Aspects

In most Courtier situations, if anyone has children, you do. Usually, he wants none or thinks of them as so much in the future that they never happen. Even if your difference is one of wealth and status, instead of age, generally the decision on both your parts is to avoid two-legged, slowly maturing dependents. You two are the primary playthings.

However, older children, in and out of your custody, might be involved. Then, the major concern is what they do with the Courtier and what he does with them. He has little choice but to hang on the edge until they like him. He figures his one and only necessary connection is to you, so he's guiltless toward others. His relationship to your family depends on what you demand as bottom-line courtesy. Often, they like him, since he's a likable fellow. He pals but rarely fathers.

As for his family, they've gotten quite used to him since childhood. He's always had his own pace, his own ways. They've never been able to make him conform. They've given up on bribes. If they grumble in quiet, that's all he expects. He's independent but distantly fond of them. He treats them like just people, not parents; the same goes for brothers and sisters.

He rarely grows close to your circle of friends, though he's polite and agreeable. He probably has and makes separate friends from you, both male and female. He may see them independently or he may bring them around; but for you to have two groups of friends is definitely not uncommon.

There's no way you can say he's everything. He's not the man on the white horse, the provider, or the chairman of your board. He's got other pluses and minuses: He's joy and pleasure, someone there, a lover; he's for spontaneity. And mostly he's there because you can't do it, feel it, and be it all on your own. You can't expect him to save for a rainy day or build formidable foundations. He probably won't lavish you with diamonds, although he may use your money from a joint account to get you some—unannounced. He's an easy rider.

What Is in Store for You?

Too many King Arthurs can try any Guinevere to her limit. After all, how much did she see of him? He was always off ruling, warring and pontificating, while she turned into a dowager. If Arthur had owned a telephone, he'd have been on it day and night. Sooner or later, almost any lady is ready for Sir Lancelot—attentive, delighting in your society, but not unambitious—or better yet, Sir Galahad— known for his courtesy, humility, and quiet wisdom despite his youth.

If you're ready to spend what you have—money, status, sex, looks—and the Courtier offers what you like—sex, looks, company, congeniality—the ride can be fine. But it's best to know consciously what you're doing. The Courtier is flattering to you. So remember the old maxim: Flatterers always live at the expense of the one who listens.

Yet if you want music to your ears, not to mention to the rest of your body, and you don't care about costs—it's nobody's business but yours. The Courtier isn't a first affair. He comes as step two—step one is you. Before he happens, you've reached a new conclusion about what's good for you. The Moguls, Picassos, and Misogynists no longer look like prime rib, rather like gristle. You've decided that hard work good income, glory, and prestige in a man are usually more crunch than munch. Besides, you've got enough in your own refrigerator— you want some salad days! All is not easy with the Courtier, but if you are confident enough of your intentions, you *can* overcome the obstacles, for Courtiers really do reciprocate. They make margaritas *and* love.

Right from the word one, your having things he hasn't presents problems, and you have to discover how you both feel about that. You go through delicate maneuvers to discover answers to certain questions: What does he want? Has he got what I want? Am I flirting? Is he swindling? Who's on top? Usually, you do this figuring-out undercover.

That first private phase has another reason: You need time to reprogram your computer, to dig down and decide just how much normality means to you and if you can disregard convention. If you can't fight the conservative streak within you, or feel that you'll always remain embarrassed in public, probably your partnership stops there. But if you can, you incorporate, go public, and take stock of the reactions. Things can quickly become no laughing matter: Potentially you face not only angry elders but nasty children. You need to band together against gossip and derision.

It's usually then that you have your first split. Bad times usually don't bring out the best in *any* couple. It's now you face pitfalls and boredom: Perhaps you really didn't have enough between you. Then there's the dead end that sophistication can bring: To handle your friends, you act so jaded you hurt your lover's feelings. Or you might discover that despite what you thought, you just can't handle the affair. Guilt, shame, or jealousy is wreaking havoc in your brain.

But usually, only very independent women go for Courtiers. So for you, fighting other people's expectations and oversimplifications is routine. What makes or breaks the relationship is what you have between you and whether you continue to mellow, for even the Courtier requires surrender. You may not be willing to lose control. You may not succeed. You might totally triumph. Even so, while you eventually outlive criticism, other adjustments continue to arise. Even friendly children can present a constant problem: They tend to switch you out of parent and into peer, since you're doing what young people do, not what an aging parent ought to. Without your old parental stance, you have to restructure discipline. They might flout convention and claim it's imitation of you. And your parents can be a problem, too. Most likely they'll put you through at least a few hoops.

You two are faced with all the problems that any couple has, plus a few new ones: Dominance is always an issue; dependence and fear can nag at you. Even if all else goes well, you've got a worse old-age problem than most. In the worst of Courtier unions, you stick together like master and dog. In the best of Courtier twosomes, sooner or later you equalize who has and who hasn't, who gives and who takes, who domineers and who doesn't. And you go long-term because you're developing, because you're in love.

What Are the Telltale Signs of Trouble?

All that glitters isn't gold: Sometimes it's gum wrappers or con games. So watch out. There's a big difference between a Courtier and a thief. Make sure you've got the one and not the other. The best way is to exercise caution.

Recently, a woman wrote a letter to "Dear Abby." A younger man, unknown to her, had shown up at her husband's funeral. He said he had known her husband and then began coming over to see her. He was charming and genteel. She started to desire his comfortable companionship, but a sixth sense told her to check on him. To her shock and her saving, she found out he'd collected off an armload of widows.

Real Courtiers don't approach you out of the blue. You meet them the way you would anyone else—through work, mutual acquaintances, and social events. They haven't lived off one single woman after another, although you may not be the first. They're just people of the moment, and somehow you hit it off. Usually, when a true Courtier flags you down, he offers a voucher: He may well be a user, but he's rarely a borrower. (Only much later, as his partner, might you lend him money.) The only odd thing about him is that *you* have what *he* should have, according to prevalent custom.

There are some definite indications that things aren't going as they should be: If he's got a wandering eye, or if you're getting restless, or seeing the green-eyed monster. Even worse is if one of you grows possessive and allows the other no breathing space. Or if someone plays games to make the other jealous. Any relationship grows crow's feet. But in a Courtier union they should look like laugh lines. No matter what your age, your bank account, or your wisdom, when the wrinkles turn downward, it means you aren't having such a good time. Of all men, the Courtier should offer some sort of ecstasy.

What Are the Chances?

Anyone for that $64,000 question? When you ask about chances with the Courtier, there's no simple answer. Is it a good thing to do?

Depends on you. Will it last? Sometimes yes, sometimes no. Odds are against it at the moment, but times are changing, and throughout history, some have always made it. Are the short-term benefits worth it? They might be and they might not be—60/40 for it.

The Courtier remains hard for most people to handle. Outside of a few super-cities and fast classes, it's still rough to turn tables on what's expected of males and females. But it's *not* impossible. In a small coastal California town, I met a woman in her forties living with a twenty-year-old man. They were open about it, which is healthy, but so defensive that you could tell their honesty was costly. She was walking the edge of outcast status. And yet *everywhere* you meet forty-year-old men with twenty-year-old women. In most places, it still takes courage for cowgirls to tell the world nobody can take away their gusto.

But think about it. Your pleasure merits holding onto even in the face of an adverse community. After all, being pushed around by custom is like acting out of guilt, shame, and fear. Social ordinances aren't really *real;* they're just ideas. And it's pretty silly indeed when a rule that nobody you know invented comes between you and how you feel.

If you're more comfortable with the socially accepted admit it to yourself. If the particular stresses in the Courtier combination are more than you care to handle, O.K., look for a man who fits your expectations and with whom you have a better chance. Keep your zest—but keep it in more commonplace ways.

Otherwise, *I'm* all for adventure. If he comes along and looks interesting, try the Courtier; see where it gets you. But only under certain conditions: Both of you have to *know* that with the right attitude you have nothing to lose. And don't forget it! You should foresee the possibility that you or he will end it. You're more likely to cut it short at first; he's more likely to farther on down the line. As in any relationship, to get the best from the Courtier you have to give yourself to it. If you just toy around or try to control him, you're probably Doe Stalking in reverse—it's called Chicken Stalking. I don't think it's any better or less exploitive when women do it than when men do. When the man is very young, it's *very* bad. But if you're both of age and both choose merely a carnal caper, it's your affair. If you aim to get something from him but keep him from getting much from you, neither of you is bound to get much at all.

A permanent Courtier alliance, or a mutually successful temporary one, requires you to give more of yourself than is usual—emotionally and in territory, money, and place in the community. In no union can you keep everything in your own hands, and only one approach is operable here—what you use and what you lose simply don't matter. If you start to fear for your property, you'd better back off.

If you come to hunger for someone whose intellect, ambition, and knowledge are closer to your own, it bodes a bleak future. Individuals don't necessarily need a lot of similarities to establish a solid foundation, but certain correspondences do help. You may drift apart because the pleasure was ephemeral—the first flash fizzled. Or you might still be getting over other types of men: You tried a new idea, but the Courtier proved transitory. Or he might be too devoted, like a child to a teacher, and the adoration held no payoff for you.

In any of these situations, you should put the whole business in a file marked "inactive" and start on a new case study. But, if all goes well and more interest, richness, and affection develop, buck tradition and fight to keep your Courtier affair alive.

Where Do You Fit In?

So Courtiers are looking luscious. But you're not sure of your own black-widow potential. Or else Courtiers have come and gone and left a bitter taste, and you wonder who's at fault.

It's probably harder than you think to do the Courtier right. It's no good if you start out a Courtier relationship in less than the best climate. You need to work for an awareness of what you're in it for. Deep down underneath, you may need to show off that you can have or can lure a young, attractive man. Then you discover that while you may desire an exciting mate to reflect on your value or provide an escort, a man on a leash doesn't make you look better. He makes you look worse. You may be afraid to look as if nobody finds you sexy. Or fearing that, all alone, your erotic desires might shrivel and die, you want to reassure yourself by having a lusty admirer. You need to realize that sexual confidence is hard to gain; it comes internally, not from alluring partners. And while you may go through periods without a bedmate, that doesn't mean you have lost your fire. If there's any coal that rekindles instantly, it's your remembrance of things past—and how to do them!

If you're separated, divorced, or widowed and the months stretch on and on, don't jump on the Courtier to avoid the mourning process. If he's the man who comes along when you're ready, that's fine, but he's no shortcut. Wait, no matter how long, until you're resilient and ready. And don't give up hope of love.

Often, women go into a Courtier affair as if on a spending spree. Then the spendthrift instinct dwindles and results in a double bind; They want to keep the relationship but want to put a lid on financial and psychological expenses. If that happens to you, consider this: Monetary and sharing problems in the Courtier are not that dissimilar to those in any other union. If you feel you must change things, you'd better discuss it honestly with him. All too often, women fear they'll lose a lover if they change any rules. But if you don't clarify your concerns, your worry is bound to surface in unpleasant ways—you denigrate your man in public or in private get sour. Rather than picking on your man and starting fights, better to announce your anxiety and hope for the best. It's hard enough for a man with less and a woman with more to maintain mutual respect. Don't worsen the situation with corrosive tendencies. Take the chance of loss and keep your policies open. You can find joy almost anywhere. Don't dispel the happiness that comes from seemingly upside-down, unexpected situations. Every time you worry about convention, remind yourself that it doesn't *matter*. Your value comes from *you*. And so do your values.

Notes and Particulars

10/ Intimate Type Two —The Oldie But Goodie

Related Types: Intimate Type One—
The Loving Polymorph
Intimate Type Three—
The Limited Partner

Positivity Scale: + + +

Man the breadwinner, woman the homemaker.

A number of the Twenty-two Types of Men perpetuate or presume the old ancestral arrangement. But of them all only the Oldie But Goodie's really got it right. So if your angle is old-fangled and you care enough to get the very best, get an Oldie But Goodie—a traditional man who wants a traditional life and wife. He's the tops of the way it used to be. And sometimes still is.

But here's where the Oldie But Goodie is special: He doesn't think men are superior to women, and he doesn't believe your household is less important than his job. Quite the opposite. He wants a good home and family more than anything, including his career. He knows the value; he just believes in the old formula. He thinks a division, but coordination, of labor works best, that different areas of interest and authority make for the smoothest partnership. So he does one thing, you another, but toward the same purpose—the formation, care, and keeping of a single family unit.

And indeed your own little corporation is the center of the universe. Together you mow the lawn and paint the walls. You spend almost all your time in the company of one another. He returns home to run the Lionel train or watch a good game of baseball. You fry eggs, patch skinned knees, and visit Fabric City. He loves you. You love him. In perpetuum. And you are both monogamous: You don't cheat on him, nor does he on you; it's part of the deal. You see, Oldies But Goodies figure it's equal. Man has no special right to philander that woman doesn't as well. If he wants you only to have one man, then by rights he can have just one woman.

Naturally the Oldie But Goodie's system works only if his lady is in agreement. So Oldies But Goodies tend to head for old-fashioned flavors in women, a blend of wholesome ingredients and down-home intentions. He goes through all the steps, never missing a procedure—falling in love, courtship, going steady, proposal, and marriage. Five layers, slow oven. Hopefully you have time to test the batter before you add the frosting.

It all sounds pretty ideal. But in truth, as with all the Intimate Men, the Oldie But Goodie relationship is hard work to establish and even harder to keep—and the most painful when it fails, because it relies so much on faith. But if tradition is your comfort zone, there's nothing to lose and much to gain from an Oldie But Goodie man. If you find him, that is, for Oldie but *Not* Goodies are are all too prevalent!

Story

My pal Donna luxuriates in family life as if she were a Queen of Sheba—for her, dishpan hands don't matter. But then she's hooked up with Hank. And for Donna, Hank is a humdinger. Nothing makes either of them happier than to meet at the table at the dot of six. Even when they have to eat their daughter's Stir and Serve.

Strangely enough, Donna's own mother was either home acting fragile and inept or she was out fitfully pursuing a concert career. Donna's upbringing was almost devoid of indoctrination in the domestic arts. While many women who come from a line of strong homesteaders seem to want to try their chance in the outer world because they know the inner, Donna followed the opposite tack: She valued every afghan and brooch from her grandmother. And she took to sewing and knitting before she could whistle or pop her Double-Bubble.

Not that Donna didn't finish her education; she did. But even then she found herself leaning toward a customary role—she trained as a schoolteacher. Then she took a job in an elementary school, in a medium-sized town on the outskirts of the state. It was there one day, at a basketball game, that she met Hank.

Hank was just a bit younger than Donna, a college dropout and a natural laborer. You couldn't keep Hank inside, much less behind a desk or on a chair, for long. But none of that mattered. Donna and Hank were like pippins meeting pastry dough. All Hank really wanted in life was a home and a wife plus a kid or two, then to install them where he could love them to death. As for work, he just wanted a job with enough interest and progress to support them, not kill him, and maybe buy a camper.

There was no question that he meant it to be forever. So did Donna. In fact, through thick and thin (for things weren't always blissful), what held them together wasn't their love for each other; it was their *commitment* to the idea of one, lasting marriage.

After a short courtship, they got hitched. Although Donna got cold feet at the last minute—she wasn't quite sure Hank was the right man for her—luckily her instincts said "go." The first baby came pretty quickly—nine months. Clearly it wasn't a shotgun wedding.

The first seven years were the hardest. Hank had his work, and since they both agreed that Donna should stay home, she had her house. It took them quite a while to work out the balance of their different realms. Hank tried to preempt the household management and overdo the "head of the family" role. Donna sometimes stepped on Hank's toes and undermined his discipline. They had each other's habits to get used to, good dust-raising quarrels, labor layoffs, different driving speeds and sets of in-laws. They also made more babies, who ate a lot and kept things dilapidated. But Donna and Hank knuckled down to raise the kids and grow old together.

Donna never feels sorry for herself because she stays home and doesn't have a career. She *likes* what she's doing and says so. She doesn't have to lie or feel guilty. Hank never rambles on about having the final word or being boss. He doesn't feel less masculine because he quits work on the button and goes straight home. Their decisions are so intermingled it drives their kids crazy. Hank always says, "I'll go along with what your mother says," then Donna sends them back to ask Hank.

Their sex life—they have to hang a "do not disturb" sign on the door—started fast and awkwardly but grew better. It never got very wild, just substantial. A lot of the time, they simply snuggle. When the day fades, they're pretty tired. But then they discovered that, for them, cuddling was almost more important than sex.

There have been temptations and near breakups. Sometimes Hank gets to flirting with other women; sometimes Donna feels isolated and fed up. Age, boredom, and monetary problems have pursued them, like any adults. And like all adults, they have had to solve such issues for themselves. But in the end, they've decided to hold on to the supposition (since they have no proof) that it's better to build on what they have than to start over with someone else.

Now they're learning the trick of thinking up new ideas to keep interest alive. Lately they've discussed early retirement, desert retreats, and trips to the Amazon. They change their minds a lot. It seems pretty obvious now that they'll make it. They have a good chance. It's not just Donna who claims she intends to stay with Hank; Hank says he couldn't go on without Donna. And they tell each other so every day.

True, they limit their entertainments and explorations in life. Their goals are circumscribed and simple compared to many people's. But they know that, have chosen it, and make no bones about it.

The tradition of man the breadwinner, woman the homemaker is, of course, somewhat specious. From prehistoric times to the present, women have brought home much of the grub. But correct or not, the old-fashioned recipe—oatmeal cookies with no chocolate chips—is many people's idea of heaven. Sometimes their recipe succeeds, sometimes it fails. The Oldie But Goodie has the ingredients— including mutual respect—that can help you win the gold medal.

How Can You Identify One?

Churning around in the Oldie But Goodie's head are a bunch of theories. He doesn't always know he's got them, nor does he check his principles for correctness, he just assumes they're right and staunchly upholds them. Strangely enough for a conservative man, his beliefs are rather liberal: He believes the family is the atom of society; he sees your alliance as the old division of labor. He believes in justice and democracy, plus equal rights for all. If he has a slight shortcoming in his policies, it's in his notion of liberty; he isn't sure just what personal freedom is, but he's sure it has limits.

He's a social scientist's delight. He believes in ideal rules that he doesn't derive from any form of logic. He lives a pristine legacy: What's been good enough for others throughout time is good enough for him, with some minor alterations he thinks of as his own.

Certainly he's a positive man. Since so much is settled and simple for him, he has time left to get *happy*. He more than expects you to be an equal boss with him—he wants it. Why should he make decisions in departments that aren't his responsibility? Isn't that what pairing is for, to divide half the weight?

He may expect you to bend to major curves in his life. But that's not because his employment is all important. Rather it's because the money he earns is simply a necessity. And an Oldie But Goodie often refuses to go along with a transfer if it means a serious breakup of family, friends, and harmony.

Outer Signs

He's not traditional only in principles, he generally dons customary dress and subscribes to the civilities of etiquette. The Oldie But Goodie is anything but rude or flashy. He likes his clothing middling, modest, and passable. Grey, blue, and brown with buttons, proper zippers, and no plunging necklines. He always wears a belt. Usually he picks a never-changing style, such as collegiate, cowboy, carpenter, or C.P.A., and stays with it forever. Indeed, most Oldie But Goodies keep two sets of dress. Formal and informal: He's a properly dressed businessman, storekeeper, or laborer in the outer world, then he comes home, showers it all off, and out comes Man of the House—tidy, casual, usually dressed in the style of his school days. He's simply not clothes-conscious enough to shift with the winds of fashion.

He is, however, decidedly clean. From his Arrow cotton-and-polyester collar down to his black (or white) socks, he's scrubbed. His hair is shortish and shiny. He's often afraid he has dandruff; even if he doesn't, he chemically wards off any errant flake before it dares approach him. He shaves a lot, though he may try a beard or moustache every now and again. He's not meticulous and spotless; he just takes joy in eliminating the presence of whatever he was doing last and drying out his skin. (He's also afraid he's greasy.) He goes through tons of Dial and Irish Spring. He doesn't drop his towel afterward; he slings it over the rod crumpled and clumped. He doesn't know a fold from his elbow, but at least he doesn't leave a soggy trail.

He likes order and he knows where things are supposed to go. Most of the time, he'll put items back where they belong. He considers himself responsible for what he uses but not for how supplies get on the shelves or what happens when they get used up. He'll take out the trash and drive in the nails, but he has to be told when and where. He thinks it's proper for you to take his last name and for him to sign first on documents, insurance, and loans, but you sign right there with him and the benefits are for all. Often he denies himself goodies so that you and the kids can have more.

He doesn't like his car too new or too old. If it doesn't last a proper time span, he feels highly cheated. He chooses square and practical autos. The car he drives, instead of being a little bigger than yours, as with the Man Who Would Be Mogul, is a bit smaller; he figures you need the seats and space. He has a second-hand Maverick or Honda, while you have the wagon or bus. He drives your car for family expeditions, after checking the water, oil, and air, of course.

Since he thinks all machines are in his department, he washes both cars, sees to their maintenance, and makes the kids help wax. He makes everybody do some of the labor. After all, he's an economical man. He thinks up work assignments for different ages and abilities. That goes for the cooking of waffles, the purchase of flea collars, and the dishing up of Alpo.

He likes to have a place surrounded by a little lawn. With you, that is; he rarely owns a home on his own. He'll go for condominiums and apartments when he must, but he usually shuns the center of town. He wants a little space, and he likes it to be his—an exclusive shelter for his group. Usually he prefers to buy rather than rent. He'd pay in cash if he could. Being moderate, he relaxes more in a place of sensible size; he's not the mansion type.

He doesn't pay much heed to walls and furniture. He might expect to come along with his checkbook for purchases, but he defers to you in the aesthetics of choice. If asked his preference, he'll opt for big and heavy items, often plaid or maple. Probably only French Provincial, doilies, and little tea tables will make him voice a veto.

In mannerisms, he tends towards pleasantries and chivalry. He says "please" and "thank you" and expects to hear some back. Gestures of respect please his fancy, and obligation is his major driving force. He works to provide sustenance even when he doesn't particularly care for his position. And deep down he harbors an instinct to guard his loved ones without exploiting others. He aims to get his family schooled, his old age secure, and his woman's wishes met, and to accomplish this with love, attention, and responsibility. As much as he may seem antiquated, somehow he's not out of date. He's just doing what he thinks was meant to be and hoping it still operates. When it doesn't he suffers.

Like all the Intimate Men, he treats himself with care and honesty. He pays attention to his heatlh and welfare, but some of his care will depend on you—he relies on your help. After all, upkeep is interdependent with the Oldie But Goodie arrangement. Without aid, he can be blind to nutrition and not inclined to lose weight (you have to bet him that he can't). He often practices a sport or activity, frequently with other men or with kids. Most likely his game removes him to the nearby park, school, or gym. He roams a wider range than you. And he may be gone more than you like. He may coach a soccer team and get involved in Boy Scouting. But his adventures are tethered. He's roped to his work half the time and his home most of the rest.

Sex Signals

He heads for moderate women, nice rather than sweet, good rather than gushy. He avoids shy ladies who don't announce their likes; he thrives on a little simple, sometimes snappy commentary. He's more comfortable when he knows what you've got to say. After all, he bases his system on interchange, not submission, though women with determined career ambitions don't suit him. Since he tends to women of substance, he often finds himself most drawn to women who have always had a home and family as a main goal but who have tried a few years out in the world.

His idea of courtship is pretty predictable. He takes you out, drives you about, and spends some, but not a lot, of money. He gleams with delight when you cook him a meal or invite him on a field day. He likes to put his arm around you almost more than kissing. Tucking you into his elbow makes him feel you aspire to a union in the future.

Sex comes at a simmer, not a boil. He's not much of a hustler, and he doesn't take sex lightly. He'll go long spells with none rather than seek sex with no relationship. He doesn't demand virginity from you or himself—that's more the Gender Ascender's double standard. Each of you may have had one or two serious involvements before; more than that on your part might give him pause. Once you're together, he caters to your requests and gives exclusive sexual access: no others for himself or for you. He sees fidelity not so much as possessiveness but as a major gesture of love.

At first, he may not be completely without sexual problems. More than likely he comes very quickly. Perhaps he doesn't show his best until he's good and comfortable. He needs time to find his pacing; good sex between you emerges from learning which versions are just right for one another.

Your sexual interaction stays behind closed doors. His moderate streak turns to modesty when things get erotic. To outside appearances, there's little amorous innuendo between you. Whatever wonderful things go on, no one knows. Later, your kids say about you, "I can't imagine them ever doing it." But you *do,* and often, too.

Money Markers

The Oldie But Goodie's money never belongs to specific persons; it belongs to particular purposes. Some goes for upkeep, some for the future, for a vacation, education, or a new car. He divides dollars up and directs them toward certain objectives for his little kinship unit. All cash is corporate stock to him. He might have a 51 to 49 vote over you, or he might have 49 to your 51; sometimes the kids win them all.

He is less than loose with money. He's not petty, but he's guarded and inflexible. Even wealthy Oldie But Goodies spend moderately, think in terms of good investments, and buy conservative items that don't depreciate.

Your money or earnings give the Oldie But Goodie a ticklish problem. More and more families require two incomes to survive, and he knows it. Your *needing* to work can punch a hole in his self-image, but he adjusts if the income serves a good purpose, whereas the Gender Ascender doesn't. The Oldie But Goodie solves the problem of pride with a clever trick: He keeps the finances separate. You file yours away for college or retirement and use his for daily bread.

Family Aspects

Oldie But Goodies almost always want children, preferably their own; but he'll adopt, too. The Oldie But Goodie doesn't do much of the child raising, unlike the Loving Polymorph. Children are still by and large your job. After all, he isn't home when many of their troubles arise. He leaves their general management to your expertise. Yet he values his fatherhood and forms his own view of fatherly interaction and discipline: He treats his sons and daughters equally but differently. He wants his girls to have the same education and rights, but he expects more, often *too* much, from his boys, just as he does from himself.

The Oldie But Goodie maintains some good male pals from his work or past, but mostly he likes to keep company with you and other couples. His active friends come from among neighbors or colleagues who live in much the same style. Occasionally he and the other men play sports, cards, go fishing or some such without the accompaniment of women, which means you can't rely on seeing your Oldie But Goodie every night or weekend.

He rarely has women friends other than his one and only lady. He even feels strange getting close to his chum's mates, though he may like them a lot, aid them in a crisis, or offer them support. The same goes for your friends: He enjoys them, looks forward to seeing them, helps them if they need it, but doesn't seek their company.

Being familial as he is, he sees relatives as friends. He loves your sisters, cousins, and nieces (if you do) and defers to your parents. He's not sure about your brother. He treats his own parents with respect and his siblings with fondness. He thinks holidays and relatives go together; such occasions usually become big family affairs. Not that there isn't some quarreling. Not all Oldie But Goodies come from happy families. Often a man becomes more familial and traditional *because* his own parents were troubled.

Certainly he has some drawbacks. He's not the world's most exciting man. He can be stubborn and resist new ideas, get stodgy. He can close you off from a lot. But mostly he has assets. He's yours. He shares. He cares. He's respectful and supportive. He's a bread-and-butter lover. He deserves three stars.

What Is in Store for You?

So the workaday world was never your aspiration. And you're just as happy to read Mother Goose as Proust. What you want is a pal, a partner, and a chicken in the pot (with you doing the cooking). Well, that's what you get with the Oldie But Goodie.

You start off with all kinds of pluses when you enter an Oldie But Goodie relationship. He's not saccharine, stealthy, or sly. He keeps his career interest in balance with his intimate life. His respect doesn't depend on a person's sex or occupation. Sure, he's a bit possessive. Yes, he's a touch jealous. Not because you're his property or because he's a maniac, but because he has a sense of tenure and he feels all the complexities of love and attachment.

But remember this: His idea of sharing—to divide and assign according to gender—is permanently fixed. He doesn't overlap, alternate, or assimilate roles as the Loving Polymorph might. Prepare for the fact that your lives will always remain somewhat apart. You spend *many* hours in different places, doing *very* different tasks. And while the Oldie But Goodie is a honey, he's no great shakes at tripping the light fantastic. If you're looking to step lively, find another Nureyev. Certainly an Oldie But Goodie can come from any walk and lead any sort of life, street corner to ivory tower. But his conservative ways and less-than-spontaneous pace always incline him to schedule his thrills and predetermine his delights, no matter what his station. You're heading for a *planned* life course. He doesn't expect alteration in his feelings, circumstances, or goals. His future vision is tunneled toward narrow, rosy, and cosy ends. Through lengthy stretches of years, you establish your relationship, build your establishment, and collect your rewards. Even the ups and downs, as heartfelt as they are, tend to come as protracted pendulum swings and not sharp, fast peaks and lows. The aspect that makes most Oldie But Goodie couples happy is that you spend most of your beginning years *preparing* your life, then in the end you're left with exactly what you worked for.

Making a lasting relationship stay alive and not just together invariably requires effort. No two people's moods, sensitivities, trust, or motives remain even all the time. And major weak spots occur. One is when you wait for all the payoffs to come in the end and don't enjoy your life *as* you go along, only to find that the fates deprive you. A second is loneliness. It's not just in the beginning and middle stages but even in the end that you spend much of your time apart. Often just as your way together is getting paved, along comes a surprisingly hard period. When he or you turn forty or so, get bored with work, or face the death of parents and friends, the waters get troubled. And the Oldie But Goodie can sometimes change for the worse not the better. Usually he gets back on keel, but sometimes he doesn't. He can lose energy and slowly decline into stodginess. He can even desert his principles and transform himself into a not-so-intimate man. Over the years, he can go through times when he's simply not happy. He can have crises and depressions. He may question why he's working and his reasons for devotion. Retirement is hard if he's left without a realm. His sexual interest can decidedly dwindle. This is a real problem when your libido stays lively and his doesn't. Few Oldie But Goodie couples deal easily with unexpected changes, particularly when their children don't come out as expected.

Still, most Oldie But Goodies make it through these storms. That's why they're Oldie But Goodies. They even laugh at themselves. After all, both he and you *work* on your relationship. He doesn't expect a union to perpetuate itself without care and stick-to-itiveness. Both of you should keep your perspective about the past, present, and future.

There's one perpetual advantage with the Oldie But Goodie, no matter what happens: Once he loves you, he always does. That's why the romantic part is short with him. He wants the loving part to last as long as possible.

What Are the Telltale Signs of Trouble?

Of all the Intimate Type Men, the Oldie But Goodie most easily and bafflingly turns sour. The others (the Loving Polymorph and the Limited Partner) have a more ironic vision of the future; they foresee that life's miracles and miseries can cause unpremeditated happenings. The Oldie But Goodie so simplistically augurs his by-and-by, he forgets about the possibility of off-the-wall circumstance.

There are various signals that an Oldie But Goodie relationship has lost its crucial balance: when he stops valuing your work in words and deeds, when he denigrates your role and upgrades his own, when he withholds his pay. Also when he gives lip service to principles and morals but doesn't keep them.

Very often an Oldie But Goodie who goes astray begins to lie a little. First he tells himself that what he's doing or contemplating doing with his time or money isn't *really* what it is, then he goes on to cover up his tracks. Most Oldie But Goodies who break promises get very guilty, so if he starts acting like a Sugar Pie Honey, you might wonder what rule he's no longer keeping. Usually he gets disgusted with himself and 'fesses up to some entanglement. But when he doesn't, he heads you toward a nasty shock. Before that happens, consider the above signals as omens.

With age, an occasional Oldie But Goodie grows into a Father Knows Best. Or, with success, some edge their way into the Gender Ascender, the Man Who Would Be Mogul, or even the Picasso. Matters get serious if he starts to think he's superior. If he turns helping into unmitigated bossing, it means he's sliding backward into purported tradition more than you should tolerate. If such occurrences happen to yours, above all don't slip into an anxious pleaser—hold onto your equal-partner status while you try to straighten things out.

What's worse is if he starts to feel that his contacts at work have left you a dullard in the suburb; in this case, he hid status ideas and pretensions about himself all along. Such late revelations are hard to swallow, but if he isn't the man you thought he was, he isn't the man for you. A real Oldie But Goodie isn't concerned with whether you match him like a sweater set. He doesn't expect you to follow his commands like a lackey. He only cares *that* you provide the other half of his life.

There's a final critical issue, rare but conceivable, with the Oldie But Goodie: Sometimes people stay together (even remain faithful) in hatred, not in love. They develop an unending bond of dislike that holds them together better than epoxy. Their perpetual quarrel becomes their very food for life. If this happens to you, no matter what money, long years, or children have kept you hanging on, you should get your walking papers. To grow inward and bitter is not just anti-life, it's not living at all.

All in all, few Oldie But Goodie relationships have abrupt and terminal crises. The prevalent problem is a slow descent into flavorlessness. So watch for it. When you start to develop the blahs, don't depend on your partner for the solution. Get yourself together and stir up some action. Go square dancing, roller skating, or join your local Save the Whale Society. Then bring him along. Just because he's old-fashioned doesn't mean you get to sit on your duff. Up and at 'em. It's life and life only! Don't live it with cobwebs.

What Are the Chances?

With the Oldie But Goodie, you have the opportunity not only to be in a snapshot but to become a daguerreotype—you seated in a velvet chair, he standing behind with his hand on your shoulder. The tone might be a little dated, the pose a little formal, but you just might grow into a septuagenarian couple. In terms of potential permanence, the Oldie But Goodie's a winner.

No good things are easy. As much as the relationship relies on him, it also relies on you. Some special areas need constant attention. But don't throw this baby out with the bathwater during troubled times— keep scrubbing. Fight before fleeing. And don't flee at all if the situation is in any way viable.

Don't forget these tips: Prize, don't spoil the balance, keep in mind your original commitment to pairing, and know the depth of responsibilities not only to your mate but to yourself. If anything starts to go amiss, add time, surveillance, and forgiveness if necessary.

With the Oldie But Goodie, you start with the *idea* of permanent partnership as much as your mate does. But obviously you also need to love and admire your partner to achieve success. Surely if you lose your love, if you enter the match with no feeling, or even if you misconceived the degree of your emotion, you doom your efforts to a large chance of failure.

When you give both affection and assurance, you have a tremendous advantage. Both of you have already implied that you're responsible for your own participation and that you're pledged to overcome what befalls you. So if life shifts the glass in your kaleidoscope into a new pattern, just remember the pieces are the same. All you have is a new perspective. Go with it. You have nothing to fear. With an Oldie But Goodie, never delve into backbiting, revenge tactics, or sleeping around. A breach of principle can break the Oldie But Goodie foundation irreparably. Better to lose the fight than lose what you were fighting for.

No relationship is guaranteed anymore. A changed Oldie But

Goodie or a new you could decide to back out of the original declaration of duality. But when you both remain pledged, your contract helps you win a long-term future together. Of course, it doesn't come without sacrifice. When you stick with one sort of experience, you give up the chance to try others. But it's worth the chance with this man—you could come out with something great.

Remember to enjoy yourself, whatever you've got. In life you don't get a trial run—so take what you get. Don't waste time on the paradoxes; don't question what you lose for what you gain. Do what seems best for you and do it thoroughly.

Where Do You Fit In?

Never give up a right: That's the best piece of advice my father ever gave me. That maxim, which applies to many situations, forms the keystone to the Oldie But Goodie association. Does that seem contradictory to a traditional male-female arrangement? Not a bit. Not if you want a healthy partnership.

It's your right to live as you want. If you want to stay home, mind a house, raise children, do crafts in your basement or whatever, do so. It's your privilege to make the match that suits you. If you prefer a traditional man, then no matter *what* your women friends and trendy magazines say, tarry with one. But keep in mind the one thing that more than anything else keeps the Oldie But Goodie union wholesome—the knowledge that you're doing what you *want* to do.

Never giving up a right can not only help you choose an Oldie But Goodie but also provide you with the best formula for *keeping* the partnership functioning. The Oldie But Goodie union works best when you think of yourselves not as male and female but as equal partners and peers. If you want a voice in all decisions, search out the mate who confers. The Oldie But Goodie association doesn't stem from deference and submission but from joint ventures and goals. If you renounce your desires and demands, you end up with something less worthy.

You're ready to fit with an Oldie But Goodie when you decide that you wish to follow the conventional female lifestyle and that you need a man who matches your qualifications. You don't fall in with any old breadwinner and hope he treats you like an equal. You know what you are, and you look for a man who's equal to you. Only when you respect and admire yourself can you select the right mate and keep your union steady. You're on the beam when you value your work and worth to the highest, even if your favorite chore is canning with your pressure cooker. The Oldie But Goodie mate never underestimates herself. Nor does she assume she's any more dependent on her pal and partner than he is on her.

As with the other Intimate Type Men, with the Oldie But Goodie it's very important that you stay in touch with yourself and your man. You need lots of lines of communication and a great deal of honesty. You have many bargains to work out: Who handles which responsibility, under whose command is which decision, how each of you feels about proposed changes. He may want to quit a job and you feel threatened; you may tire of home and want to go to school while he thinks *work* should come first. Remember, you're a corporation. Make appointments with one another. Have conferences. Schedule times to talk. Even write letters.

You can go wrong with an Oldie But Goodie if you expect him to solve all your problems. Just because he brings home the bacon and puts his body in your bed nightly doesn't mean he's father, brother, uncle, or repairman to you. You're still on your own in life, no matter what your domestic combination. Daily disasters ranging from broken dishwashers to depression remain yours to handle. Don't lose your capabilities and turn into a weeping willow just because you're coupled and have a shoulder to lean on.

His role as household supporter, husband, and father is where he holds self-esteem: Keep your hands off it. Get your rewards from what *you* do and not from being his sidekick. Yours is *not* a Limited Partner contract; you're a *full* partner who does half the work. You should know his business, what he's doing and how things are going.

It's most important in the Oldie But Goodie relationship that you enter and stay with no nagging doubts. Don't become a mate and mother because it's expected of you, forced upon you, or considered *normal*. It's not an easy relationship; you literally have to stick through thick and thin, good and bad, sickness and health. So you'd better be sure it's worth it—for you.

Notes and Particulars

11/ The Idle Lord

Related Types: The Picasso
The Minimal Misogynist
The Gender Ascender

Positivity Scale: + − −

He leaps onto your stage like an outlaw or a trickster. He knows what's wrong with the whole wide world—or at least his half of it. He can show you how what seems right to others is most definitely in error. He disdains compliance with the norm and common toil, so he's going to set an example. You see, he believes the world owes *everyone* a living; he's just the first to collect.

Round and round goes the wheel of fortune; where it stops, no one can tell. Some of us get diligent men and some of us get Idle Lords. When your needle stops on the Idle Lord's slot, the question is—do you win or lose? The answer is—neither and both. He's quite a confounding spin. In your twenties he's a renegade, in your thirties he's a bum. When you meet him, he's a rebel; when you leave him, he's a layabout. How can he make such a drastic switch? Because while he's a mesmerist, he's also irresponsible.

Certainly not all of the Twenty-two Types of Men labor relentlessly. Some are a little lazy; some are content to live off the land or the cash in hand. But most pull their own weight one way or another. They may get a little drunk or land in jail, but all in all they keep their upkeep up.

But not the Idle Lord. He refuses occupation, never sees things through to the end, makes up projects and doesn't produce them. What he does mostly is play philosopher king. He talks about what he is or will be and harps upon the sins and errors of society; meanwhile he commits himself to little useful and he leans on other people.

Ah, but he *can* be entrancing. He's certainly not your everyday fellow. The only misfortune is when you mistake him for a mate. But

159

it's hard to tell a player fiom a partner when you're feeling mutinous yourself.

You see, the Idle Lora heads toward women who recently took a turn in life or asserted some new independence. He's aware that a brave new world makes you vulnerable, emotional, and ready for something different. When you're in that state, there's nothing quite as romantic then as a free-thinking man. If you're Mary, Mary Quite Contrary, watch out for the Idle Lord.

Story

In the many Idle Lord tales I've collected, the men range from do-gooders to drinkers to demons. Yvette's story is average. I think it's a good one to tell.

After going through teenage intractability, insurgence, and sexual rebellion, Yvette had just gone out completely on her own when she met Phillip. Phillip was certainly different. He was free, charming, confident, and sexy. He astutely criticized the powers that be, the old ways of life. He *was* a truant, but a most lordly one. Besides, he called himself a jack-of-all-trades and Yvette had never met one before.

Yvette felt she had to prove herself to Phillip; she went to bed with him right away, which clinched the attraction. To say that Phillip was erotic would be an understatement. For the first time, Yvette felt knocked asunder by a man's sexual presence. Almost overnight they began living together.

Yvette told me that over the next few years she felt like a runaway gypsy. Phillip wanted to be a kingpin in his domicile, so they decamped from the house where he had a room for a place of their own. For a while, they lived out of a truck, then they skedaddled south to the beach for a year or so. Eventually they returned and took a flat in the old part of the city where they met. They moved away from each place because of his malaise—he complained that the locals wouldn't offer him the right position or buy his services. Yvette worked almost everywhere, and when she didn't, *she* had to go for unemployment, food stamps, and welfare in order for them to survive.

Although both Phillip and the different lifestyle captivated Yvette at first, she began slowly but surely to grow annoyed that she had to take the jobs and buck the lines. She also noticed that any tidiness depended on her. Disarray was fine up to a point, but the laundry and the dishes always ended up her job; Phillip simply claimed he'd just as soon wear dirty clothes or eat with his hands. He didn't care *how* high the piles grew. He left his tools and clothes everywhere, his scattered projects never got finished *or* picked up, and nothing got repaired.

She began to realize how greedy Phillip was. His anti-money philosophy certainly didn't mean he didn't want his share—and more. He spent their funds mostly on himself. He wanted to marry so they could cash in on the wedding gifts. They did. He resented it when Yvette used the car or when her mother sent her a ticket home and he didn't get one—he wouldn't let her go unless someone sent him one, too. Ultimately, when Yvette found herself pregnant, Phillip thought the baby would prove a financial advantage to them despite the child's own costs.

Phillip managed to keep matters depressed mentally as well as physically. He had always stipulated an open marriage, but his most pointed and blatant affair was during Yvette's pregnancy, the time she needed him most. And after the child arrived, he not only brought in no money but was gone a lot and gave no help at all—he didn't alter his personal habits one jot.

At a certain point, Yvette began to want to live a little better—some ease, time for herself, and loving care. It wasn't just her labor or Phillip's selfishness taking their toll; she simply changed, and she started to assess Phillip very differently. What Yvette had not foreseen and now saw was that as circumstances changed, Phillip would not. His evasion of duty was permanent. No matter how many years passed, in Phillip's eyes all of his and Yvette's personal problems would remain someone else's fault and someone else's job to fix— namely the person who tried to make a life with him. Roaming with a rogue had been marvelously free and contrary at first, but as time altered Yvette's desires the returns not only diminished, they almost disappeared.

A lot of tongue-rolling words exist for the Idle Lord, so many, in fact, that only someone as compelling as he is annoying could attract so large a vocabulary: "free spirit," "individualist," "libertarian," "maverick," "lazybones," "lounge-lizard," "laggard," "loafer," and "shirker." As different as these words are, you can apply them all to the Idle Lord at one time or another.

How Can You Identify One?

He emanates originality and noncomformity, but that doesn't mean he's actually uncommon: Idle Lords have been around since the days of the Scarlet Pimpernel. For all we know, there may have been moochers among Cro-Magnon Man. The term "Idle Lord" used to refer to the son of a quality family who came to no good, caroused around, caused various fiascos, broke hearts, blew fortunes, sniffed the winds for his advantage and never made the most of it. And why should he have? He always had Mom, Pop, uncles, and cousins by the dozens to fall back on. He could stay well-heeled while living as a reprobate. He's much the same today. Only his relatives have changed. Nowadays the Idle Lord depends on Mother Earth and relies on Uncle Sam.

The Idle Lord has every reason, philosophical to religious to political to healthful, to explain the folly of diligence. He *claims* to lack ambition, but it isn't quite so. He *longs* for power and glory but won't run risks for them. So while he squelches major aspirations, he remains an opportunist. The Idle Lord doesn't hang loose just to hang loose. He does it to stay ready for whatever comes along; when it does come along, he can't hang onto it. He keeps all his options open: residential, financial, temporal, spatial, sexual, and occupational. He won't commit himself to Saturday Little League with Idle Junior or to your wedding day, because something better might come up. He expects success and notoriety to walk into his living room like guests who don't have to telephone first. In fact, he generally acts as if they've already arrived.

Outer Signs

His dress is both a statement of policy and a description of his philosophy. He defiantly shows he's not run by society's usual cogs. Sometimes he wears only things from Goodwill or a freebox; sometimes he dons drawstring pants and Indian chintz holy-man pullovers. He may attire himself in such extremely hip fashions that regular people dismiss him. He speaks loudly through his socks: He wears thick red ones, mismatched ones, green silk ones, or none at all.

His dress is more than uncommon; it's also provocative. It's hard to
tell how immature he remains in certain respects because he makes
such a bold announcement that he's anything but a child.

He *hates* to be treated like a kid. Early in his teens he declares he's
adult and autonomous; to demonstrate, he becomes sexually active as
soon as he's out of his Toughskins. His style continues to evoke his
sexuality. He's sensitive, almost narcissistic, when it comes to his hair,
which some say is a sexual symbol. He acts as if, Samson-style, his
power lies in his silky strands, which he wears very long or very fluffy,
waved, braided, beaded, styled, or slick. He carries combs or
headbands and likes to have his locks touched. He frequently grows a
full beard or a mustache.

If he has a car at all, it's more than likely an old heap. Well, maybe
an old heap of a Cadillac, spiffed-up. He likes to sell and trade cars,
which are the closest thing to money when he's down to zip. He carries
no car insurance, but if anyone hits *him,* he gets outraged and sues.
The condition of his own vehicle constitutes a highway menace. He's
prone to getting tickets for parking, exhaust, and reckless driving. He
spreads army blankets or fake fur over the car seats. Beads or amulets
hang from the mirror, cans roll around on the floor. He converts the
back seat into a bed or the whole rear end into a trailor.

The Idle Lord has an amazing capacity for picking rundown home
surroundings. When on his own, he seeks free or dirt-cheap housing;
he inhabits the seemingly uninhabitable. He makes a home out of a
Sears prefabricated tool shed, or he rents a garage and brings in a
mattress. He house sits or shares a dilapidated mansion in a commune
with numerous others, some of whom he has slept with. Sometimes he
remains at home and irritates his parents.

When he hooks up, he quite likely moves into his lady's abode, but
if he wanders with his woman, five will get you ten he picks decaying
areas. Sometimes he heads for isolated rural acreage with hardly a
path to drive on. Almost inevitably, he settles on a place lacking at
least one modern convenience. There may be no plumbing or no
electricity; perhaps the roof leaks. The place is dusty and hard to keep.
There are no shelves or cabinets, only Sunkist orange crates. Legions
of termites and cockroaches think they live in the Galapagos Islands
instead of a house; they sit around and evolve new species while
getting suntans.

The Idle Lord keeps unpacked baggage about or scatters belongings
like Hansel leaving a trail to get back out of the woods. You can
unravel events much like geological ages when you plow through the

strata on his chairs and couches. If he decides to work, he selects the most inconvenient site possible and yells if anybody touches his tools.

The Idle Lord is surprisingly self-indulgent; often he's just plain greedy. He's always watchful that he doesn't get the short end of the stick—in cash, clothes, food, or anything. He also cheats, but only when he can justify the cheating. If he doesn't pay taxes, it's because "the government is bad." If he shoplifts, it's because "stores are capitalistic." He claims a suitcase he didn't start with because "airlines are huge companies." He never gets caught without his American Express travelers' checks; he "loses" them to a friend who cashes them while he gets a brand new set. His blanket rationalization is that he deserves to live as well as anyone else.

While an occasional Idle Lord claims perpetual illness as a reason for his exemption from labor duty, most rarely get sick. He insists he need not exercise, he "stays fit naturally." While some Idle Lords are health nuts, many are heavily into drink and drugs; the Idle Lord is frequently an alcoholic or addict or both.

Sex Symbols

He likes rebellious and independent women. But he doesn't go for the long-term individualist who's strong-willed and demanding. He goes for the lady with the learner's permit. She takes second place.

His approach is a fast and very effective hustle. He pushes you farther in the direction you were heading anyway. You might have been dressing with less than ever before, but he'll say, "Do you always wear so many clothes?" You were becoming *very* erotic, but he'll ask, "Don't you ever do anything to men?" You were trying new things, but he'll come up with even more offbeat adventures. He'll offer a new drug, a whole day of street theater, or a whole day in bed—something that you've never done before.

Sexual power is his high card. He turns himself into a walking, talking aphrodisiac. Sex with him is more than lusty and passionate, it's sensuously carnal. He plunges in everywhere and likes a lot done to him as well. He often manages to lie back and get more than he gives. He turns you on to the point where you never say no. He likes devices, mirrors, odd places and positions. Your body seems to belong to him, and you aren't sure you want it back.

While on the one hand he renders you rapturous, he proposes a no-

strings attitude. To him sex is just one of life's little pleasures that
means nothing in itself; he claims sex has nothing to do with
relationships, that it can't be controlled or limited by partners. And
you know what that means.

He may even like two women in his bed.

Money Markers

While the Idle Lord purports to share money and support, he acts
quite differently. He most likely contributes very little or no money,
and when he does earn something, somehow it always slips away
toward his own "development" before it hits the common depository.
Either you become the financial mainstay or you manage to live on
nothing. When someone has to stir up money, almost inevitably the
task falls to you.

He certainly uses the money when it's about. And the nickels he
doesn't spend you seem to end up spending his way anyhow. The Idle
Lord is a skinflint. He has strong ideas of how money should be
used—often for pleasures instead of needs. If your ideas are different,
he condemns them until you agree with him. On top of obtaining
money, you have to make the pennies stretch. You buy beans instead
of bacon.

Family Aspects

Somehow the Idle Lord manages to leave any decisions about
bearing children entirely in your lap. That way he can claim that any
offspring belong to you, not him.

You're the one and only parent; financial support and childcare
ultimately rest with you. He may haphazardly help out, but he can
come and go when he wants and never make payments. He may love
his kids, but he doesn't want them to interfere with his options. And
even when he does occasionally take over the care of the kids, he hauls
them along on what he does instead of doing something with them;
he'll shoot the breeze with strangers or fiddle with some project while
they play around unattended.

He almost always claims detachment from his own parents and
family, but in truth he harbors hostile sentiments toward them. He

feels his parents did wrongly or not enough. He blames them far longer than the normal rebellious stage most people go through. After he consistently shows himself unable to step into their shoes and see their side, they finally give up on him and get mad back.

Probably he's closer to his brother than to any other man, but still the tie shows strain—they can't talk spontaneously but have to engage in discussion. If he has any intimate family bond at all, it's probably with his sister. She often adores and defends him, if not vice versa. He certainly spills a bitter version of past history into her ear.

The Idle Lord often has a brusque attitude toward your own family. He seems to tell them, "Take me as I am and then like me if you can. But if you can't, too bad. You haven't got a choice." He likes to put himself between you and your parents, although he might demand you go to them for aid more often than he will go to his.

The Idle Lord doesn't really seem to care for other men, perhaps because men more quickly than women spot him, dislike him, and dismiss him. And although he is definitely friendlier to women, he rarely has a female pal that isn't a sexual intimate at some point in his life. He often chooses women who are mated to other men. He seems to use other people more than he esteems them.

He has his assets and they sure can hook you; he's complex and interesting. Like the Minimal Misogynist, he's a verbal enchanter. Like the Picasso he seems to be special. And when the lights are out, he's a close encounter of a very alluring kind. You can collect on eroticism, if nothing else. That may be enough and well worth the price. But in the long run you realize he's a negative influence. He dwells on what's wrong with the world, not with what's right. While he offers a new vision, he's fatally short on action. He sees himself as a bird of paradise but is actually a bit of a parasite.

What Is in Store for You?

There's hardly another relationship that so suffers from the ravages of time as that with the Idle Lord. More than any other twosome, it has foreboding age stages. It appeals in your twenties because he seems like a change; it becomes boring in your thirties because philosophical reward grows thin when faced with hundreds of dirty socks. It can easily turn you into a shrew in your forties and dry you up in your fifties and beyond.

But it's mighty hard to see the road ahead when you're having your daily delights in the spring of your romance. Almost nothing feels as delicious as doing what you shouldn't. The Idle Lord tastes like thrillingly forbidden fruit. You're together a lot—after all, he doesn't depart to the tune of the old clock radio. Everything you do seems different from your previous life. He marks a turning point, and somehow that period will always remain very special to you, no matter what transpires.

But few flings last forever, and sad to say, the Idle Lord is no exception. As maturity means more responsibility, the Idle Lord becomes as burdensome as he once was liberating. For his upkeep, he relies upon his Adam's Rib; he becomes your total dependent. And what few women consider until they're well into an Idle Lord relationship is that his ideas on survival tend to make more rather than less labor for his partner. It's well known that monetary stress makes more work and eats up a person's time. Cheap food requires lengthy preparation; sewing, altering, and rummaging for used items take hours. Lines take standing in.

Still, work and a meager existence can look like gold if your man plates them. If the Idle Lord appreciated what you did and praised you occasionally, you could certainly say, "What the hell?" But unfortunately the Idle Lord is not one to acclaim anyone but himself. He not only doesn't acknowledge your contribution, he thinks everything he does for you is utterly magnanimous of *him*. The favors he does for you eclipse anything you do for him, in his eyes. He's determined to have his way, and when you cross him he condemns with a razor-sharp tongue. He wins all the arguments because he overwhelms you with verbiage.

Since he perceives of himself as very much a Man, he demands all the privileges that presumably follow: By rights, his feet are loose and his fancy free; he's surely his own boss. It's not that he *denies* you the same rights, but since his options come first and yours second, you have a harder time putting yours into action. He even gives you the same sexual freedom he claims for himself. But you get the feeling he does so in order to keep his own license clear. Besides, when can you exercise yours—on your trip to the grocery store?

It's no wonder that an Idle Lord spouse often finds that in a few years she's fed up. All along, he has taken your attempts at sensibleness and mutuality as a policy of resistance. Now you no longer attempt to be sensible. He treated you as an obstacle; now he's the same to you. Your freedoms gnawed away at his liberty; now you turn the tables.

Unhappily, any measures you take to make him change his ways rarely work. He simply doesn't begin to face obligation. Instead, matters grow even worse. The ultimate Idle Lord partnership is when he not only thwarts his own successes but spoils yours. Every time you work for a goal, your partner blows your savings. You have a child and he has an affair; you plan a holiday and he picks a quarrel. He makes sure you know of his brawls, his lost jobs, and his flirtations. He has a grand eye for messing things up.

A great deal depends at this point on how magnetic the bond between you is. Present circumstances give you every reason to leave, but memories of passion past provoke you to stay. And it's hard to see that the relationship may grow yet more barren.

Usually at this point you begin to retain your own money, form your own goals and stop considering his. To stay with him means you begin to treat him worse and worse over the years. You oust him in almost every way but physical. You take over and become a matriarch. You strive for yourself and your children without any regard for him. You think you tell him to "take it or leave it," but he stays—and you still take it.

But to leave also has a strange aftermath. He bestows a bitter wariness that can make you seem tough, stubborn, and anti-male. And while you may have some short romances, usually you don't trust love for quite a while.

What Are the Telltale Signs of Trouble?

If a man comes on sexy and bewitching, claims he's exempt from work, but thinks that you should work—you might taste his tallow, but don't sell your soul for his candle, no matter *how* big it is.

A man who's dependent on women almost *always* has a woman around. His relationships go back like a steady stream, starting in his youth. He goes very quickly from one woman to another, sometimes within forty-eight hours, but certainly in no more than a few weeks.

He always has a small collection of single lady friends, so some new nest is never far off. And if he has shirts made by one lady friend, gifts from another, and embroidered jeans from a third, you know he picks caretakers every time.

Pay attention when the quality of your man shifts in your mind's eye. The very first time you mumble "good-for-nothing" should ring like a five-alarm fire signal. You've begun to disrespect him, and when you disrespect anything about your man, it doesn't bode well. It's time to consider the decade ahead.

You get an especially loud signal of serious trouble with the Idle Lord that women in other types of relationships rarely get: You don't want to leave, you want to get *him* out. You figure the place is yours. He earned little and deserves less. Whether you notice or not, your sense of injustice has grown ominous. All too often when you get in that position, you hang on to win when you should simply end matters without more losses. Better stop and think, which do you want— freedom or the Franklin stove?

What Are the Chances?

When it comes to the Idle Lord, the chances are high that he won't change. What's most likely is that *you* will become different from what you were. In the first glow of an Idle Lord pairing, it's so hard to see the future that in all probability the only women who will recognize the truth of what I say will be those looking back. Considering that fact, my advice is this: Do the Idle Lord if you will and must, but don't think in terms of forever and a day. Think of him as an event. When it's over, say so long. Most likely you will start to take life seriously somewhere along the line.

The Idle Lord relationship causes an irreversible shift in you. If you stay with him, you experience one of two changes. In the first kind, you stay close to your own path while you foot his bill. In this case your transformation is inward, not outward. Perhaps you live much as you always did, but your outlook turns pessimistic. Certainly working becomes your permanent condition. The combination of work and a gloomy outlook is poisonous. If you remain with the Idle Lord in this frame of mind, you suffer malcontent. And if you leave him, all too frequently you join the type of women who seeks a man to support her "this time." And that's bad; such a bitter ambition not only goes against love but often works exactly contrary to your desire—men recognize ulterior motives and quite rightly retreat very fast. In the second kind of change, you stray far from your previous road. Your modification is quite visible. You live very differently from the way you did before you knew him. Usually the transformation comes to suit you.

Yvette's case was lucky. Her new lifestyle eventually not only suited her but aided her. When she found herself bickering with Phillip, plotting not to leave him but to get him to go, having affairs and mocking him, going back and forth between two men because the other man "met a different need," she decided to separate—to think things out. Yvette realized rather fearfully that a nonconformist life was now the only one in which she would ever fit. In certain communities, her case was more the norm than the exception: Support systems were available and a lot of caring people were around. But she also recognized that she had a long time ahead before she was ready for another alliance, because she acted like a black widow spider.

When you meet an Idle Lord, my suggestion is *Look Ahead.* The fun and games of an irresponsible mate simply don't go with every stage of life. Also, if you find the break with an Idle Lord miserable and seemingly impossible, don't rush to the decision that you can't do it. Usually a split from him takes a long while, and during it other men don't seem to come up to the old one's snuff. After an Idle Lord, one of the healthiest things you might do for yourself is to withdraw from all sexual relations for a while. Once you distance yourself from passion, you can better return to a more caring love. *Then* you can retrieve the sex!

Where Do You Fit In?

Often when a woman chooses a man who's loose in every way, she's every which way *but* loose, only she doesn't know it. She seems free and easy, but deep down she isn't the totally unrestrained soul she aspires to be. Instead of being an escape from social constraints and upbringing, her fling with a ne'er-do-well is in part an escape from herself.

Many a rebellious earth mother is a dutiful caretaker. Sadly, the Idle Lord is often an attraction to your projected self and not a match for the real you. In time, when the real you crops up again, so do the irreconcilable differences between you and him.

If you are prone to the Idle Lord, you most likely have strong ideas on how life should be led. Chances are you're responsible, ethical, loyal, and honest. As your ideas lead you toward independence, you mistakenly believe that you aren't bound by rules, at least not the *old* ones, and that's where you go wrong.

For a clue to yourself, just examine the motivations you have for falling for the Idle Lord; I'll bet you find some righteous principles involved. Did you choose the union because of love? Well, after all, "for love" is a *very* principled reason for mating. Did you desire a new, more *real* kind of life? Are you stubborn? Then a commitment to duty and obligation probably isn't far behind. The trouble is, when you pick a man who lacks responsibility and you have it, you end up picking up his slack.

When you're with the Idle Lord, it's not that you can't change him, but that you can't always change *you* either. You may kid yourself for a while. You may reveal to yourself only slowly exactly what you are like. You may ignore the evidence that you and your mate differ greatly, but the ways in which he seems remiss in your eyes reveal as much about what *you* are as they do about him.

When you select someone you'd like to be, only to find out that you can't be his way at all, it's hard to face. But you are not to blame for a lack of self-awareness—if you grow with your errors. You can only get knowledge by the process of life itself, and to do so you have to live it, miscalculations and all. You didn't make a *mistake;* you may have lacked insight and foresight, maybe at worst you held on too long. But you did try. You'd regret it more if you hadn't done it at all.

Notes and Particulars

12/ The Romper Roomer

Related Type: The Instant Barricader

Positivity Scale: + − −

Love? There's no such thing. There's only Lust. Talk? Waste of time. Why not just pull down the blind and take off your Levi's? But make sure you leave all the lights on.

For some of the Twenty-two Types of Men, sexual surrender is only *part* of what they want. For the Romper Roomer, that's the beginning and the end of it: no attachments, no deep conversations, just good old ho! ho! And lots of it. He may go from bedroom to bedroom, or he may fill up his own house with bedfellows. He may like it one by one, or he may think groups are groovy. He's a combined voyeur and people collector. He's good at talking to strangers.

Just as some automobiles are exercises in sensory deprivation (cushions to keep out bumps, tinted glass to keep out glare, air conditioners to keep out heat and odor), the Romper Roomer is an exercise in emotional deprivation—no tears, no fears, and certainly no jealousy. A ride, yes, but please—no extra feelings! He gets all his highs and lows from sexual encounters. No wants and needs, no real contact. First-name basis.

Story

My neighbor Rhonda recently reported this incident to me.

Kids out of her hair, bikini in place, she was out at the beach. A man approached her. "Hello," he said. "You're twenty-eight, aren't you?"

"No," she said.

"Twenty-seven?" he asked.

"No," she said.

"I'm going in the right direction, aren't I?"

"No," she said.

"How old *are* you?"

She told him.

"You're certainly in good shape," he said. "Do you jog?"

"No," she said.

"How old do you think *I* am?"

"Are we playing twenty questions?" she asked, annoyed.

"No, really," he said. "How old do you think I am?"

She brutally scanned him and added five years. "Forty-seven," she said.

But he was undaunted. Within three minutes, the inquiry had progressed to whether her kind of woman had ever had group sex.

"Every Tuesday for the last five years," she said.

"Good!" he responded, as if cheering her on in some campaign. And would she come over for a martini? He announced his name, something very rhythmic with lots of L's and R's, but didn't ask hers. Then he gave her his phone number and asked her to call him.

She didn't, but the indications were fairly ample—after all, he had already indirectly accused her of being old-fashioned—that she had met the local Romper Roomer.

Rhonda really suited the type of woman the Romper Roomer heads for. She's cute in the proverbial sorority-girl way, very athletic. And she's married. In other words, energetic and not innocent. She looks like a good sport.

Rhonda didn't happen to fancy a frolic, but she appreciated that he didn't leave her guessing. Though he didn't directly state it, his questions made it clear what he was offering: That she could come and get it.

By being transparent, the Romper Roomer expects to deal only on the superficial level. Then, he assumes, if you're at all willing, your intentions are the same. No underlying motives are allowed with the Romper Roomer. And no one has responsibility for anyone but himself or herself. He thinks he operates on a basis of free will. But the kind of free will he gives you implies that he won't take the buck or anything

that happens. And not every woman knows exactly where it all leads
when she sails in his regatta. When it's said and done, a relationship
with him is not much more than sport. A sack race at the start and
squash at the end.

How Can You Identify One?

The Romper Roomer likes lots of entertainment. Life for him is a
parade of passing people and trappings. Safety lies in numbers, escape
in variety. There's simply too much happening to do much thinking.
Good times is his philosophy. It's also his geography. He thinks you
meet a lot of easy women in Europe. Even more in Asia.

All in all, he's a pretty literal fellow. He doesn't go for depth in
meaning, in feeling, in relationships. If life is a wave, then he's a body
surfer. He doesn't reveal complex stirrings or thoughts to others or to
himself. He loathes the idea of psychotherapy, though he may
participate in encounters and "enlightenments," especially on weekends. He's not your most sensitive man. He takes all that internal stuff
and puts it in the deep freeze. He nibbles on trifles. The minimized,
external self.

As a result, he reduces reality with one of two mottos: 1) Everything
in life is so wonderful you ought to have a good time. Or, 1)
Everything in life is so awful you might as *well* have a good time. A
singular optimistic or pessimistic stance. No explanations. He probably subscribes to other hip but prosaic policies: Freedom. Owning
yourself. Open marriage. No monogamy. No jealousy. Space. When
he wants to persuade you, he can rally all of these as criticism of what
you aren't and what you should be. He can flip them over and call you
uptight, old-fashioned, and hung up.

Outer Signs

The Romper Roomer takes care of himself. He's the only person he
has to take care of. He leads a sort of stripped-down existence—
unencumbered emotions go with unencumbered apartments, sleek
cars, and scanty dress. He doesn't wear undershirts. You won't find
him buying underpants, either, except perhaps tiny nylon bikinis. He

can`. always be bothered to get a pair of socks when he puts on his shoes. He goes for half-dressed—or undressed. Because no matter what, he wants to look sexy. He owns lots of shorts, but he wouldn't be caught *dead* in boxer shorts. Nor does he *ever* combine street shoes and swimming trunks.

He's a very casual, fairly good dresser. Semi-silky print shirts worn unbuttoned to the navel. Tight jeans. Butter-soft leather loafers, boots, or boat shoes. If he has to don a suit, it's Frenchified, and probably has a vest with a paisley back. He has a running suit that has stripes and is tight across his bottom.

When he's a little older, his garb becomes a bit looser and more hippieish, your basic comfortably sexy appearance. He probably sports a beard and tunic tops with plunging necklines. Under the neckline glows an inordinately deep suntan, flashing like a neon sign saying *Nudist Colony Ahead*. (He'd call it a "discovery center.")

Perhaps he adds a touch of rococo. A puka-shell choker, a gold chain, an I.D. bracelet, an onyx ring. A big, flashy turquoise belt buckle. And recently, and even more likely in the future, you're liable to find just a touch of makeup.

Youth means a lot to him. He can't envision sex without it. He has unspoken but obvious worries about age. He will try to stay and to act very young. Yet he probably looks older than he is. His life doesn't wear easy on mind or body, despite his seeming leisure—his skin, eyes, and neck reveal it. He plays too hard and thinks too soft, and it shows.

The Romper Roomer's style extends to his automobile: It's meant to please him, and it's definitely not family oriented. It looks game. Often he drives a sports car, especially the more manly type—M.G., Triumph, or Corvette. Sometimes a little more suave and seductive, but still not too expensive—a Mazda Z-type. In any case, sleekness and image mean as much to him as function. If he thinks big, he thinks Pontiac or Mercury.

He would like to own a boat. Sometimes he does. He sees yachts and cabin cruisers as going with carnal picnics and orgiastic clam-bakes. He likes to take small batches of people to out-of-the-way places. He doles out drinks and bologna. He tells everyone what a good time they will have, are having, or have had.

His apartment is in the center of the sporty, singles-y part of town, located in a complex of buildings. His pad is a little bit modern and a little bit expensive. It probably has a pool. Sun or no sun, it boasts a steam room and Jacuzzi. If he has a house or condominium, it lies near the beach, hills, or woods. The backyard is *very* private. The closet has been turned into a cedar sauna. The deck supports a hot tub. He *always* has a couch—a big one. The tables are blond wood, the television color and portable. The mirrors are everywhere and curiously placed—often on the ceiling. A king-sized bed with no bedspread fills one room. He owns a supply of huge towels and a couple of spare terrycloth bathrobes.

There are a few paperback novels about. He reads John D. McDonald and Dick Francis. Heavier ones than that appear, but he doesn't quite finish them. He subscribes to *Playboy* ("for the articles") and *Hustler* (for the obvious).

He uses services to make his existence more convenient—he sends clothes, sheets, and towels to the laundry. Young Romper Roomers might go to the building laundry room, though, to meet girls. He knows the way to the delicatessen blindfolded. He has a charge account at the liquor store. They deliver—and deliver.

Surprisingly, he doesn't eat out much except for breakfast. He centers his activities around home; all *kinds* of things can happen over dinner. His eating habits are Spartan; he does steaks on his hibachi and tosses salads in a Danish modern bowl. He derives his more elaborate cooking from the *I Hate To Cook* book. His refrigerator is bare except for juice and iceberg lettuce. He makes quick runs for food when he needs it. He thinks of chips, dips, and cheeses when having company over—less fuss that way. Basically he provides only one regular meal—and it's not soul food.

He *does* stock a lot of ice cubes.

His bathroom cabinet is his real pantry. It contains abundant and diverse supplies: Tampax, Vaseline, body oil, baby oil, Close Up, and Scope. But no condoms. He considers birth control *your* responsibility.

He equips one other department—the liquor reserves—for every preference. In general, he purchases the cheaper brands—gallon jugs of Ye Olde Wolfbreath vodka, quarts of Uncle Unknown bourbon. And whether or not he likes marijuana himself—he's tried it, for sure—he knows it can make you merry. He's inclined to pass around lots of not-so-good grass. Say, Tijuana Tan.

Some Romper Roomers live on an inheritance, but most tend to have a job that requires regular hours and a certain amount of attention. Usually they are not the boss, but they manage a good enough position to allow for free time. They might be sales manager or computer representative. Some are doctors, dentists and professors.

While he may not treat his soul terribly well, he treats his body all right. He cares about physical fitness. More than likely he jogs, exercises, lifts weights, or plays tennis. He can be swept away by new ideas on diet and nutrition. He might eliminate sugar and red meat for a while and try alfalfa sprouts, lecithin, and bran. Cardio-vascular systems intrigue him. Cancer is a forbidden word.

Sex Signals

He aims for youthful, solidly built women. He'll try anything, but he'd rather avoid bookish, intricate, fragile types. He prefers those who have been taught to appeal to men, those who make themselves available and not intense. First choice is sportsy women who don't burst out with too much analysis, who have a lively interest in activity. He hangs out where such women hang out—at hangouts.

He's not shy about meeting women. He easily talks to people in fern bars, sports shops, and swimming pools. He gets you to establish who you are and what you do right away, usually by asking impertinent questions; he doubletalks his way around telling much about *himself*. He engages you. Hooks a response. He hopes to spear something more tangible. He challenges you to prove yourself. A lot of women seem to need to rise to it. He may query you on your habits to see if you are "old-fashioned" or, better, "hysterical." He gives you his policies on freedom and "our times." He offers to cure you. Not too much footplay comes with his offering; dinner and theater are not on his agenda. Once you've met, the next step is his place or yours—preferably his. It has more mirrors.

Sex with the Romper Roomer ranks beyond proficient—it's *acrobatic*. He's read the *Kama Sutra* upside down and backwards. And that's some of the ways you'll find yourself with him, too.

He insists on getting himself, as well as you, well attended to in bed. He shows you where to apply yourself. He expects the whole thing with added extras right off the bat. Hesitation signifies hang up.

In performance he gets excellent marks. He has lots of acts down pat. If you prefer prowess to profundity at the moment, he's right down your alley. Cuddling and cooing are not in the bag of tricks.

Money Markers

He spends quite a lot of money—on himself. He's unable to accumulate much. He lives just a little over his means, or just a hairsbreadth under. He has a pretty sizable monthly tally to pay for his easy way of living. He often owns items that are big and expensive, like boats and cars. He likes skiing trips and Mexico. He flies SAS.

He doesn't use a woman's money. Moreover, he entertains women without coughing up much of his own. After all, he doesn't take you out. To him, women are a common commodity. He's attached to none; they're easy to get. So why pay?

Family Aspects

He seems to have no family. You rarely hear him speak of them. Phone calls from them never interrupt you. No pictures with them seem to exist. Wherever they are, they're distant. Their world and his rotate in different orbits.

The word "friends" can't quite be applied to his acquaintances. He plays tennis and eats lunch with his regular chums, but they're more like a parade than partners. His acquaintances lead him to other people (especially women), to parties and picnics. They use each other like an entertainment circuit. Some men find that the Romper Roomer strikes up a friendship with them only to meet their women friends. When he gets their numbers, he disappears.

He's a textbook case of self-centeredness. He cultivates mindlessness in most aspects of his life. He is not only hard to get through to, he pretends there is nothing there when you do. Whenever you reach for him, he's like Casper the Friendly Ghost gone invisible. He has his assets. He comes equipped with light entertainment, serves up physical gratification without strings attached. Perhaps, however, the best plus he offers women is one of which he is unconscious: He provides you with a way to experiment and learn about yourself. The size of your emotional and carousing needs becomes clearer in his crucible. For that reason, it can be worth walking into his laboratory.

What Is in Store for You?

You can't exactly say you have a *relationship* with The Romper Roomer. You can meet and greet, talk and make love. But you can't see each other, go together, or head for the altar. He will put your name in his black book and call you for parties, but there's no emotional bond. He's not even a telephone buddy like the Instant Barricader. You can only call him for a feather-bed bender.

You can only stay on his list if you participate. He scratches edge-hangers. If you ask for more than he's giving, he'll disappear fast. Sex is the only ante to his game. If you don't pay, you don't play.

In some ways the Twenty-two Types of Men are like horse racing. You have to learn the odds, study the form, then pick your horse. In the case of the Romper Roomer, he's a fast starter at the gate, but he's only good for a very short run. If you're looking for a quick sprint, fine. If you're looking for distance, choose another number.

When a man asks you over, not out, at your first encounter or begins to talk about sexual prowess, group gatherings, and swinging before you exchange names, the underlying invitation is pretty obvious. Most Romper Roomers carry you as far as they can get you to go, until you stop them with a very form *whoa!* As far as the Romper Roomer is concerned, a no is still a yes unless you back it up. He's hard to rein in. If you have him over, he'll put the jump on you; he'll assume you meant to run the course with him.

Most women use certain ploys to protect themselves until they get to know a man. Consciously or unconsciously, you will choose to meet somewhere away from your bedroom, a little in the public eye, with open avenues of escape. A Romper Roomer will try to circumvent these protections—they mean time and trouble. His intention is singular. Why fuss around?

He expects sex and makes it seem like you agreed. So *you* become the remiss one when you withhold what was understood. If he gets his way and you seem upset afterwards, he will use guilt tactics and call it choice—you wouldn't have done it if you didn't want to, right? He has a firm rule he never wavers from: If you've taken one or two steps you *have* to go all the way. It has a variant: It's not fair to lead a man on; if you mean to back out, you must do so at the beginning. And so on.

Don't buy it. It's bunk! Whatever there is between you, it's short. If you say no, he'll move on pretty quickly. If you say yes, that's it, the whole schmere. The event is over. You might be offered occasional repeats and escapades—adult field days—but his track runs in a circle; it's not a highway.

He doesn't want you to call unless you want to come over. Hanging on the telephone is not his idea of fun. Physical contact is. You don't go on gradually to learn more and more about each other. No introductions to family follow. Once around the course, usually the Romper Roomer moves on to another track.

Since you can't go anywhere with him, what's important is how you end up yourself. Win, place, show—or lose. You may meet other people through him, but only to encounter the same horse of a different color.

What Are the Telltale Signs of Trouble?

The Romper Roomer flashes his calling card pretty quickly. So if you have any suspicion that you'll come out with losses, don't place your pennies on his pony. His outer signs pop off like so many firecrackers—all in a row and in speedy succession. You reach a critical point of decision often within the first few minutes. His Mae West act ("Come up and see me sometime") is a definite storm warning. So is a barrage of questions that get more and more personal.

If you do go up, or have him over, a set of irregular ripples crisscross your pond. He stands just a trifle too close. You feel as if you have to keep from backing up. He brushes by you when it wasn't really necessary. He pats your rear and nuzzles your neck, as if you were already intimate, when you are not.

He's waiting to see your reaction to all these things. No reaction means he moves one step farther. If you do react, he'll try again to see if you really mean it. If you've gone to his place, he might grab you behind the bar, slither up to you on the couch, or head you to the bedroom. Crossing the threshold means going all the way—he'll try.

Balking on your part produces a bombardment. He'll question your with-it-ness. If you say you have another man, he'll accuse you of being property. If you say you prefer to love the person you have sex with, he'll say you aren't liberated. Refusing is utterly *neurotic* of you. It's certainly self-denial. Who but a disturbed person would turn down such pleasure?

If his maneuvers unnerve you, it's time to take a stand—a negative

one. If you definitely say no, a Romper Roomer tells you that you're
"nice." It's his way of saying he's decided to jog off.

Any point can be critical with the Romper Roomer. You may find
yourself out of curiosity, or whatever, having gone along with him
pretty far. The idea that you can't back out, that you're "mean," is
ludicrous; you can say no any time! And you never have to put up with
grabbing. If the usual gesture language—taking his hands off, moving
away, staying behind the kitchen counter—doesn't work, then muster
up every way you have of saying stop. In fact, *yell: STOP IT!*

Politeness is his greatest advantage and your greatest disadvantage.
So toss it. Your mother isn't looking.

What Are the Chances?

Let's be serious. There's not much chance of turning *People*
magazine into *Time*. And there's not much chance of turning a
Romper Roomer into a scout leader. He has no respect. Sharks have
little regard for the spirits of the tiny fish they scoop up, devour, and
excrete. The same goes for the Romper Roomer.

Considering the all-around rewards, my advice is to say "so long."
You can find more intimacy in other versions of short relationships
meant for sex alone. Certainly you can find more things to do and a
wider variety of communication elsewhere. At the bottom line, what
the Romper Roomer offers soon gets boring. Personally, I think a spin
with the Romper Roomer means you aren't taking care of yourself too
well. I read even a cool, calculated go-around with him as a sign of
depression. In so many non-words, the Romper Roomer says you
think you can do without love. In most cases, I just don't buy that.

For pure physical contact, with no friendship or commitment
attached, at least he's safe. You can try him and if you get tired of him
or find you don't like his ways, you can cancel him with ease. Also, at
certain points in life, you might want to test your survival equipment.
If you can take the Romper Roomer for what he is and come out fine,
you'll know you are guaranteed to survive arctic conditions.

But please—only do him if you're in the same frame of mind as he, if
you too want sex and no attachment, if you want performance. Then
also see if he just wants to get pleasure or is willing to bestow some as
well. Some Romper Roomers only want to get massaged, not to rub in

return; they hate feeling they have to do anything. After all, they aren't good sharers to start with.

When you romp in his chambers, your chances for a good experience are best if you have good eating habits: Stop when you're full. If you do too many of them for too long, the uncomfortable feeling that results can take a long time to go away. You can't find an Alka-Seltzer for too-much-Romper-Roomer at your local drugstore.

If he uses shame to persuade you, he's not the one who ends up guilty; *you* are. He'll take advantage of your shady areas—what you think you should do, how you don't want to make him angry, how hard it is for you to say no directly. He doesn't suffer your confusion when he's happily getting it on.

As for group sex—it can be fine; it can incorporate love and care for all involved. Or it can be forced by social pressure and have a circus atmosphere. You certainly ought to be the one who decides on your own participation. You might derive more satisfaction from a strong no than from a muddled yes.

Where Do You Fit In?

If too many men who just want sex come through your door, you might need company so badly you will take anyone and anything.

It is possible to find yourself entertaining and sexual enough not to require provisions from the outer world. Your life doesn't have to be a parade of people, jokes, and good times just to fill it up. Think about sitting down with just you. Make *yourself* your favorite date and go to your own living room. Admittedly, it isn't always an easy task; it can be hard to break through loneliness. But, once found, the world inside your own head can be spectacular, multicolored, and infinite.

That means taking personal charge of your sex life, too. You can fulfill your own desires, say, during those long in-between-men spells, without frantic forays in search of someone, anyone, to satisfy you. To comply with something you don't want just to answer a sexual drive means you allow a need to become a blind compulsion, if not a fetish. It means you're admitting only one solution where there are actually many. Abundant techniques for loving yourself sensually and sexually exist. Masturbation can be healthy and delightful. You can explore it as a stop-gap measure if not as a full-time pleasure. That way you can hold out for the partnership, not just the anatomy, you crave.

Check out just how far you will go to prove you are (pick one) liberal, liberated, not hung up, guiltless—or whatever other definition unnerves you and is important to you. Demonstrating or not demonstrating hip modes does not make you good or bad, right or wrong. Zero in on your *own* comfort zone—what's right for you according to when it starts to feel wrong—and set your limits accordingly. Otherwise other people's definitions will push you around and their terms will intimidate you At least let the things that threaten you be *real*. The fear that you won't be with-it isn't real. Tell anyone who manipulates you with accusations to go and shove it—where it's at. If he can find it.

Romping with the swinging set could indicate a backhanded way to get attention. Do you have a history of repressed rebellion? Is doing something shocking important to you? The high of a "they'd never guess" secret? Did you smoke in the bathroom at sixteen, knowing that, despite opening the windows, some scent remained when your folks came home? Or did you wait till you left home and you've been on a surreptitious free-for-all ever since?

Sex tends to be one of the very first forms of rebellion for women, the first break away from parents and childhood. But it doesn't have to remain a continual way of announcing your identity. Once you've run down that street, you can try others. Graduate from adolescent ways. When you learn to tune into *all* your needs and not just your nocturnal ones, you'll leave the Romper Roomer's one-track, boring mind forever.

Notes and Particulars

13/The Man Who Would Be Mogul

Related Types: The Instant Barricader
The Disaster Broker
The Picasso

Positivity Scale: + − −

He is (or will be) famous. He is (or will be) wealthy. He is (or will be) president, senator, producer, director, general, magistrate, or potentate. The Man Who Would Be Mogul has career madness.

He seems smooth and suave on the outside. But inside he's the engine on the Rock Island Line—a nonstop express that moves a mile a minute. They named a dance after him: the Hustle. Only he's too busy to learn it. But he sure can talk it—it's his native tongue.

He's hooked on *getting*, not being, so there's no end of the line. As soon as the last deal is sealed, he moves on once again—often to the neglect of what he just accomplished. Many times he has a hidden self-destruct button to make sure the ultimate coup always eludes him. Only a few become *real* moguls. The rest remain ever would-be. But even when he fails, he always fails upward. And he never quits. On his way up to Mikado, he becomes Lord High Executioner. He axes associates and even mates. He also acts like Lord High Everything Else. He overrides contributors, helpers, and staff members.

First in his life is Ma Bell. Nothing is as important to him as the telephone. When he enters the door, he never fails to walk directly to the nearest Touch Tone and ring his answering service. And always just as you're about to leave for somewhere he says, "Wait a minute while I make one more call." He lives solely for business. All other things—women, children, friends, ambulances, firetrucks, paddy wagons, floods, hurricanes, holocausts, baptisms, bar mitzvahs, and funerals—simply come second.

Since he always makes deals, you might be one, too. He spurns the domestic side of life. He claims he "could handle it more efficiently than you" but doesn't have the time; he has "better things to do." What he wants in a woman is an indefatigable keeper-upper, a backdrop and a buttress—installed in some interior, not flying around without him. And since you always are less important to him than any business of the moment, once he takes you as a consort, he turns you into a lady in waiting.

Story

When my sister's school chum Marlene wed Jack, she also married a master plan—Jack's. He aimed to ascend a conglomerate tower by way of Babel—he could talk anyone into anything.

Jack's father had a small air-freight service. But Jack wasn't content to glide. He wanted to fly high, world wide. Nothing short of tycoon would do. From the minute Jack took over, he was wheeling and dealing, dividing and diversifying.

Marlene never knew whether she had a silent partner or was one— Jack was always conversing, but to somebody else. He considered her perhaps his only transaction that was totally signed, sealed, and delivered. Not that Marlene wasn't ambitious and competent herself; she was. But she thought she should disguise such "masculine" traits in order to become a wife. Jack looked like the perfect mate. He proudly showed the ambitions she closeted. When she hooked her sidecar to Jack's motorcycle, she thought they would make a good combo—like Batman and Robin. She considered herself an equally active partner, just smaller in stature.

Jack didn't see it that way. In his world of "big fish eat little fish," he judged women's talents as sardine-sized. The Man Who Would Be Mogul swims upstream for himself; Jack didn't want Marlene leaping in with him. Jack decided things so quickly and gave his opinion so bluntly that Marlene found there was little dialogue between them. At one point, interested in the law, she wanted more schooling and a career. But he pooh-poohed it. Then—Catch 22—when she couldn't prove her competence by means of success, money, or degrees, he judged her as lacking the stuff.

An originally self-assured woman turned into a tortoise who confined herself to a wifely-motherly world. She falsified a sense of family around an absentee husband and father. And while she professed contentment, she suffered constant, nagging boredom. Marlene waited endlessly for Jack. He was always at an appointment or in a meeting; he delayed the dates she asked for. On Sunday, supposedly his day at home, he inevitably had to go out "for just an hour or two." She spent years biding her time and hoping for her turn, but it never came. Other, more "important" people always had priority.

When Jack and Marlene were together, everything they did was business-related. They gave no dinners except for clients, took no vacations except to inspect facilities (the company paid), attended no party without potential partners present (and then not even Cyclone Cindy, not to mention Marlene's dislike of parties, could keep them away). Sometimes Jack went alone, telling Marlene she "didn't fit." Back at the ranch, they lived beyond their means, causing Marlene acute discomfort. Jack considered their lifestyle an investment; Marlene lived it even though it went against her grain.

Sex came and went on a predictable basis; it was reasonably steady and well accomplished, but it just wasn't Jack's preferred intercourse. Often he was too busy or tired. Marlene asked for a lot more than she got. But as his corporate power really began to swing, so did Jack. He was away a lot and met many people, women included. And in his constant search for advantage, he wondered if perhaps another woman might pay off better than Marlene. After a few flings, he slid into another contract: He took a mistress.

After a time, Jack dropped on an unsuspecting Marlene the news that he wanted out, or at least a separation. At first she couldn't believe that after all those years he could mean divorce. He didn't; he just wanted free rein for more assets. She clung on. For a while, every time something went wrong with his affairs, business or romantic, he was back, and she welcomed him. But the more she struggled on her own, the more she changed her mind. One day when Jack wandered home, an unsure and shaky Marlene said "no more."

While most women hang on in the hope of the eventual returns some decide to split from the Mogul early. Jack's partner's wife took a different tactic from Marlene's: She got tired of marking time, photocopied every paper in the office and walked out. One of their pals took a third road—she decided to keep the real estate; an on-again, off-again husband for her was better than none. Besides, what she did when he was gone was her own affair.

The Man Who Would Be Mogul looks like fame and fortune. Sometimes he can make life Wonderland. His life moves as fast as a game of craps. In the meantime, you stand by and breathe on *his* dice—not taking a chance on your own. And since he gambles on roll after roll after roll, any jackpot he wins is always in his control.

How Can You Identify One?

With the Man Who Would Be Mogul, what looks temporary is permanent: The way he is now is the way he will always be, how he acts about business is how he acts about life, and how he treats others is how he'll treat you. He's not hard to spot. He stands out like a Porsche on a Nicaraguan freeway, madly accelerating, endlessly passing.

He believes in Time. He thinks you can waste it, kill it, lose it, stretch and certainly use it, but not put it aside until later. He's more than prompt—he's four minutes early. He yells at you to get ready, makes you wait for a call, and still you arrive too soon.

He has faith in space and substance. He likes things massive, talks big, thinks big, and chooses big. For him, bulk means he can back up what he says; so he likes huge homes, large cars, grand music, king-size beds, and enormous desks. Naturally he subscribes to the theory that might makes right, although he doesn't necessarily say it. He sees people in two categories: winners and losers. He deals with the one and discards the other. He judges the successful not by their feelings of personal achievement but by public image—money, power, and fame. He equates talent with "getting it on." If it's manifest, it's real; if it's latent, it's of no account. He hates muddles and speaks his mind in direct speech. For him it's "I don't like it." You never hear an "I don't really care for this, do you?" out of The Man Who Would Be Mogul. He doesn't elicit your response or tell how he really feels; he just makes lightning judgments.

He's as sure of things that flop as he is of his brilliant success. Just because he would be mogul doesn't mean he gets there or always makes good moves. It's his *style* that makes him his type, not faultless achievements.

Outer Signs

He's just aggressive and dominant enough to be taken for a kingpin. He dresses in a look of *slightly* conspicuous consumption—a look of substance, not quite ostentation. He's not fashionable as much as comfortably expensive. Quality is his style. His suits, jeans, or shirts are exactly right; his one or two pieces of gold jewelry (not to mention his flask) are subtle; his shoes look hard to find; his scent whispers "Men's Boutique."

He drives a sleek, heavy, often spacious automobile; the older he is, the larger or more costly it is. It's dark grey, dark maroon, or dark *something*, usually. It has automatic transmission and power steering. Sometimes the windows are ever so slightly tinted. Smokey, austere, significant. Low level or high level, it's a luxury car.

He likes bricks and rocks, especially in walls and fireplaces. He wants his abode to be back from the street, sheltered by some expanse of greenery and with a solid front—traditional English, brownstone, modern mansion, or high steel and marble. He longs to cross thick, endless carpets. His black leather chairs turn into lounges and outweigh the Washington Monument. His couch looks like the Great Wall of China. He wants his own private den.

He never likes the table he's given at a restaurant; he always picks a better one. Or else establishes himself with the maître d' at one special place he always goes to.

He's inordinately fond of communications equipment—ham radios, Betamaxes, T.V.s, Stock Quotation Video—but especially the gadgets of A.T.&T. and Western Electric. He wants *all* their latest goodies. He likes his extension cords long and his wall jacks frequent. He has an in line and an out line, one or two numbers, and phones of all shapes and sizes—in numerous places. He prefers buttons to dials—they connect faster. He has (or is about to get) a car phone; he's thinking about one for his briefcase. He uses the operator a lot, and he's a regular on information. He hooks his T.V. to a cable. And he can unflap a lovely folder of colorful credit cards: The gold ones for special privileges show above the others ever so slightly.

The cards and equipment aren't for display alone. He's a frenetic user and doer. He acts like a man on the edge of starvation. He develops long, sensitive antennae directed toward a men's world. He derives his packages and prizes from other men's kingdoms, so he aims his ears for men's talk. He goes to all-male lunches, to the men's circle at parties. The social affairs he attends resemble solar systems: Big moguls stand stationary like planets while little moguls circle them like moons.

The Man Who Would Be Mogul treats himself to lots of things, but not to leisure. He gets no relaxation. He creates no privacy away from his employment. Wheelers and dealers call him at home, during meals and in the bathroom. A last-minute phone call, no matter how vague, can scuttle six months of your arrangements.

He overuses his engine. And while he makes sure he has nice things, he may not have a very good heart, brain, liver, or bladder. He exercises irregularly, though he may join a men's club. His stomach gets upset and he has headaches. He's prone to a huge mid-life crisis. Failure to him is like death. Often he's afraid of airplanes. He's sure the next crash is bound to be the flight he's on. He studies the odds. Some Men Who Would Be Moguls carry guns—from the paranoia bred of self-importance.

Sex Signals

In a woman, The Man Who Would Be Mogul seeks a supporter, a social secretary, and a good piece of scenery. He has to shine big, so he looks for a lady who will defer to him and help toward his promotion. He needs a helper. Because he only creates superstructures, he can't survive without some underpinning.

He sets his sights on a female Sherpa fairly early in his career. He could hardly scale Everest without one. As usual, he doesn't want to fuss around—he zeroes in and courts with intensity. He vibrates with a personal, compelling excitement. He pays attention to you—until you sign a merger. He paints a picture of gains and glory.

And he merges very well in the beginning. Sex at first is abundant, becomes sufficient; finally, it gets scarce. It has to slip between the schedules, not just the sheets.

He thinks of himself as sexual; probably he began early. He knows some razzle-dazzle techniques. But lovemaking with him is rarely leisurely after the first thrilling months. In time you realize it's more surgical than cozy. Sometimes he goes for spontaneous quickies; mostly, he's as functional as a sleeping pill: bed, sex, slumber.

The Man Who Would Be Mogul likes control in sex as in everything else. When you're aroused and interested he often says no—as a consequence, you always want more than he does. He's happiest when he gets something for nothing. He nudges for new positions and would rather win a contortion than achieve orgasm.

He *does* relax with women, whereas he can't with men. Since he doesn't view females as competitors in his economic war, he can almost let go in their company, at least for three minutes or so—and after the switchboard's closed. He gets tired at home because it's the only place he can. Perhaps that's why you can often sympathize with his plight.

Money Markers

You would think money is property to the Man Who Would Be Mogul. It's not. It's *proof.* He doesn't judge himself by how much he has, but by how much he can "swing." He might stockpile a little money he isn't using, in order to attract more, but most of all he plays with his currency. To him coins are simply chips to risk and flirt with. He skirts the edge of financial ruin. And he'll use your money without a second thought, forget what he borrowed, and try for even more.

The Man Who Would Be Mogul is related to the type I call the "You Send Me To Medical School" Status Seeker. The "You Send Me To Medical School" Status Seeker uses a woman's contribution to aid his own progression. In fact, one woman after another. One woman may put him through school only to be dropped later. Another may labor like a silent partner to get him business connections or clientele. After a certain point, he may seek yet another woman whose gentility offers him pure status.

Each woman expects some reward to come later, perhaps her turn at advancement. But the "You Send Me To Medical School" Status Seeker leaves her behind and doesn't pay her back. He tends to desert a partner at life-transition points, just as he has achieved a goal that they worked for together. She's not good enough to move him to the next level, so he goes on alone.

Beware of the "You Send Me To Medical School" Status Seeker.

He could happen to anyone. He seems to be "all for one and one for all." You trust his good intentions. Don't. Don't assume anything that isn't specified and don't take turns—especially when you come second —*without a written agreement.*

Family Aspects

The Man Who Would Be Mogul usually doesn't have children for a long, long while. Some expect to have two quickly and get it over with; others want to bear a platoon. Among his progeny, he prefers the verbal tykes with congenital con artistry. He doesn't participate much in their raising although he thinks he does. Children are for lower members of the staff—such as mothers, sitters, and live-ins—to oversee. He insists on keeping his freedom from them; either you have plenty of substitutes available or you stay in alone with them. He must get to those appointments.

Some Moguls view their families as dynasties; some cast off all blood ties. The dynastic ones get patripotestal: They try to incorporate parents, children, nieces, and nephews into their company. Other Moguls treat all relatives so offhandedly, they soon dismiss him as a distant acquaintance.

He negotiates contracts, but he exchanges little in human relationships. As a result he rarely cultivates, much less keeps, any friends. His judgment of winners and losers is so harsh and changes so quickly, he excludes many people who would honestly help him. He ends up surrounded by those he deals with and who don't care a hoot how he feels. And since he moves through collaborators along with collaborations, he rarely has any comrade of long standing.

Obviously, behind that drive, the Man Who Would Be Mogul hides some serious liabilities. He intends to rise at any cost. He uses people and sees you as a silent constituency, not a partner. His vibrancy never reflects on the moment he's living but rather feeds on what's coming; while he's seemingly after booty, he never stops to enjoy it.

But he has his pluses: He provides you with a glittering vision that makes life seem exciting. He's quick to sweep you off your feet; it's attractive to see yourself as his lady. Especially if you can cohabit the heights he wants to reach and cavort with the funds he aims to throw around. There's always the chance he might make it.

What Is in Store for You?

What's it like to live with high rolling and hot talking? To consolidate with Trans General National Universal Incorporated?

With the Man Who Would Be Mogul, his dream has to mean a lot to you, because his presence is scarce. He means long spans of little affection and short spans of irresistible magnetism—just enough to keep you hanging on. Some are basically affable men who are simply so obsessed with personal progress they battle onward, oblivious to your needs—with them, you face a future with lots of time on your hands, but no malice. Others build their kingdoms in a more cold and driven manner, kicking whatever gets in their way and leaving behind what doesn't, even their lady friends. Each kind thinks the grass is greener somewhere else.

Once the Mogul sets the wheels in motion, he generally wants a permanent alliance. The steps ahead are pretty predictable. The thrilling preliminary trance passes in a whirlwind. Then, very quickly, he makes it clear that he does his business alone. What he defines as "business" grows and grows. He finally comes to the realization that some honors come more quickly to the loner than they do to the family man. So he develops two profiles: one single, one paired. Soon the occasions for which he wants to show he's mated happen far less often than those where he wishes to appear alone. He starts to exclude you: first by day, then by night, weekends, and trips. He goes lots of places; you stay home. Even when he promotes the reputation that he's a solid spouse, you're heard about but rarely shown. You become a mystery woman about whom people say, "Have you ever met her?" Others don't know that you exist.

That doesn't mean you never join him or help him; you do, but within limits. Most likely you serve as a memory bank and computer: You record dates and places, do books, groom appearances, eye the winds for coming trends, put on dinner parties for close associates. He expects you to be as silent and regular as a monthly bill from the gas and electric company.

When you do escort him in his paired manifestation, he talks only to men; you sit silently or chat with other moguls' abandoned paramours. He gives you instructions on how to behave and what to talk about; any role other than that of unwavering cheerleader is definitely out.

It doesn't take long to realize that your Man Who Would Be Mogul is a gambler, and a compulsive one at that; you have to tighten your seat belt and pretend the ground beneath you won't suddenly disappear. If he's not incessantly putting all your cash on the line, he risks other tangibles and intangibles that have to do with your security. Naturally the subject of money looms more than merely prominently in your daily dealings—it takes over. The getting and keeping of money becomes a leitmotif weaving its way into every concern. Almost all conversations and quarrels soon wind around to the topic of cash. You could write a *book* on the subject. And your children turn out to be very materialistic little creatures.

Your man also turns out to be a fighter, and a dirty one at that: He has to win just for the sake of winning, even when his opponent is you. He pulls out all the heavy guns, no matter how petty the argument. He holds an ancient, ever-ready list of sins and errors and uses them as evidence, whether they're relevant or not. He may even lay the groundwork for imagined future battles—he may leave you out of titles or get your signature on obscure documents that forfeit all your claims.

From moment one, he wonders if perhaps he couldn't have found a better sex partner. No matter how hard he worked to get you, from the instant you say "I'm yours," he begins to view your union as somehow not all it could be. The thought that there must be more to this relationship business, that maybe he cheated himself, gradually nags him to death. Occasionally you find him scrutinizing you; then he'll sigh and carry on. He ponders whether associates get something he doesn't from their mates; he envies single men and those with new, young wives. He treats you more with toleration than with affection as time goes on; he starts to look around.

Aging (both yours and his) becomes your nemesis. Most Man Who Would Be Moguls try to counteract decades with affairs. Quite often they go Doe Stalking: They turn back to younger bodies. He says a man under as much stress as he needs a less complex relationship in which he can get some peace and rest.

You *can* enjoy the way he keeps things hopping. Yet, your belief in his golden accolades *has* to dwindle sooner or later. No one knows what didn't happen and what doesn't come through as well as you. Any consort of the Man Who Would Be Mogul lives with his past all through her present. If you're his first round, there are all the things he does on his way up. If you're a later mate, part of your fare is the paperwork, lawyers, and half-truths about the first. And don't neglect the fact—with this man you run a high chance of widowhood.

What Are the Telltale Signs of Trouble?

Even if you can't see the Man Who Would Be Mogul from up front, you can certainly hear him. He sounds like an airport control tower. All day long he radios in and out, issues takeoff orders, gives landing instructions, and radars new sightings. He's always checking his messages—he's crushed when he has none. And he tells people where he is now and where to find him for the next five hours.

The more he leads a separate life, the more you're heading for troubled times. As soon as you notice you're left out in the cold more than your liking, you should call his secretary and make an appointment, then lay what you expect in a relationship on his table. Unwanted isolation has a way of breeding stopped-up feelings: You feign all is well while you grow bitter. With the Man Who Would Be Mogul, you shouldn't let the topic of what you need slide away beneath his other conversations.

You might ask him what reasons he gives for your lack of attendance at his happenings and wonder what they show about his intentions. Consider the age-old signs of affairs: late appointments, frequent business trips, odd Visa charges, and a toothbrush kept in the trunk of his car. He doesn't answer the phone where he said he'd be (how *unlike* him!), and his address book lists certain last names without any first name.

With The Mogul, the more you don't know, the more critical the situation. What you know can make life stormy, but what you ignore can spell impending disaster. It's probably better to keep things turbulent and alive than to make like the *Titanic* on its way to an iceberg.

What Are the Chances?

There's no way to have a close companionship with the Man Who Would Be Mogul, and the chance of change is slim. If he does change, either he modifies his ways so late that the onus of irretrievable neglect is far too weighty to overcome or else he changes for the worse.

I suggest you pass over the Mogul and seek a fellow with better balance. Even when drive and ambition attract you mightily, try to find the achiever who has another side to him. Many men who constantly strive for further accomplishments combine their pursuits with warmth and attention toward their loved ones. With the Mogul, even though you double up, you still live alone. In such circumstances most living beasts, especially female ones, tend to shrivel up. Far too many Mogul spouses substitute material goods for lack of companionship; but when baubles, bangles, minks, and Mercedes take over the soul, little spiritual development takes place. In the end, you cut off all avenues to emotional rewards. The only thing left is visions of bigger and better Moguls.

If you are already with the Man Who Would Be Mogul, or see him on your horizon and can't stop yourself, I wouldn't say you should necessarily flee forthwith. You might approach him with an attitude of caution mixed with common sense and a good sense of timing. And I recommend you begin, without fail, a program of self-reliance. Quietly and independently fill your life with your private joys. You'll be taking the risk that he might fault you for lack of support, but at least you won't spend your days shelved and suspended—the worst state to be in. Try to size up just how much intimacy you require. If you find closeness crucial, don't do the Mogul. But if your need to relate to your man is moderately low, then you can try to approximate a Limited Partner setup, at least from your end of things. Then you can catch what you can with your Mogul between both your doings.

If you want him with you and don't want autonomy, be warned: Very few devices will attract him or reverse a growing rift. There's not much use in getting sick, causing scandals, or throwing fits to get him home. Of course if you enjoy such things, you might as well go ahead! Just don't expect results. It's also not a good idea to try to get involved in his work, to compete in his field using his associates, connections, or companies. Better to develop your own standards than try to buck his.

You might consider dwelling with the Man Who Would Be Mogul only on a temporary basis. When the fascination ends, you can prepare for a civilized end. Even in the midst of a total involvement, keeping track of diminishing returns can tell you not to hang on past a point of detriment. Everybody has a certain tolerance quotient: So much neglect, so many affairs, so little time, a mistress, or bad partners' underhanded business practices may eventually top your T.Q. You don't have to live with him; you *do* have to live with you. When your self-respect and your Mogul no longer mix, it's time to call it quits.

If you stay for better or worse, stay for love and no other reason. And then, for the love of him, remember this: Try to get him to live for now; don't wait for retirement or some far-off finish line. In the first place, he never retires! In the second, his supertension leaves him prone to heart attacks, strokes, and other catastrophes. Enjoy him while you can.

Where Do You Fit In?

A woman afflicted with a case of the Man Who Would Be Mogul— even one time is a suspicious symptom—should examine herself carefully for vicaria. Vicaria isn't exactly a virus or bacteria, but it's a malady just the same—the desire to achieve your own ambitions through someone else.

Vicaria tends to derive from fear. It's not just the fact that you hide the aspiration for a more prestigious and affluent life—that's bad enough. The real cause of the Man Who Would Be Mogul affliction is the secret apprehension that you can't cut the mustard on your own. So you deposit yourself with some acquisitive partner who does your succeeding for you.

Your secret apprehension may or may not be justified; almost certainly it's learned. Women, until recently, have had little access to games of power and position; they are generally taught to assume personal status from men rather than achieve their own. And if the difficulties of becoming a lady mogul alone aren't enough to fill your heart with trepidation, the negative connotations ambitious women receive can give anyone qualms. To call a man "tough" or "hard as nails" is somehow a compliment, but when such appellations apply to a woman, everybody's noses curl up. Don't forget that sticks and stones may break your bones, but names can never hurt you.

Most women have not only learned to fear, they have even learned to deny that they are afraid. "I wouldn't join that rat race for anything," they say. But when you refute that you have ambition, the age-old formula looks doubly good: First hook onto some man's wagon, then claim you have no aspirations. All belongs to him; you just go along.

But there's a catch. A partner who fulfills your own cravings almost inevitably becomes the center of your existence. And although he occupies the most important spot in your life, the kind of man who seeks to conquer rarely holds you as the central focus in his; so you develop problems he simply doesn't have. Everything he does pleases or hurts you some way, but he hardly notices you.

The vicarious vision that once seemed attractive turns disastrous. The mates of the Man Who Would Be Mogul tend to hang on for dear life until he walks out on them. Then the material goods acquired in the relationship start to become substitutes for him. Property, homes, shares, potted plants, vases, paintings, and ornaments take on life-and-death consequences. Things get very messy when the relationship ends. Sometimes the defunct bunkmate of the Mogul jumps acrimoniously into an aggressive career just to show him what he lost; others suffer such loss their depression never ends.

Too often your own self-care comes second. You devote yourself to waiting, while he lives actively. With the limited amount of time we all have to live, there's *nothing* as wasteful as suspending your own animation. Then you get hooked on judging yourself by externals, just the way your Mogul does, you size up your worth by what you possess. To evaluate yourself according to outward paraphernalia is like asking to swim in quicksand. Putting all your eggs in one basket— no matter how bulging (and it often is at first)—causes you to cling desperately to your high cards—your beauty, youth, figure, or zest— and forget to develop others. When the trump is played and starts to fade, a big crisis is in the making. You shred yourself up inside hoping for his sign that you're still O.K.

If you're dwelling with a Man Who Would Be Mogul, ward off vicaria before it gets critical. Work on your own ambitions and achievements. Then your mate can constitute a blessing, not a possession.

Notes and Particulars

14/The Father Knows Best

Related Types: The "But I Really Like Women"
Manipulator
The Doe Stalker

Positivity Scale: + −

What do daddies do? They protect you and provide for you. If you make a dodo of yourself, they fix it all up while saying, "Tsk, tsk." They know everything *so* much better than you. They tell you where to go and *just* what to do. And they like their little girl. So much so, in fact, they don't let her grow up.

The Father Knows Best relates to women only as a parent to a child. He never acts as if you were an adult. He refuses mature communication with you. With an unwavering belief that he's so much older than you, whatever his age and experience, he turns into an imperturbable despot. After all, everybody knows that fatherly authority is as close to unassailable as authority can get. Upset your daddy and you're bound to feel bad; you can also get in big trouble. By inherent rights, no matter what transpires—father knows best.

As a spouse, the Father Knows Best takes his part so to heart that he turns himself into your benevolent protector. You can't question his opinion without his getting riled. Refusals equal rebuffs and confrontation is contradiction, and pretty soon you're left with little choice: You turn your affair into a game of Daddy, May I? You sugar and spice your way to rewards and pout over punishments.

The Father Knows Best knows enough to head for particular women when he molds his relationships. He finds some women aren't malleable to him, so why attempt the impossible? He looks not so much for young women as for women who stretch a girlish demeanor beyond the girlhood stage. He notes unchaperoned ladies who still act sequestered, those who hesitate to relinquish a precious kind of charm, and those lazy about self-maintenance who would rather lean on a maintenance man. He very often meets his mates just as they are facing a big transition from family, home, or school into the outer world. Such transitions tend to heighten both damsel-like distress and the desire for feathered nests.

Story

I once had a student named Ruth who was a number of years older than her fellow classmates in my introductory class. Ruth was a returnee to college who had recently emerged from a long-term cocoon with a new life and new wings. It was quite a difference from her previous existence as perennial princess in training.

Ruth grew up as one of four daughters, all doted upon and all owning every kind of stuffed animal, canopy bed, and dust ruffle possible. Her father so adored them, he acted as if his wife and daughters were a personal treasure. He could only let each daughter go by throwing a truly spectacular wedding in which he zealously gave her away.

Her last year in high school, Ruth started going with Lester, a man six years her senior. She didn't question the fact that, rather than go with a college woman, he preferred the company of a high-school girl. Ruth's father sent her away to an out-of-state university, but she transferred right back to attend the local women's college. She dated other men; she even broke up with Lester. But as her two-year course neared the end, she decided to marry him. She spent her last semester majoring in engagement and showers. She never even finished her last Incomplete. Lester didn't see why she should.

Despite his youth, Lester made life anything but unfettered. He knew the only "right" way to do everything: He directed Ruth's shopping, didn't approve of her cleaning, patronized her cooking failures with an "I told you so." He only wanted Thanksgiving stuffing the way his mother did it. He insisted the Fourth of July always be spent at the lake, as in his childhood. He didn't like anything *new*. He turned into a grumpy monster when he got sick. And he would get in such a huff when Ruth tried to fight with him, she found she was better off wheedling.

With little else to do—certainly not work—Ruth became thoroughly preoccupied with what they needed next. She got into spending money. She bought clothes, picked new furniture, and planned vacations. Lester would hesitate, talk budget, and refuse; Ruth would beg; then he would go ahead and get her what she wanted, with a pat on the head. He led Ruth to believe that "no" meant "yes, but plead first." Soon, "Oh *pleeeese*, Lester," was part of her every sentence.

Lester never told her the limits of his salary or the meaning of his budget, so she never knew whether funds were tight or loose. He always said things like "We'll find a way" or "I'll manage it somehow." On every level, he treated Ruth as an unreal and ineffectual being. He acted as if, other than providing entertainment and decoration, she had few capabilities and even less consequence. He teased that she would never learn, so she had to follow his more knowledgeable and more rational instructions.

Except when it came to sex. Ruth kept waiting for tutelage, but it never came. He was *more* than gentlemanly about sex: He was bafflingly restrained. He used her naïveté, her hesitations, even a yawn, to "free" her from sexual obligation. And when she clearly wanted sex, he would indulge in only a little foreplay and then turn over to sleep. They had intercourse, but what was satisfactory to Lester was utterly empty to Ruth.

In a few short years, Ruth found herself disappointed, frustrated, and out of love with Lester. But meanwhile she had grown up so little that her attempt to end the union came out like a thwarted child's. Rather than formulate clear actions, she began to flirt with other men. One was particularly consoling; he sympathized with her and offered her shelter. He had a home and salary all ready, so one bright day Ruth sashayed away from Lester and over to Wayne.

It was out of the frying pan into the fire. Ruth went right to another all-caring, all-capable, all-controlling parent. Wayne was so composed and complacent that despite her attempt at scandalous behavior, Ruth reverted to an innocent child-bride. Wayne acted more like a school principal than a mate, so Ruth acted like a buoyant bubblehead who needed remedial reading. Meanwhile, their erotic life became almost as dull as that with Lester. Wayne seemed to get aroused only when Ruth played babyish, sat on his lap, and called him "naughty."

Years went by as Ruth puttered around her new doll's house. Wayne was growing ever more fussy; Ruth felt cut off. Women friends often lost patience with her. She grew lonely and bored; she felt pointless. She began to have problems with envy: She either loved or hated every woman in *Vogue* and *Ladies' Home Journal*. A depression set in that seemed so close to a breakdown that a friend suggested Ruth seek therapy. When the vacation he suggested instead didn't work, Wayne grudgingly agreed. He didn't want her unhappy but felt threatened by her change.

Ruth found therapy uncomfortable and distressing, but she wanted to keep it up; something was happening to her. She was clamoring for an adult demeanor and liked the way it felt. But the more she changed, the more Wayne resisted. When he didn't begin to bend as she had hoped, she realized she didn't have the strength to fight both for herself and for him. She had a difficult choice. She could remain a partial child in the guise of a wife forever, just as her mother had, or she could leave and try to stand on her own. Ruth decided to separate. She was afraid, but she felt if she didn't make a break she would stay under someone else's care for the rest of her life.

The Father Knows Best is usually a good, well-intentioned man. Unfortunately, he knows no other way to love than to emulate a parent. Many women hate him. But to those he attracts, his bearing seems so natural they just glide right under his wing without a second thought. You see, more than any of the other Twenty-two Types of Men, a relationship with a Father Knows Best is a two-way street. When you check his signs, check yours, too. If yours are the opposite of his, take heed. You might *think* you're heading for romance and end up with adoption!

How Can You Identify One?

Dos and do nots, how and how nots, shoulds and oughts, right ways and wrong—somebody has to know just how things are done. And the Father Knows Best thinks he is the one.

When he was very young, someone or something got into his central computers and tried to make him perfectly socialized. He got programmed with responsibilities and regulations, systems and means: He was told the *one* right way to celebrate a holiday, the *one* proper hour for supper, the *one* efficient method to mow the lawn, the *one* sensible approach to buying a car. He learned that you don't jaywalk, wear shoes without socks, forget clean underpants, close the window when you sleep, that rarely should you weep. And while you claim you aren't prudish, you believe in modesty. He found he got approval when he followed all the rules like a little man. Since then, he's equated affection with regimentation. Now he does the same to you.

The Father Knows Best is a kindly man, but his kindness comes out as concern for your welfare. He's giving, but his giving is like philanthropy to a helpless charity—you. Much of any parenting is in the pose. And the Father Knows Best has the pose down pat. He doesn't quite tell you what to do, but always acts as if he knows. He doesn't say that he is right and you are wrong, but he seems to convey that he's more O.K. than you are. He hands out rewards and administers punishments.

Outer Signs

His entire carriage implies he was grown up the day he was born. There's hardly a snip, snail, or puppy-dog tail left in him. You, on the other hand, have a little curl right in the middle of your forehead. The Father Knows Best tries for the look of years and experience. He likes venerated apparel, utterly conventional and unflamboyant styles, as well as the clothes that he bought ten years ago, from which nothing can separate him. His look is not unlike that of a bride at a wedding. He wears something old, something new, perhaps something borrowed, but *always* something blue. If he hasn't got a penny in his shoe, you can bet he's got one somewhere. He always carries a pen, maybe two or three; sometimes he has a pocket guard to protect his clothes from ink stains. His socks are black, his shoes Florsheim—laced, resoled, and four years old; he also has bedroom slippers. All of these things have a closeted, unaired but not unpleasant smell.

As he grows old, he's terrible to buy for. His needs are few, and he's got them covered with items from his past. Besides, his taste is fussy, and you can't find what he wants because they don't make them any more.

He likes his car stodgy; he takes factory regular (blue, green, or tan) right from the showroom. One color and no extras is good enough for him. Unleaded gas appeals to him. He uses S.T.P. and any other additives that makes his auto run better and last longer. He keeps his car for at least four years, usually close to ten; he doesn't play the radio when he drives around.

Before he hooks up with a daughter figure, he takes care of himself for a while. He lives in some very compartmentalized apartment. He cooks on a hot plate or small stove or goes to some nearby inexpensive restaurant. He works part- or full-time even when in school. He has his clothes laundered but irons them himself. His lifestyle isn't expansive or exuberant; he likes the standard provisions.

He likes to do what he thinks is sensible and reasonable. Later, when you pick a residence as a couple, he goes not so much for design as for affordability. He prefers conventional, conservative, and small-ish shelters, and he heads either for moderately nice residential areas where one house is pretty much like the others or else for huge, square apartment buildings where the flats are endless, square repetitions of each other.

In décor, he shuns extremes and "different" things; he avoids spindly antiques and super-contemporary furniture. He plants himself in a standard, comfortable chair that bespeaks no particular style. He likes the arrangement of things to stay static; he gets displeased when too many pictures hang on a wall. He likes each picture hung at the same height as all the others. The few vases and statues go one per table and stay just so.

Though some Father Knows Bests are quite worldly and like formal gourmet dinners, others get testy about garlic, onions, and vinegar; they claim to have sensitive noses and stomachs and like their cooking plain, their lettuce iceberg, and their pie apple. They fuss over your cooking enough to make you feel that you're Holly Hobbie at a baby Betty Crocker Mini-Wave Oven. Under such scrutiny, you start to burn things. All the more reason for him to take you out.

He watches sports but rarely plays them. He tends to get thick and lose body tone. He's more and more inert as time goes on; his skin gets soft, and he starts to go for cardio-cholesterol checkups. He turns into a terrible baby whenever he gets sick.

He's very, very cautious about what he does. He says "don't," "watch out," and "be careful" a lot. He aims them at you but lives them himself as well. Occasionally he says "I forbid," but he's well aware that he steps pretty far out on a limb when he goes that far. His first response to anything is more than likely "no." Then, with time, prodding, and careful examination he grudgingly allows what he once rejected. If you go through channels, plead, reapply, meet certain conditions, and wait ninety days, you can get a charge card for Saks Fifth Avenue.

He carries on like a living bank: He watches his input, output, and rate of flow. He says he needs his sleep; he believes one can have too much sex. Sometimes he's a hypochondriac and thinks of drafts and germs.

He follows an internal rulebook for all his actions—as if he might get a bad check mark from the boss, the neighbors, or Big Brother. Then he treats you as if you were an extension of him, as if you reflected on his record. If you don't behave well, others will think it's his fault.

Sex Signals

The Father Knows Best heads for hesitant women or fledglings—or better, both. His opening approach comes in the guise of help; he takes care of a mess or a problem that you've been having trouble with. Then he offers more assistance, then some more. Pretty soon, he's lifting lots of weights off your back and becoming a necessary resource—and an easy way out. He pampers you in a way that makes you almost indolent. He encourages you to be superfluous but decorous. He makes it seem you can have an existence almost like a vacation if only you stay with him for good.

He paves his way to bed with small maneuvers; he adds food, care, and nice events. He seems to be the better judge of the two of you of when the time is right, so you don't have to decide. But once the union is established, he's so cautious and so diplomatic about sex, you wonder who really didn't want it. You realize his courtesy may well cover his own lack of interest. The edge of rejection makes you all the more childlike. He makes you feel modest; he almost always waits until you're in bed before anything starts. He approaches under the sheets and often in nightclothes. But sometimes he has a totally unexpected weird streak: He might like to spank, get spanked, or wear strange clothes. Even so, his rate of intercourse is slow, his desire low, and his performance short. Somehow you end up frustrated, and you don't know why.

He's not one to carry on affairs. After all, he doesn't encourage one whole, grown woman, so why two? And he thinks you won't fool around either. But he may well be wrong.

Money Markers

He holds the purse strings. The Father Knows Best always works and almost always saves. At least, he uses savings as an argument. He applies his earnings to both of you, but since he expends funds less than moderately on himself, he puts you in the position of being the money spender. He allows you to purchase, but he makes your access to cash seem like a weekly budget you always run over. He doesn't give you an actual allowance, doesn't tell you the limits; he wants you to ask for money so he can give it.

Even though he both earns and pays for your living expenses, it's uncanny how often he marries a woman with at least some money. The Father Knows Best partner often has steady family handouts, trusts, or an inheritance, and frequently your family has a higher status than his. Since you live on his cash, he expects to supervise yours; he doesn't let you spend your money, but he feels he has to let you to run through his.

Family Aspects

It may seem paradoxical, but the Father Knows Best hesitates when it comes to being an actual parent. He puts off having a family as long as he can and permanently if possible. He has all sorts of reasons. He may use your frivolities to prove that you're not ready. When he does have progeny, he often allows only one or two children, who are very carefully brought up. As a father, he lacks the necessary sense of fun. He dislikes play and overlikes instruction—through words, not demonstrations. He rarely lets the kid in him shine for his own child.

Perhaps his attitude toward parenthood comes from the fact that not many Father Knows Bests look back on their own childhoods as happy times. They have a few delightful memories, but the rest seems to fade into a sense of oppression. Often, one relationship was particularly difficult for them. Someone required the young Father Knows Best to mind his p's and q's too much. As an adult, he remains

attached to his family but not in an expressive way. They love him as
he does them, but no one ever quite says so. A degree of disapproval
always seems close at hand between him and his parents. As his mate,
don't expect his family to adore you.

His feelings for his brothers and sisters combine a protective desire
and a wish that they were really better friends. They are never as
friendly as they try to be.

Although the Father Knows Best had several long-term friends in
his youth, once he hooks up, those friendships fade away. Once mated,
he no longer has individual friends; rather you two pair up with
couples. He occasionally meets the man from the opposite twosome
alone, and you see the woman, but mostly you do a lot together as a
foursome. Within your whole social circle, with the Father Knows
Best you have few unattached persons around.

The Father Knows Best has many great qualities, both obvious and
buried: He means well and has good motives. He loves you; he also
tries to love himself, but he tries to through you and that never works.
He doesn't know any other way to care for the child part in him but to
turn you into it. And that's bad for you. If you can ever get beyond his
patripotestal armory, there may well be a delightful man in there.
Though maybe never a lighthearted sprite.

What Is in Store for You?

Instead of well-defined stages, a slow but steady process of involution
takes place with a Father Knows Best relationship. You most likely
initiate what becomes your later interaction early on in your romance,
you just let it get more and more thorough as time goes on. When the
Father Knows Best begins to take care of you, you fall into being taken
care of. As he grows custodial, adult, and proud, you get giddy, silly and
young. Rather than having an equal-partner stance, the cute game
between you develops into a tie of utter dependence.

Three insidious things happen to you when a Father Knows Best
plops you into a permanent playpen. He removes you from serious
activity or meaningful consequences in life. Having freed you to play,
he feels it's part of his job to oversee and guide your amusements. And
he makes the games hard for you to win.

Like a toddler stuck forever in a cell with only a Fisher-Price Busy Box, in a partnership with a Father Knows Best you become totally involved with the intricacies of getting along with him, getting a response from him, and getting what you want. As a consequence, you steadily get out of tune with the outer world. You get very good at games that only two can play. And some for only one. You turn into his "good girl." The Father Knows Best is not like the heavily adult and masculine Doe Stalker or the seemingly equal "But I Really Like Women" Manipulator, against whom you can rebel. Nor is he the utterly compliant Sugar Pie Honey who somehow turns you into the Wicked Witch of the West. Instead the benign, always "for your sake" control of a fatherly type evokes too deep a memory and seems too hard to buck. So you take the opposite tack: You go so far as to believe that he dominates you more than he actually does. You lead yourself and others to think that you need his permission to go to the drinking fountain. You ask him for your allowance in dribbles and request him to limit your Pepsis.

Soon he acts as if no matter how much advice he gives you, you never profit from it; you agree. You come on like a novice who will never get promoted. Everybody knows that you lack grey matter. When he gives you *some* information, duties, and understanding but never *all,* you assume that total accomplishment is simply beyond your ken. He enacts a reward and punishment plan, and you try to test but not break it. He becomes a benevolent missionary who nurtures the savage. To get in good with him, you seemingly follow his good book, of which he owns the only copy, since it isn't translated into Girlish. When you go wrong, he holds back on goodies, mildly reproaches you, and takes it personally. If you are really bad, his reaction can be very frightening: He asks you that since you can't take care of yourself, what would happen if he deserts you? They don't have orphanages for full-grown waifs.

You find you start to use the age-old tactics of disenfranchised, unpowerful, and half-grown people: You get petulant, you deal in manipulation, and you start to use sex for favors. You flirt, with him at first and maybe others later. You get secretive. You do things behind his back: You store chocolates under the bed or bury a bottle of bourbon in the oatmeal. You make purchases and then subtract twenty dollars so he won't know the price.

When you directly confront a Father Knows Best or your cunning gets too obvious, he has a way to tie you into a permanent knot. He fights resistance with instant role reversal: He becomes the baby and brings out the mother in you. If nothing else gets you stuck, a surge of maternal control over him almost always does.

Boxed in, the mate of a Father Knows Best tends to take a much more dangerous kind of escape than actual flight, one that removes her from the external world even more. Quite likely you start to dwell in a fantasy world: Daydreams, like soap operas, start to take over your mind. You conjure up dramas and disasters. You begin to take too seriously the things people nonchalantly do. Perhaps you disappear into magazines, paperback romances, scandal sheets, and T.V. You become idolatrous and envious of people you don't even know. You imagine utterly ridiculous ways to gain approval: You dream you will walk up to someone's Steinway, sit down, and play Chopin's First Concerto. No one ever *knew* you could play piano so magnificently.

It's likely that you drift away on the wings of sexual fantasy, too. Since your mate doesn't surprise you in bed, perhaps some superstar will see you and do it for him. Or maybe a swashbuckler will kidnap you and whisk you off to his seraglio. He's nameless and faceless and incredibly erotic. He never hurts and he does just what you want, even though you protest.

You can glide through years with a Father Knows Best. Then with age, two changes head your way. Both are part of your process of involution and isolation. You reach a time when you begin to feel the loss of your most important assets: youth and attractiveness, both necessary for the ingénue act. The more your behavior contradicts your decade, the deeper the crisis gets. You become prone to more than one mid-life crisis. As you age, even fantasy offers little solution; divorce certainly does not. Quite the opposite—you feel you have nowhere to go where you can still be babied.

Meanwhile, rather than having a crisis, your partner reveals more and more of what used to show only occasionally—he demands more and more care. Instead of being an imperturbable despot, he becomes an incapacitated one; he gets needy and testy. He took care of *you* when you needed him; now, like a well-raised offspring, you should take care of *him*. And he *still* wants you to do it his way.

In some extreme cases of the Father Knows Best, the childlike mate finally gets even in older age. She uses the money, deserts him at home, bosses him around, even abuses her man like Buñuel's Tristana.

What Are the Telltale Signs of Trouble?

Alert yourself when a fatherly hand keeps saving you. Beware when a man deals with romance in an advisory capacity. Caution yourself when the lap you're sitting in seems as if you've sat in it before. Otherwise you may be the owner of a proud new parent. Take heed if your mate keeps his head and face somehow above direct eye level, so when you approach him it's always an interruption; he's behind a book or a newspaper plus maybe glasses. He's always preoccupied. True, he puts down what he's doing and turns to respond to you, but he acts a little put out, shows a bit of noblesse oblige, and he sighs before he speaks. He expects to deliver full speeches and expositions without disruptive queries; if you have anything to say, you must save it to the end. Of course by then, the plans you offer tend to look silly, because (he'll point out) he covered that ground before. If you had only been listening! If you dare to inquire why this way and not some other, he gets quite annoyed that you should contradict him.

The other storm warning comes in you. You suffer repeat pubescent growing pains, only they're worse the second time around; you slip back to even more immaturity. You start to lose self-esteem. With the Father Knows Best, the storm warnings mean you're off the changing table and into the crib. They should make you sit up, clang on the bars, and realize this is *not* the start of something good.

Unfortunately, all too often these warnings pass so slowly and evenly that you never notice them. But you may still get one of two types of growth spurts. The first and not so hot one is when you bolt from your foster home but do it out the back door. You felt growing exasperation, seemed stunted and stifled. You didn't quite know what was wrong, but you knew something had got to give. But you fixated on a change of mates, houses, or happenings—not the whole pattern. You set yourself up for a repeat or worse.

The other type of growth starts with resistance as well as exasperation. The exasperation wanes and the resistance grows; you begin to see your situation clearly; in time you force the issue and demand change. But you're faced with a problem: You can alter yourself, but you can't necessarily alter your mate. You're at a turning point. If you want change, you either bridge the generation gap or leave the nest.

What Are the Chances?

Back in the days of yore when most unions lasted for better or for worse, when women had less freedom to exercise options, and when parents heavily influenced choices, Father Knows Bests were legion. Now, Fathers (or partial Fathers), while still common, hold a less popular slot among the Twenty-two Types of Men. It seems many women who meet parental men simply don't stay for long.

I rather agree with the modern trend. Despite the fact that the Father Knows Best is a long-distance runner who loves, cares, and provides, I don't feel he provides what's right or beneficial—not for today and maybe not even for yesteryear. After all, Nora had to leave the Doll's House, and because she lacked a sense of her own significance, Emma Bovary created quite a mess for herself. My general advice for most women is not to tarry with a Father Knows Best. I also advise that you tell him why. If he's going to change, he has a far better chance to do so if he has strong evidence that a parental approach is counterproductive.

Once paired, the Father Knows Best allows for little development. Stalemate is in his interest, change is not. Just watch his reaction to the idea of therapy or even transcendental meditation. Especially when it's you who wants to try such things.

Occasionally a woman spots the potential assets of a particular Father Knows Best, stalwartly refuses parenting, and still manages a relationship with him. But it requires a great deal of effort. He instinctively avoids adult women, and he's resistant and tenacious.

The best guarantee you have of a perpetual relationship with a Father Knows Best is to remain in the same parent-child framework. If that's all right with you, well and good. If not, the odds for permanence dwindle fast.

If you become intent on change in this relationship, a lot depends on whether you desire to modify *yourself*. There's no denying the most expeditious way to alter your own condition is to go out the exit door. If that's your goal, remember there's an easy and a hard way out; I suggest the hard. As difficult and uncomfortable as it may seem, don't slide from one man to another, don't take family housing or handouts, don't even take helpful but obligatory favors. Get professional aid if you can, definitely get work, make your own decisions, and pay for all the aid you get with cash. Then spend a good stretch taking care of yourself before you form an attachment again. Don't be one of those for whom once is not enough. Repetition costs time and energy.

If you have it in mind to grow yourself up and at the same time shrink your present partner down until you end up on an equal plane, you'd better get some protein powder and build up your strength. You're going to have to be the adult for the two of you. In order to rearrange a Father Knows Best while staying together, you have to be utterly determined to stick to the change and stick to him, and you have to let him know it. The shock of that is about the only thing to get him moving. Don't make threats with a Father Knows Best; threatening to leave is bad strategy with him. For one thing, threats are childlike and assure him that you're still his little girl. And he takes menace badly: He'll retrench more firmly than ever.

He needs love and affection, but he fears his need. To give him alternating childish and motherly attention, you may meet his desire, but you perpetuate his fear. You can make a healthy turnabout only if you take a steady, mature stance. Give him concern without dependence; constant but objective compassion. If all goes well you might get . . . say, an Oldie But Goodie?

Where Do You Fit In?

It's even played out in a ceremony: A man passes one of his ladies over to another caretaker in front of the altar. One man asks for your hand, another gives you away. So you're never unprotected. As much as we *think* we base our unions on love, the old pattern of being exchanged from one man to another hangs on more than you think. In a study I once conducted, none of the women interviewed said she established her permanent partnership because of love. Rather the women's main reasons were: 1) Some inner sense told them it was time to couple up, so they picked a likely mate and settled down. Often that was toward the end of high school or college or after one year of work. The inner sense seemed to indicate they couldn't make it without marriage. So no matter what their supposed career plans, they dropped everything else and did it. 2) They wanted to move somewhere or travel away. But they couldn't change space without another home base and male protector all arranged for them. So they zeroed in on a suitable relocator. 3) But the most startling, poignant reason was that they married because their father had just died!

Obviously a couple of decades of social change don't automatically wipe out several milleniums' worth of deeply ingrained patterns. Even today, fears of growing up can make many a woman find a Father Knows Best attractive: He fits an age-old stereotype for men, and she has been inculcated with the age-old imagery for women which relegate her to permanent juvenility. Consider even some of the rather contemporary images: "Chicks" are baby fowl, "dolls" are fake babies, and "babes" are infants.

We still have automatic time buttons that tell us we ought to couple up. We have trouble making our own space without a man. Like the women in the study, all of us are prone to old beliefs, expectations, and behaviors. For some of us at all times and all of us at some times, the pressure to fall into ready-made grooves is particularly strong. It can seem more than handy to go from father, home, or institution right to the shelter of another male.

There's nothing wrong in picking a traditional union or even a fatherly mate when you do so consciously and choose the life ahead, but to do so unconsciously is called leaping before you look. All too often it ends you up where you don't want to be. Stop and consider any union carefully. To remain a colleen with a parental mate may look like an easy path and in many ways it is, but it's like being given a bicycle and never being allowed to ride it without training wheels.

Here you are with a *life*, a *mind*, and a *body*. If someone comes along to hold you up every time you use them, in the long run, the results can be catastrophic: You just stop using them at all.

Notes and Particulars

15/The Disaster Broker

Related Types: The Intensely Intimate (But
Crazy)
The Man Who Would Be Mogul

Positivity Scale: + + − −

Death, doctors, and injury; crimes, courts, the law. One more roll of
the dice, on the brink of losing it all. One more try for the trophy; one
more campaign trail. One more fire; one more war.

Imagine yourself attached to Batman, Napoleon, Sam Spade,
F.D.R., Evel Knievel, Mario Andretti, General Patton, Butch Cas-
sidy, Al Capone, Bruce Lee, and the Six Million Dollar Man. At the
same time. High-pitched action; always the big event. And the next.
And the next.

The Disaster Broker runs on risk; jeopardy is the breath of life to
him. He pits himself against huge, unwavering outside forces—law,
loss, disability, catastrophe, stigma, bankruptcy. He threatens himself
with the heavies—hospitals, prisons, blacklists, and oblivion. If the
stakes aren't real, he can't feel.

But who's Clyde without Bonnie? Or Julius without Cleo? The
Disaster Broker likes to have a combination moll, decorator piece, first
lady, and avid fan attached to him, someone who shines for an
audience, stands with him against adversaries, works for him, and lets
his cohorts intrude endlessly. But she should still have spunk. Then
the woman herself becomes a trophy: He can lose her and try to win
her back. And rewinnable she is. For while the Disaster Broker's lady
is noteworthy and tempestuous, she also tends to be unflaggingly
devoted and full of grit. In the name of dedication, she bends her
ultimatums and gives in to his every trip.

Story

Take the case of Sky. Sky grew up on a small ranch as a tomboy through and through. But fate played a trick on her. Tough as she was, she also took on good looks, feminine urges, and lots of natural class. By the time she was sixteen and eyeing the horses at the local rodeo, the horsemen were eyeing her.

Monty was one of them. Monty rode broncos and did stunts, but he already had his sights set higher—or faster. He had tired of horses. He now wanted speed vehicles: cars, motorcycles, and anything else that moved like white lightning, including ladies. At first, being charming and a little bit fatherly, Monty "let" Sky hang out with him. But he knew that as a conquest and sidekick, she would be a feather in his cap. Pretty soon his saddle went into the back of the pickup, Sky went into the passenger seat, and they were sharing rooms in motels "by the month."

Sky heard all of Monty's plans. But she had no real idea what doubling up with a daredevil could turn into. In time they were no longer a couple; they were a caravan. As Monty struck out for ever more spectacular events, they needed trailers, more trucks, then more trailers again; Sky became ticket taker, second driver, hand shaker, errand runner, mopper upper, and mascot. They took on mechanics, agents, and managers. In addition Monty added advisers, helpers, and hero worshippers. Soon they were never alone.

They also had another ever-present, invisible companion—danger. Monty not only flirted with disaster, he tampered with the odds. He wasn't just after the win, speed, and prizes, he was after *peril*. He ran races in ticklish circumstances, added hazardous devices. He managed to crash one craft after another on a regular basis. Sky spent more hours than she could count escorting stretchers, following ambulances, and sitting in hospital corridors. She would nurse and feed Monty, then watch in dismay while he sawed off his casts three weeks early so he could ride again.

She also sat in jail houses and legal chambers. Since money was like the rest of their life—all or nothing—Monty had a sideline: He dealt drugs. He claimed he just needed a big score to back his racing, but Sky suspected his motive was risk and melodrama. Not satisfied with simple sales, Monty awaited shipments from Lima and Thailand. He so feared a rip-off that their trailer looked like the Alamo and every stranger became a potential "Fed."

Almost everything Monty did had to have a critical edge. Even sex took on a frenzied aspect; with Sky and Monty, every amorous event became a marathon. They were on the bed, off the bed—all over the place. They were upside down, inside out, and halfway killing each other. They climaxed like trains crashing. They played at sex like a bomb team carrying TNT. Monty liked it best when he felt there was the danger of getting caught. He would pounce on Sky just as people were coming over or a race was due to start; sometimes they would fight in a restaurant, then make love in their car in the alley behind.

Unfortunately, getting caught occasionally meant his getting caught by Sky. Once in the cycle rig (after a triumph) and once in her own bed (after a loss), Sky found Monty naked and entwined with someone else. Lord knows there was reason to suspect other times. Sky flew into a fury and departed on both occasions, but Monty chased, charmed, and persuaded her on his knees to come back again. He also sent his friends to urge her home. Sky switched from beer to Seven and Seven.

They lived traveling, crashing, and racing for six years before Sky announced she was pregnant. But only when she was three days overdue did Monty drive her to a Justice of the Peace. She got married in her jeans, fly open and with Monty's shirt as a maternity smock. They produced yet another baby ten months after. And still they trucked around from one race or stunt track to another.

Both kids were still preschoolers when Monty pulled his final crack-up. He wasn't even racing. He was running a tryout lap. With his usual bravado, he refused to wear his fireproof garments. He burned to death before they could remove him from the wreck. Sky became a sudden widow. And although she was always aware of the possibility it might happen, her recovery took quite a while. Monty's death came at a strange and poignant time for her.

A few years before, she might have gone on to another rash prodigal. But Monty crashed just as Sky wanted out of the whole affair. On the one hand, Monty left her alone a lot and ignored her on the sidelines. On the other, they had so many fights to clear the air, their air was as pure as a bottle of Canada Dry Club Soda. Sky could no longer stand the pace; she scarcely spent a day without a Valium or a drink—or several. She wanted to enjoy the children and was intrigued with real responsibility. She wanted occasional peace and quiet, relief from the constant worry. She didn't like the liquor and drugs, but no matter what she said or did, Monty would not quit. At least not for long. On the day Monty died, Sky had been examining her wrinkles and telling herself it was time to call it quits. It was hard to accept the truth as a widow, but Sky knew her feeling for Monty had died before his crash.

Not all racers, sportsmen, gamblers, warriors, or politicians are Disaster Brokers; only the particular sort who seem to goad disaster. With such men, kicks come from playing brinksmanship, not from loving and living. There's no doubt they kindle constant excitement, but the price accumulates. You suffer wear and tear. Your emotions and your body play tit for tat. When you don't leave, your sacroiliac does. Sadly, the Disaster Broker is so intriguing that he becomes just as addicting as the habits he leads to. It's not spotting him that's difficult, it's trying to quit.

How Can You Identify One?

Instead of tinker, tailor, soldier, sailor, the Disaster Broker is burglar, stuntman, gambler, candidate. They're also foreign correspondents, doctors (emergency or surgery), lawyers (defending against a lynching), or truck drivers (of big rigs going breakneck). Also C.P.A.s who fake tax returns. Then there's the man who is so trouble-ridden or accident prone you *know* something is going on; you just don't know what it is.

Sometimes the Disaster Broker only dabbles a bit; sometimes he's a full-blown pro. But whatever peril he prefers—war, arrest, or high steel—and to whatever degree, one fact remains: What he has going makes him an ultimate barricader as opposed to an instant one. He's so preoccupied with crises, he obliterates almost everything else there is to feel.

Not only does the Disaster Broker turn his life into a cliff-hanger, he often sets things up to lose. He's never satisfied; no one event is ever good enough. That way he has to keep on keeping on, do what he did once before all over again and, take the next step forward, or he's more frustrated than ever. Some Disaster Brokers manage to just stay over the edge of victory the whole way along, but even they push their luck one more time.

The Disaster Broker whips prosaic events into critical ones; he can't participate unless a situation practically screams with tension. He frets, strategizes, analyzes, and spends hours talking about what hasn't happened. He lives in the not-here, not-now until triumph or disaster smacks him with the present. Even then the effect is short lived. Sometimes his surface is seemingly serene, but behind his eyes he operates on a constant red alert. He has trouble with the fact that he's alive; he tests his existence with peak experiences so he can prove to himself that he's real. The trouble is that as long as he *stays* alive, his testing has no end.

Outer Signs

He dresses to be the center of attention or else in such a way as to dispel suspicion. Notoriety confirms his existence; he either seeks public recognition, both positive and negative, in which case he holds a public celebration, or else he plays the game of getting away without being seen, in which case he celebrates in secret.

Those who go for pizzazz might don studded show-stoppers, satin shirts, or expensive, impeccable business suits that twinkle like stars. He's very blatant in some regard; he's hard to miss. He has a way of showing up in costume. If you don't recognize the meaning of his outfit, ask the kid next door watching T.V. Sometimes he wears a helmet that slopes down the back and red suspenders. Sometimes his garb is blue and he wears a metal badge. Sometimes his outfit is striped and has a number on the pocket. Or it's a body stocking with red boots and a red S on the chest. It's a ski mask for daytime urban salvage (that is, robbery). Or it's racing skins, diving tanks, epaulets, or riding chaps.

The more surreptitious sort wears clothes so perfectly suited to his job that he fades into the wall, or he dresses so ragtag casual that he defies distinction from the surrounding populace. But every Disaster Broker—hiding or shining—has a little personal touch in his dress that becomes his trademark: It might be a scarf, a cat's-eye signet ring, a special jacket, or an eye patch. He has some kind of lucky piece he carries everywhere. He absolutely *always* or absolutely *never* wears one particular color.

He tends to go for large cars, sports cars, special cars, or limousines. He owns a type of Lotus of which the factory only made three, or he alters his vehicle so that its maker would never recognize it. When he's a policeman or fireman, he adds some individual attachment to the dashboard. His vehicle always makes an impact; it has speed, luxury, hidden power. He may own a boat or plane in addition to a car. He gives them all names and puts on his monogram.

The Disaster Broker home can be anything from hotel room to mansion; it doesn't seem to matter. He is his own housing wherever he is; everything goes with him wherever he goes. He can turn any room or show wagon into a momentary residence as soon as he occupies it, because he doesn't really have a home—he has a hub of activity. Even when he gets a house, he alters the space until the rooms don't make sense: Parlors become workshops, bedrooms turn into supply cabinets, kitchens get reorganized for random conferences. Private life and business for him are forever jumbled. Try as you might for separate space, you and your room are just part of the mixture. He doesn't give a hang about décor as long as there are plenty of chairs and ashtrays around.

He thrives on interruptions. His concentration span, although intense, lasts only two minutes before he needs new input. He loves to handle about fifteen actions and conversations—some overt, some covert—all at once. Voices in his head are always talking to him; one is ever mindful of the next scheme he's planning. The only time he's totally present and focuses is when he's just lost, just said "Fire," just realized he's escaped, just tossed in the towel, or just proclaimed a win. The attention he gives people is permanently superficial because only *events* really capture his imagination.

He wears himself ragged. He doesn't always know it, but the dark areas under his eyes definitely show it. Sometimes he breaks his bones or overuses his adrenaline; sometimes he gets thrombosis, strokes, and tics. Sometimes he simply kills himself. Often he uses drugs, smokes, drinks like a fish, and womanizes mindlessly—he plays his body out to the limits.

Sex Signals

Usually he has a very good eye for women. He has a fixed idea of the type he likes and tends to pursue duplicates; when he spots the likely ones, he moves in on them fast. He wakes up when he gets a snappy, sassy response along with a pretty face. And he knows when a woman has heart and stamina underneath; often he goes for the lady with more quality or looks than he has—in other words, a *prize*. And he recognizes those who find his circus exciting. He picks you out in an offhand manner, as if he weren't looking. Then he scoops you up, whirlwinds you, and sometimes scares you. At first you're liable to stay up all night and be spontaneous to the point of wildness. Often he brings all his male helpers so you're the only woman and it flatters you. Later, you become his aide. You carry his silks and files, put on bandages, and brew coffee during long nights. You become one of the guys, with a special distinction and an occasional kiss—you're a mascot.

Sex is like a version of life against death or a race against great odds. He makes love as if you're climbing over rocks, cliffs, and glaciers, maniacs are chasing you, and there's no way back. He drags you along, eggs you on and on. He won't let you get stuck on the ice, and he'll be damned if he'll let you fall behind. He'll go on forever until you get to the top—so you either climax or fake it.

He seeks these arduous adventures at strange hours, on the spur of the moment. He also has a penchant for public places and unprotected situations. He'll try it standing up in the airplane toilet or on a theater stage before the crew arrives. At home he goes for bathroom floors and kitchen tables. He enjoys a chase and being a little too noisy; he likes guests to guess that they just interrupted something. Sometimes he does it while talking on the telephone. You don't exactly get a regular sex life with him. You get it anywhere, anytime, five times a night five nights in a row—and then get abstinence while he's off on devious doings.

He likes to play the flower to which the honeybees flock, and he also likes the role of the bee. He's extremely aware of all women, yet he feels more complete when he has an official consort. He doesn't necessarily care about marrying you, although he will. But he does maintain a permanent alliance, after his own fashion. He may well have one-night stands or short affairs with others, especially when all else is quiet—he usually does them just messily enough for you to find out. Still, he tosses you just enough exhilarating moments to keep you attached and, in the meantime, gives you the company of all his pals. You're never exactly *lonely*.

Money Markers

To the Disaster Broker money, like everything else, represents a means to create hazard. He uses it to promote risky ventures, or he merely risks the money. He's a real spender: When he has it, he burns it; when he runs out, it's down to the very last dime—and lower. He runs through cash so fast, he doesn't even know where it went. He feasts (which to him is either health food or a steak) or he starves (which to him is a vitamin pill, upper and/or downer and/or drink), but he rarely saves unless he has a family inheritance—and then he probably dips into that.

But *your* cash hardly seems to enter his mind. Financial advantage is not what he seeks in a female. He may eat in your kitchen when he's down and out or he may take some of your bucks in need, but mostly you both ride along on what he's got. Like the Gender Ascender, when he's flush he loves to toss you a big bill and tell you to spend. He rarely minds your expenses. In fact, he uses the need of money to excuse his dangerous business.

Family Aspects

If he collects anything, it's cohorts; he keeps a troupe. The Disaster Broker allows his friends constant access to himself; those who help him or hang out with him have open channels to his attention anytime—even before you. He relies on constant intrusions to bring him new and crucial data. "What's up?" is the first thing he says to chums. They tell him the bad news; sometimes they invent it.

His legions are mostly men. The one or two women he befriends are separate from the crowd and are probably on their way to a potential affair with him. He *is* brotherly to one or two of your women friends and the wives of his pals. In some ways his buddies, especially his best one, and maybe his brother will always be closer to him than you. He calls *them* when he's injured, lost, or arrested; they break the news to you. You stay by his side till he's over the crisis; then they come back when he starts up again.

He wants you to have children, yet he hardly seems to want any for himself. Once they're born, he treats his offspring like trophies on a shelf: He coos at and glows over them from across the room, shows them off as if they just got polished, but when it comes to real care they're *yours*. Later, his version of fathering will include putting toddlers on his lap behind the wheel and letting them steer, plunking them on a pony and slapping the horse's behind, or letting them hide under his podium and calling over the cameraman. When they're older, he tries to make them equals, friends, to get them to follow his calling. Parenting is foreign to him; after all, he's still playing hide and seek himself. But if you break up, suddenly the loss of his children becomes a drastic event. He'll try almost anything to get them back, especially cross-country kidnappings.

He has a powerful attachment to his blood kin. Sometimes it's loving, sometimes bitter, sometimes open, sometimes secret, but family ties bind him one way or another. He may distance himself from his relatives and try to forget them, but more frequently he incorporates his parents, siblings, and cousins into his keeping. He does favors for all the relatives he can, as long as they come to him. Even when he rejects his family, he allows them strange ways to find him. He uses his feelings of guilt, responsibility, or anger toward them as another reason to take chances.

He can lose his name, his fame, his life, and his money. He can go to prison and take you with him. He makes ordinary satisfaction impossible for you. But if you like drama, the Disaster Broker is everything you ever wanted. He's as close as you'll ever get to making life into a movie screen: He's a thriller, an adventure, a living, walking chase scene. You don't have to sit on a seat in the dark to watch him—he's there in Sensurround and you can join him.

What Is in Store for You?

Did you ever want to run away and join a circus? Not to become a juggler, not even a clown. Instead, to wear a little tutu, climb up a rope ladder, and hold the trapeze for some daring young man. (In tights!) Somewhere during his act you would get to take a swing into his muscular arms. When you told your mother, she clucked her tongue and said, "Darling, what looks like fun when you're young isn't so enjoyable as time goes on." Somehow you knew she was telling the truth.

Everyone likes an occasional crisis, a little touch of danger; they add zest to your life and take top billing in the stories you collect about yourself. But a steady diet of them is liable to do to your psyche what three meals a day on Godiva chocolates is liable to do to your body. When all your hours are zero hours, you wind up badly under-nourished in spirit, with cavities in your self-control.

With a Disaster Broker, unlike most of the Twenty-two Types of Men, the transformations and stages you go through as a couple largely emanate from *you*, not from him. The man who plays footies with fatality can rarely hide himself for long. He's not one of the obscure sorts who seems one way during courtship and then changes when all is said and done. Nor does he often change his ways. That's the trouble. If the Disaster Broker is anything, he's perpetual. He may shift the kind of peril he pursues; he may go from firefighter to financial phantom or free-fall parachutist. But he hardly ever gives up *all* temptation for calamity.

At first you get to play moll and adjunct thrill-seeker. You meet adulthood in a captivating manner; all they ever said about being young and free seems true. Without set schedules and regular expectations, you cut yourself loose, throw yourself into life, and enjoy an exciting man.

But even in the first stages of a Disaster Broker affair, some less-than-pleasant aspects start to appear. Like it or not, you become part of his act. In some cases your role is to stand just outside the spotlight, show a lot of leg, or wear a perfect pillbox. In other cases you're less obvious: You wait at home or at the finish line and appear only at certain times. You may even be in the dark about his doings. But mostly you serve as the net when he takes a spill. And you worry, fix up, and clean up the mess.

Sooner or later, three things happen. First, you realize that to entertain himself he needs external excitement provided by someone or something else, not himself or you. When the two of you are alone, without a sexual episode or quarrel, you can hardly keep him amused. In fact there's nothing much at all to your relationship except for the times you play to an audience. *Somebody* has to see you, check on you (and maybe not discover you), know about you (or get fooled by you) for you to have togetherness. Part of the reason he always has his pals around is to take up the slack of what he hasn't got going with you.

Second, you get tired of the hollowness of the thrills: When he's around, he's exhausting; when he meanders off, you get the emptiness and the hole he leaves behind. Soon, your energy runs out. You lead a draining life on every level. You never know when disaster will occur. Even quiet spells are ominous, because they might be the prelude to twisters. Tension comes and goes in waves; you get weak. You spend a lot of time in places with pumped air and Muzak. You sit on a lot of benches. You reverberate around another person's actions. His dealings may cause drastic events to happen to you as well—you could end up anywhere from the White House or San Quentin to the grave. And when you seek some nurturing from him to compensate for the strain, it just isn't there.

Everyone knows that when you're under a lot of pressure, something's got to give. It does. Enter stage three: You begin to fall apart. You increase your cigarette consumption from ten to sixty-four per day. You get virus-prone and go from colds to double pneumonia. Your bones get brittle, your muscles grab. Pills get handy and so does wine or pre-mixed Tequila Sunrise. You deal with things that distance you from other people. With the Disaster Broker, most often you talk in codes, have insignias for friends and strangers, use cryptics for telephone calls and hand signals for commands in public. You talk to those that know your language and cut off outsiders. Every person you meet is in or out. All emotions are black and white to the Disaster Broker. *You* may feel greys and in-betweens, but you can't tell that to your man. He assumes you're loyal. Quibbling puts to question your faith; outright fights are allowed because he thinks you're just letting off steam and afterwards you'll comply. With your devotion so expected, you just go ahead and give it: to leave would be to become a bad guy. Soon you get so removed from reality, you seem a little crackers.

He's always doing things to push you away and then reclaim you again. And you let it happen rather than leave the strange and marginal world you know; you're afraid that there's nothing left for you anywhere once you've gotten used to his extremes.

What tends to happen when you stay on is that you add to the action. You have crises of your own, stamp your feet, break glasses, and throw tantrums. You get sick, weird, and drunk. You almost leave—but not quite. That always kicks up dust. You become a semi-invalid with chronic problems.

Fun in your twenties, dreary in your thirties, weary and withdrawn from forty and on: That's the program unless something happens: One is an actual disaster, an event that alters your life and relationship conclusively; the other is that one day life just gets more precious to you. You decide to stop playing "Let's run the gauntlet together," leave the ranks of the superstuff, and join the ordinary crowd.

What Are the Telltale Signs of Trouble?

The Disaster Broker doesn't have telltale signs—he has air raid sirens and seismic warnings. The trouble is, you're probably the kind who hears the rumbling and says, "Gee, an earthquake! I'd like to try that once!"

If a man comes around who's got on a costume, perhaps you should stay behind closed doors, or at least think twice. And reconsider if: he slips in the door in the middle of the night and the first thing he says is, "Pull down the shades," then peeks out the window to see who's watching; he builds smuggling holes in his hand glider; he adds fourteen gas tanks to his overloaded racer; he keeps dangerous trinkets: submachine guns, plastic explosives, high-octane fuel, blackmail evidence, heroin, and spying devices; he doesn't tell you his name at first, or he tells you one but turns out to have six others, all with different mail drops; he sands his fingertips; or he has a permit for a regulation gun but carries a snub nose in his boot.

Once the consortium is established, the storm warnings for trouble come in two big ways. The first is when he reveals a tendency to lose instead of win. *Professional* gamblers, soldiers, and climbers—the ones who succeed—like as little messy action as possible. They keep their situations simple and tidy; compulsion, complications, and carelessness spell risk to them. So when your mate goes after too many wins, take heed. When he shows he's accident-prone or when two out of three times he comes home with losses or injuries, you'd better realize he's aiming for peril despite what he says.

You're at a critical point with the Disaster Broker whenever the stakes get too high for *you*, regardless of him, or when it becomes obvious that he's slowly committing suicide, when he's on drugs, rides too dangerously, does stunts too precariously, deals with assassins and killers, or runs the line of fire. Yet his obsession holds you to him and so do his injuries. If you feel compelled to watch him fall, perhaps it's time for you to consider that your presence abets his flirtation with death.

Certainly when what he does endangers you bodily, financially, or otherwise—*STOP!* You might become responsible for his disasters in ways you hadn't even considered. If you like a dangerous aspect in life, why not at least pay for your own actions? Become a fireperson, policeperson, detective, or stuntwoman. Go legally, get pay, benefits, a support system, and most of all—get it for yourself.

What Are the Chances?

Can you stay with the Disaster Broker? With no other of the Twenty-two Types of Men is that question as hard to answer. Luck plays such a heavy hand in the Disaster Broker future, luck is almost more his mate than you are. You have to consider it a silent partner who can keep you together or interrupt you forever.

Can you change him? No, you can't. The Disaster Broker could be likened to a hurricane. Once he's started, nothing can turn him back, unless another extreme front comes along and blasts out all his punch. When he comes your way, you can either weather him, ride him out a while, stay on his edges, shelter yourself as he passes, or just get out of his way. It's up to you. Once he's sucked you in, he may toss you about, but he rarely spits you out, so what to do about him is in your hands. Let me tell you, a lot of women leave at first glance and later.

My advice concerning the Disaster Broker is also multiple choice. If his scene is very dire, if he indulges in truly dangerous drugs for use or sale, practices serious crime for fun or profit, gambles with heavy losses, or does life-endangering stunts, I strongly suggest that you stay far, far removed. You may need a lot of things in life, but those are items you definitely can do without.

On the other hand, if he seeks thrilling action and perilous challenges with some sense and precaution, and you like him and find him exciting, why not join in while you're young and free? But just for a spell. Then when you desire more substance in your life, make like Wendy: Leave Peter Pan to the pirates and crocodiles, fly home, and grow up. If you follow this course, do it with honesty and heart. Make the terms of your commitment clear to him up front. Most likely you can see the future well enough to know that he won't change and you will. Say at the beginning that you will stay until the time you want something else. You don't mean to alter him, pressure him, or torment him; you merely mean to be true to yourself.

If you *don't* think you can enjoy him for a while and take off with a fond farewell, I advise that you don't do him at all. The conditions that come with him are hazardous to the health. I'd certainly shun the game of leaving and getting re-won. As long as you stay on a Disaster Broker's invisible tether, you never become free.

If you remain with a Disaster Broker, it's very important for you to create an eye in his storm where you can rest, a calm center within you. In order to maintain your mental and physical well-being, insist on your own space where trespassers are prohibited. Then—and I can't stress this enough—learn techniques for inner peace. Try meditation, self-dialogue, or prayer until you find that very quiet place within yourself where you can gain repose and strength. Make rules about how you will live, who can come and go when, and keep the rules despite what's going on. You may even consciously choose to remain ignorant of his actions. Since you are his number-one sidekick, he probably respects you more than you think. He'll heed your conditions if you insist.

In order to weather him, you will need not only to keep up the spunk and ability you started with, but to learn not to overload, to limit yourself. Perhaps you should relinquish the thought of having children. Possibly you should only take on certain well-defined tasks with him, or none at all. Maybe you should develop a career attached to, but different from his, then stick to it and nothing else.

Whatever way you choose, when you link up with a daredevil it's bound to be tough. You're probably more of a survivor than he is—he knew that instinctively the minute he met you—so trust yourself, whatever happens to him. If you end up alone or with a disabled companion, you will manage. Instead of fretting, believe in yourself and cross bridges when you come to them. Never forget one thing: You can always decide you've had enough and get out, at any point. With the Disaster Broker, quitting isn't necessarily losing, it's staying well. You don't have to carry through with everything you start just because you handled it once. Whenever the costs mount up beyond your scope or the peril is more than you're willing to risk, cut your losses and part. Throw loving kisses, cry if you must, but don't end up in some dire place or condition just for the sake of sticking it out.

Where Do You Fit In?

So you want to be a pistol-packing mama? Lois Lane? Marie Antoinette? The smuggler's moll?

Usually that means one of two things. It may mean you're from down-home, nothing-happening land; with him you tasted your first thrill and now you love it and don't want out. You have an addictive streak, and you found your drug in an exhilarating life. Maybe you also discovered booze, cigarettes, the roar of the crowds, an occasional toke, hit, or snort? And maybe those habits are growing?

Or it may mean you too are a crisis-monger. You perpetuate zero hours, and if you don't get them from him, you create your own. He's just an easy way to have them without doing your own inventing. Ask yourself how many walks you've taken, only to come back. How many threats and scenes have been replayed? How many fights? How often do you get ill? How much do you really like it when he gets busted and you have to bail him out? How exciting do you find it when you have to hide from the law, trick opponents, set up a con, call ambulances, use codes, keep score, and destroy evidence? If this comes too close for comfort, maybe you yourself are afraid of ordinary life.

It's true that routine life can appear quite appalling. To some it's like an endless living death so, rather than face it, they manufacture extremes or develop addictions to keep their lives different from routine nothingness. Do you dislike silence, so you play the radio from dawn to dusk? Do you feel nothing when nothing's happening?

If plain life seems too dreary or if you show escapist patterns, you might want to explore the subject with outside counsel. Self-recognition is a big step. These are the sorts of issues that counseling really helps—if not to alter them, at least to understand them. Such aid is available almost everywhere. But if you're on a race circuit or in the underworld where help is hard to get, at least keep a notebook in which you religiously jot down your habits—when they happen and how. Note everything: cigarettes, the radio, drinks, mad expenditures, gambles, headaches, broken bones. How frequent are the flirtations with danger? When you read your notebook, you'll see predictable patterns you never knew existed, and with that knowledge you can often call a halt.

Sometimes, however, the Disaster Broker doesn't match your own tendencies. You just thought his craziness was a phase of youth, but he kept on. Or the adventure looked great to start, but very quickly turned old. Then you need to examine what continues to hold you. You fell for something that wasn't so. The man in your imagination may have changed, but the real one didn't. If your illusion has long since passed but you're still around, better ask why. I'll bet you find that it's a fear of routine life.

And you may fit in simply by choice. I once heard the story of a woman who died very young. Everyone grieved her passing, for she had marvelous wit and charm. Yet she had often said she would rather have a short, bright life than a long, dull one. She acted on that choice, even though unconsciously. The people who really loved her knew that she would not have wanted them to mourn.

Every human being has the right to decide how to utilize his or her energy. Some go for slow, steady, and long. Some want to be like fires that consume every coal; they prefer to burst forth and kindle fast even though they know they may quickly die out. If that's the way you want to burn, the Disaster Broker may be the best fuel for you.

Notes and Particulars

16/The Sugar Pie Honey

Related Types: The Father Knows Best
The "But I Really Like Women"
Manipulator

Positivity Scale: + −

Think of marshmallow syrup. Or creamy nougat. Now lead your thoughts to more sublime tastes. Imagine chocolate-covered care. Sugarcoated sensitivity. All pouring forth from your man. The Sugar Pie Honey. He's a sweet, sweet guy. But take him too far and he becomes a Cool-Whip nightmare. Endlessly giving way. You gobble, searching for the shortcake—at least the strawberry. Something. *Anything!* But dig as you might, you can't find the substance. There's never any resistance. Quick calories, but nothing to stomach. And somehow, it never tastes quite *real.*

The Sugar Pie Honey thinks he deserves love so little that he has to be extra good to get any. So he devises a plan, the way cereal companies do to get kids hooked on oat flakes. He adds an addictive ingredient—sweetness. The cavities follow.

He seems always to understand, to forgive. He wraps you in a coat of gentle, smothers you with nice, kills with kindness. Terrible at measuring cupfuls, he glazes over with abandon, figuring if a little T.L.C. is good, a lot must be even better. Shades of a little boy told too often to behave, he comes on like a blessed archangel.

But since he restricts himself so obsessively to beneficence, you wonder if he really loves or if he resents the object of his saccharine attentions. Sooner or later he turns his partner into the mouthpiece of all his repressed ire; the more honeyed he is, the more spleenful she. He wears the halo, she the cloven hoofs. And he takes closet offense at not receiving better treatment, although he never asks for it.

232

He picks women who are looking for a port in the storm, ladies fighting some inner war and pretending it's peacetime who, rather than shore themselves up from the inside, succumb to an outside buttress. He heads for anything wearing a fragile, handle-with-care, or just-come-out-of-a-horrible-home label. He offers a hand hold, a pat dry, a place in which to break apart safely; he'll stand by.

Story

For a long time, my colleague Brian was the Sugar Pie Honey to end them all. A little short and definitely not built like a male model, he wore heavy glasses. His hair had a mind of its own. Too shy and too unnoticed for anything except answers to exam questions, he didn't even attempt dating till he was almost through college.

Secretly, he thought that the only way he could gain his own woman was to compensate for all his failings, so he used his keen mind to discover just what women were looking for. He hit upon all the things he assumed jocks were not—sensitive, gentle, and attentive—and turned himself into the deal you couldn't refuse. At first, he gained a lot of lady friends, yet none wanted to be his lover. But sooner or later he knew he'd score.

Enter Martine. An actress. Basically well intentioned, she was unable to face her own character. Her family, who acknowledged only saintliness, were austere, troubled, and very much into guilt, so she couldn't admit to aspects of herself that weren't nice. She was very confused. Martine was having trouble facing a cold, harsh world. She was caught between lack of money, lack of friends, acting aspirations, the competition her career involved (for which she was ill-equipped), and family duties, which were laden with false responsibilities.

Along came Brian. A human fur coat. Small wonder he looked like a little log cabin, complete with pancakes and hot maple syrup. She fell for the someone-to-watch-over-me aspect of him and ignored the instinct that told her that on a diet of permissiveness she might go sour.

For while Martine wanted to be Extra Select, it turns out she was just regular—sometimes nice, sometimes not so nice. She had a streak, perfectly normal but repressed, that made her want to kick up dust, be free, and be mean when she felt like it. With Brian, she opted for safety. But he offered no restraints. He proffered money to ease her existence, sympathy for her problems, and a business sense for her ambitions. He gave massages, foot baths, and hair brushings. And he *never* got angry. Not even when he should have. He never said no and never even showed annoyance. Martine had free rein. With every liberty to be nasty, she couldn't find her own control. The devil within her got out of hand.

She began to try to provoke Brian. She became quarrelsome and critical; she broke promises. But no matter what she did, he'd only comfort her. So she got worse. And he got even more understanding. She soon realized he was withholding any response other than acquiescence. He was showing one side of himself and keeping the other hidden with a vengeance.

He even held back sex. Not that he didn't make love to her; he did. He just came so fast that she couldn't. And while he tried to please her in every way, if she caressed him back, he'd go limp. That's when she *really* got mad. She went beyond insult and zoomed to injury, started having affairs, first clandestinely, then cantankerously. Brian just got sadder and sweeter, so she stayed out all night. He greeted her with orange juice. She left for a week. He took her back.

The diet of Sugar Pie was killing them both. Martine could hardly bear how horrible she'd become, and Brian was slowly fermenting. Between them they had too many hurts to overcome. They suffered a long withdrawal. But finally, for their own survival, they parted.

You've heard of blessings in disguise. Well, the Sugar Pie Honey is the opposite. What seems like a charm is a curse. He plants the seeds of his own disrespect; you are the one who reaps them.

How Can You Identify One?

It's easy to see his potential but hard to see that he goes too far. The Sugar Pie Honey is a good man, marvelous to women, but he doesn't know how to make women care for him. Nor, more importantly, how to care for himself. He's usually a smart man. He got the way he is by analyzing and coming up with strategy. After sizing up the data, he discovered that goodness endears him to others. So he made it his M.O.

His thinking is fallacious; he's not as objective as he thinks. But it's not so much the plan as his faulty execution that really gets him into trouble. He makes two errors: excess of kindness and blind neglect of his anger. He lives in terror of his own temper, so he never tries it out. He doesn't know how to be grouchy and still have friends, and he never learns that you'll both survive it if he gets mad.

This combination of errors makes a messy mixture. His plan backfires. For his own rage is there, all right. He says everything is okey-dokey, but it *isn't*. He wants to be real, but he won't give a response other than comforting. He's mild-mannered and unpretentious. He's bright and makes good conversation but has an endless stream of queries that all center around you: Where do you *come from?* What do you *do?* How do you *feel?*

Outer Signs

The Sugar Pie Honey is not very interested in clothes; he doesn't buy them often. He claims he's concerned with people, not trappings. He likes hand-made and ethnic items, embroidery but not jewelry, huggable textures and soft weaves, suede shoes and Hawaiian shirts. He likes rather long, unfussed-with hair, and beards. He's not flashy, but he's not staid either.

The same goes for his car. At first, he's not very interested, then he works up more involvement, and each model gets a little more attention. Still, nothing with spectacular value. Always a common car, good and functional or old and funky: a Ford, a Pontiac, an old Toyota, or a Mazda with terry-cloth seat covers.

He heads for vintage houses in folksy neighborhoods where old and young both live, with community centers, hangouts, little grocery stores. Certainly not a rich area, but a place where he can be just one of the locals, a routine, acknowledged presence, a good Joe. Sometimes he shares his house or apartment with another man, very much of his type. His place is partly clean and partly not, partly decorated and partly not. He prefers photographs to prints or paintings and doesn't get around to rearranging furniture. His idea of warming up is lots of color, whole rooms of yellow, blue, or red.

His concern for human beings manifests itself in a modest political stance: He's for cheaper bread, medical clinics, more jobs. Parks and libraries. But ' s politics are not usually carried much further than his conversation. He does support local campaigns like Stop the Freeway, Open the Bikeways, the bottle bill. And he drops money into the hat of the streetcorner fiddler.

He likes animals, music, especially guitar music, and one favorite sport. He doesn't like to stand out but doesn't like to fade out either. He wants to engage people on deeper levels, to 'elicit personal problems and talk about feelings. He isn't devoid of pride. He admires his own brains, his sensitivity, and how much niceness he's achieved. He treats himself all right. But just . . . *all right*. It's part of how he semi-devalues himself. He goes to no great lengths for delight. He will buy something that he really, really wants, but only after a great deal of deliberation, and he hesitates on items he would only kind of like to have. It's the same treatment he gives his emotions. He'll recognize the one he thinks he ought to—love—but will sweep away the others— greed, lust, revenge. He thinks too much about how he should feel, about how he can make *you* feel. He lives in his head. It takes him a long while to disconnect his overactive frontal lobes enough to have fun. Drugs and alcohol often scare him because they short-circuit his synapses.

While the voices in his head talk too much, the muscles in his legs don't run enough; he exercises irregularly and inadequately. Yet surprisingly, he is not a bad athlete; he just looks more awkward and clumsy than he is. Perhaps a lack of grace is his way to get sympathy.

Sex Signals

He's not sure what he thinks about women. He doesn't quite trust them. He heads after women he views as more interesting and less stable than he; it's their fragility that attracts. These women may cover fissures with an ambitious façade, but with his seismograph, he knows they're there. The Sugar Pie Honey's woman is always under strain.

He approaches her through conversation. He spots a loner who's doing something a little unusual and seeks out the details of her life. Not shy about meeting and greeting, he knows he's good with words. Quickly he nice-talks and nice-times a woman into dependence. He becomes a special pal. The theme is "What difficulties did you go through today?" Despite resistance (which he gets because the ladies he chooses love his sympathy but not his physique), he eventually gets them into bed.

Sex is a giveaway clue of his slumbering emotions. He has a hard time staying hard, and he climaxes very quickly, almost before anything has begun. So to compensate, he continues the same pattern he finds operative socially. He is so solicitous, you feel like the guest on *I've Got a Secret*. Lovemaking with him is a cross between an amorous quiz show and a checkup. He asks, How do you like this? And that? What do you want done? Which side do you want up? Does it hurt? And (especially) did you come? He elicits your verbal response to ensure that he's getting your other one; it calms his nerves. Under his seeming curiosity about your orgasmic aptitude, he's very anxious to make up for his lack of one. He would love to become a good lover. But when it comes to basics, he's not. His anxiety grows. So does your disappointment. You talk over your problem, seek books and techniques. Beyond that, no one rocks the boat. You don't discuss anger and resentment; there's too much to lose. Day by day, he's still a sweetheart. Massages, hot chicken soup, an ever-ready ear for your troubles. They make up for a lot, or so you both pretend.

The Sugar Pie Honey bears some resemblance to the type I call the Entrapper, but the Entrapper has a far more extreme method of approach. He offers wonderful evenings that are hard to resist. He starts bringing gifts, each one more desirable than the last. Finally, he switches into guilt. He pleads that you can't leave him because he loves you so. He threatens suicide until you agree to be his for good. Using greed and implying your responsibility, he traps you. Entrappers will even get a woman pregnant on purpose.

Don't get caught by the Entrapper! Remember, gifts don't magically appear without a price tag. Another person's proclaimed agony is not your imperative obligation. And above all else, protect your *own* body.

Now, back to the Sugar Pie Honey.

Money Markers

The Sugar Pie Honey is equally sweet with money. Usually his mate isn't quite as capable of earning a living as he is, or she doesn't want to earn one all the time, day in and day out. But the Sugar Pie Honey is a worker; financial support, all or partial, is part of his package. It's not that he won't use your money or combine it with his, but *his* is primary. To keep your finances on a par, you always borrow a cup of the old granulated from him, never he from you. Quite secretly, he keeps track of whose and how much went where.

Family Aspects

The Sugar Pie Honey wants children. But he usually has to cajole one out of the union, as his co-generator wants motherhood less than he wants fatherhood. He likes to raise the children, be there for their wants and needs, be sweet to them. He'll fight for custody.

He's heedful of his family, kind to his parents. He sees his mother as cordial, his father as bittersweet, and does what they want most of the time. When he doesn't play the good son, it's away from home, then he presents his deed to them in the most palatable way. He doesn't use their money even when they have lots. He's a good boy. Often, he has only a brother. He's never learned to squabble with a sister.

Just-plain-friend isn't his style. *Super*-best-friend is. He's very close to one or two men and spends a long time on the phone with them, or they watch hockey together on T.V.

Obviously, he's an overzealous friend to you, almost parasitic. But *any* woman in his life, past or present, lover or not, is earmarked as a pal. When he's not attached, lots of women call him to commiserate. Not too many want to hitch up.

The Sugar Pie Honey's liabilities aren't legion, as with some of the Twenty-two Types of Men. He can't see why anyone gets mad at him. But that's because he hides his real self; his one-sided presentation causes distrust. Few people can believe all white with no black. He certainly has assets. In a generally crass world he shimmers with positivity. Over-sincerity is a relatively minor sin, even when you suffer the consequences of it. He's real nice; if only he knew it was nice to be real.

What Is in Store for You?

Too much sweetness isn't healthy for anybody; it certainly isn't nourishing. What lies ahead with the Sugar Pie Honey is a steady process in which satisfaction lessens and maladies grow. Three major troubles occur with the Sugar Pie Honey. First, he makes you the source of all odious emotion. Second, you're cut off from loving yourself; he's too fast at doing it for you. And third, you fight off what seems to be the obstacle between yourself and you—him—a false enemy perhaps, but too good a target to pass up. A spiteful and divisive side of yourself, which you repress and he encourages, arrives to stay.

It begins with growing grumpiness. The "so what" syndrome sets in, usually to cover the fact that you feel at fault. A little Hitler is in the making, and he's living inside you. You push the experiment farther. More and more obnoxious, you hope for a result: Will he get angry? Will he protect himself? Will he finally say, "Now you've gone too far?" But he continues to fall back and redefine what's acceptable to him, while you go ape and get zapped with guilt. The Sugar Pie Honey stays just nice enough to make you ashamed. A serious bad guy/good guy situation sets in. Only he's Shirley Temple and you're Jack Palance. The worse you abuse his curly little head, the more you confirm your creeping fear that you're not a good person. Fairly early on in the relationship, he begins to withhold but then, so do you! It's fair play to get frigid along with everything else. Later, you can give your orgasms to someone mean instead of someone kind.

Under that saccharine skin of his there's a record keeper who keeps a list of your every sin and injury. Eventually, he lets you know your marks. You and he both establish your no-goodness, but he'll forgive you, once, twice, seemingly, nauseatingly ad infinitum. His forgiveness has its limits, however, and also its conditions. He'll forgive you if you act better. He'll watch you, no longer simply sweet, until finally something snaps. You may pull away, but surprisingly often it's he who finally says you can't come back, when his forgiveness gives out.

Leaving this type almost always involves a long and arduous recuperation. It's hard to get over sugar poisoning. You had to have a sweet tooth to want him in the first place; it's tempting to turn back to him—again and again—for quick calories. You two can stick together long after the breakup, but you won't get on with your life till you wash your hands of him.

What Are the Telltale Signs of Trouble?

With any man, when you hear no nos, you should perk up your ears. Notice if there are no fights to clear the air, if he thinks out catastrophes instead of yells about them, if he coos at your disasters without an occasional "Well, it serves you right." These signs mean you're heading for gumdrop land.

When a man sighs, but doesn't say what's wrong, gives poignant looks, but grows more distant, it's a sign that his resentment is growing. He's waiting to unload his grievances and ask for contrition.

When you *take* kindness but react to it disgustingly, you're in for trouble. If you ignore your reaction and still accept more, things are going to get worse. It's a dicomforting indication. If he doesn't think he deserves care, why should you think so?

Take a hard look at what constitutes a healthy, happy atmosphere. When you feel disrespect because he's so nice, but stay because of guilt, right then you should question remaining, no matter how cozy it is. Maybe you should scoot yourself to a counselor. Why is sweetness a sign of weakness to you?

When you begin to perceive that his constant approval is a lie, it's time for you both to run for help. Nothing good ever comes of being false.

What Are the Chances?

Only rarely can you and the Sugar Pie Honey eradicate the history you stack up between you. The sins against the other result in the kind of hurt that never goes away and provides a source of reproach that can only lead to an inevitable parting. My feeling is that it *should* end, and probably the sooner the better. The Sugar Pie Honey provides a self-defeating system—a tailspin of diminishing self-esteem. With him you may grow fat, but you don't grow tall.

While the relationship is rarely saveable, you can salvage a good aftermath: The Sugar Pie Honey makes a great ex. He can stay sweet enough and involved enough to be more than civil, even more than fair in the financial settlement and childcare.

Besides, you both change. The Sugar Pie Honey's smarts ultimately save him. He probably oversweetens a relationship only once. When it doesn't work, he does some quick recalculations, adjusts the seasoning measurements, and tries a little ginger next time around. And few women are willing to repeat their part of a Sugar Pie Honey twosome again. They may head for the same sort of man but break up quickly when it starts to go bad. You will probably go through a number of short relationships after a Sugar Pie Honey; they'll keep getting better.

Meanwhile you treat your old Sugar Pie Honey better; and he you. But while you can become friends, he will never quite understand why you got mad at him; nor will he really forgive you.

If you *do* attempt to rescue a Sugar Pie Honey relationship, I suggest you first start with yourself, then go on to him. Set your own limits. Gear your behavior to how you *know* you'll feel afterward. Don't do what makes you feel bad or allow what makes you feel bad to be done to you. Remember to return your man's attentions equally. Then help him learn that love does come. Even to those with tempers.

Where Do You Fit In?

Do you need outlandish support? A living crutch? Do you choose men who give it to you, but think less of them for it?

When you're hooked on the Sugar Pie Honey, you're not looking to find out who you are—only what you *should* be or, maybe, *shouldn't* be. You're probably asking, "Am I good or bad?" But when you settle for approval, you end up not knowing what you're made of. To grow, like it or not, you need heartier victuals—criticism with compliments, anger with joy. They can be hard to digest in the short run, but they're good for you.

You have to let your friends be true and tell you what they really think. Take their bitter with their mellow. If you have trouble accepting their bad opinions, you may be missing out on their real affection. If you're battling with guilt and select a situation in which you can behave without reproach, you lose their affection and your own. Don't pick the perfect spot to wallow in self-condemnation; wallowing rarely helps you win. Stop relying on indiscriminate acceptance and unending support. Clinging to the Sugar Pie Honey is almost like saying, "It takes somebody extra good to love me." Then, since he doesn't see how awful you are, it follows you can't like him. Through your nasty actions you confirm that you have a bad nature.

But there's a secret about your "bad nature." The secret is not that you have a deeply hidden malevolence, but that you don't. You're normal! Every person has a wide range of emotions and responses. You can be special and rotten at the same time, good and bad, nice, mean, and everything in between. There is no such thing as the consistently rational person. All you can do is try to strike a balance. And forgive yourself.

Notes and Particulars

17/ The Maximal Misogynist

Related Types: The Minimal Misogynist
The Gender Ascender

Positivity Scale: − − −

The Maximal Misogynist is a physical abuser. He hits and he hurts. He comes from all walks of life—upper, middle, lower classes, different races, all religions. But he has one common denominator: He takes out his frustrations violently. And only on weaker people. That means women and children.

He's public enemy number one. And yet he never looks the part. Who would ever guess he's a wife beater? He seems just a little *more* than a regular guy—a little more ambitious and driven. He appears quietly contained, thoughtfully assured, decidedly masculine. He reeks of admired traits. But sniff a little longer, and you'll find out his confidence is not comfortable—it's assertive, and despite his drive, he's stymied. Under that extra-crisp exterior lies a half-baked chicken.

He usually hits where it doesn't show. And when nobody is looking. He twists arms, pulls hair, locks you in the closet, socks you about the body. At home, at night, or when the company is in the other room. Closed doors and clothed bodies provide his shield.

The secret is known by one other, of course—the victim. He contrives to keep you as a co-conspirator. No bean-spilling allowed; he coddles you with elaborate apologies, frightens you with threats of further abuse. And he plays on the theory that if he is "more of a man," it makes you "more of a woman."

He believes that you too think it's manly of him to let you have it when you're out of line, that he's a tamer domesticating the lion in you. He thinks that's why you stand for it. He depends on your silence. Even if the battering shows, you cooperate—you tell people

243

you fell down the stairs or slipped in the tub. And you don't wear bathing suits in public. He needs a woman whom he can threaten, to whom lack of a caretaker, lack of money, or lack of a he-man spells disaster. A Maximal Misogynist's favorite date is Snow White. Without the Prince, she just can't make it on her own. He prefers women whose upbringing included a heavy dose of female despondency. As a result, she buys the bit that she should take *anything* to make a marriage work. She heeds such garbage as "That's a woman's lot" or "You may never get another chance."

The Maximal Misogynist makes a special deal. Unlike the Father Knows Best, who wants a child to control, or the Oldie But Goodie, who wants a stay-at-home-but-equal pal, he offers care and feeding in exchange for a whipping woman. It's a bad deal.

Story

When Jeanine from my high school married Bennet, we all thought she had made a hit. Hit was the right word, all right. Only years later did we learn she took a quick trip from blushing bride to battered wife

Jeanine had completed only one year of women's college. She was biding her time, waiting for Bennet to graduate. Then she dropped out of school and into a "perfect" marriage. When he took a job as the new go-getter in a real-estate development firm, they walked down the aisle.

People called Jeanine a living doll. It was an accurate assessment. She never picked a major in school. She never held a job more serious than McDonald's French Fry Packer. She could hardly spell "insurance policy." And it never failed to surprise her that checks could bounce.

When Bennet held the purse strings, signed all the documents, and bought all the big purchases, it didn't seem fishy to her. He was taking *care* of her. Life was a queen-size polyester comforter. Not that she didn't work. But they never considered what she did as valuable labor. She kept the house clean and cared for the little cadets; *that* wasn't called work.

While Jeanine produced two children, Bennet came up with no promotions. Despite the early promise, his flash fizzled. And while he managed a very capable exterior, which had made him the envy of his high school, Bennet was *fragile* underneath. He couldn't keep a lid on his frustrations and envy. In private he flew into rages and flipped into uncalled-for jealous fits.

He thrived on man talk, he thought the love-'em-and-leave-'em philosophy was the way to go; he resented he hadn't tried it out. His father had been concerned that Bennet should be raised like a boy and become a *real man.* He had hit Bennet when he was a child and often struck his mother. Even though Bennet feared his father, his parent's "masculine" strength impressed him; he translated violence into power. So once he was in his own driver's seat, he began to attack Jeanine.

Each time he took his rage out on Jeanine, he made up to her. Ever so romantically and sweetly, he seduced her back. Soon they really got good at their fights. Together they would accelerate some little fuss until she got hurt and they could kiss it all away. But then the beatings got more brutal.

One day Jeanine realized she was making up with him out of fright instead of for the subsequent fun. But now her protests were stifled in a vacuum. He expected to kiss and make it better. Why should a broken rib be different from a slap? She was his property, and property took whatever you did to it. Once he even threw her out of the car and threatened to run her down. Jeanine was terrified. But by now Jeanine had a problem. She was ten years out of high school and, since then, had a one-sided score board: Employment record—0. Children—2. She had no money and nowhere to go.

One night, Bennet knocked her unconscious. Concerned that he had gone too far, he called an ambulance. Unwittingly he dropped the drawbridge that gave entrance to his kingdom. Outside authorities marched onto the scene. One by one, counselors, social workers, police, and legal advisers visited Jeanine's hospital room. She resisted their efforts. But only until she got back home. It seems in her absence Bennet had turned on the children.

When he went to work the next day, she mustered her courage and made for the telephone. She quickly packed up and moved out. Luckily for her, an age of social enlightenment was beginning to dawn. She found many agencies ready to help her. It took a while, but now she is on her own.

I cannot avoid giving opinionated advice on the Maximal Misogynist. My strongest sensibilities lead me to say without qualification—

LEAVE HIM THE FIRST TIME HE HITS YOU AND DON'T GO BACK. If all women everywhere walked out *immediately* when struck by their men, wife beaters wouldn't have the chance to practice their perversion.

Having given my advice, I will continue for those who don't follow it.

How Can You Identify One?

Where the Minimal Misogynist thinks he likes women but probably does not, the Maximal Misogynist does not even think of women as something to like; he never learned he was supposed to. A woman is something to show other men, to want for sex and servility.

The Maximal Misogynist is almost as hard to identify in the beginning stages as the Minimal Misogynist. During the mating dance, his ultimate abuse remains obscure. It's not so much when he thinks you are his as when *you* think you are his that he changes. By becoming jealous, forceful, or possessive, he announces you belong to him; if you don't protest but comply, you play Pandora. The ghouls pop out of his box.

He shows some early warnings: jealousy, perhaps a forceful, he-man heat to your romance. But also note these: his competitiveness with other men, his pursuit of women as part of his public image, his tight hold on emotions, his blaming others, his need to appear the dominant member of your twosome in the eyes of the world. He might strike before the wedding. If so, he works quickly to seduce you into a romantic parody of passion. Any "Tarzan is sorry he hit Jane and to prove it he will give her fifteen orgasms and a bouquet of flowers" line should ring like a five-alarm fire signal in your ears.

The Maximal Misogynist covers up serious problems of self-esteem with a veneer of storybook masculinity. His doubt mostly is in such areas as success and failure, strength and weakness, respect and disrespect. In each he measures himself against men, not women; he fears how he stands as a man among men. A submissive wife, maybe some side affairs, confirm his manhood. He is blind to the challenge and the rewards of knowing women. He blocks out much of the vocabulary of emotions and is left with largely negative feelings. You rarely find a Maximal Misogynist radiating joy or overcome with awe;

he considers that "feminine." When his emotions do erupt, he blurts out anger, often rage that astounds even him. His fury covers envy. He agonizes over a secret measurement chart of other men whom he cannot control. What other men get and he doesn't—sales, promotions, prestige, money—he considers things his wife has lost or mishandled. She flirted, spent too much money, nagged, gave hospitality to some bum. Soon her body comes to symbolize his rotten world. When he wants to kick the world, he kicks its representative—his old lady.

The Maximal Misogynist needs order and regimentation. He wants his women to walk in all the squares, on time, in place. He keeps a code of criminal offenses in secret so he can constantly revise it; it's more fun and provides an excuse to hit if you slip up without knowing what you did wrong. Forewarned is forearmed, and he doesn't want you that way, unless he can depend on you to start the fireworks for him by conveniently forgetting or infringing on the rules.

Outer Signs

He dresses with precision. Whatever his occupation, bus driver to lawyer, he usually wants his uniform in order. He may drop towels everywhere, but his drawers must contain neat stacks of shirts like so many toy soldiers in a row, his jockey shorts clean as flags of surrender, his pants creased as straight as laser beams.

To say he is not a very flexible person is an understatement. He doesn't like unexpected company. Chance meetings make him agitated. He resists parties. He cuts off conversations with strangers. Especially *your* conversations with *male* strangers.

His life runs on schedule, according to routine. Breakfast traditional, dinner hour set, children sitting down. Relaxation planned, exercise rigorous. He likes sports and plays with other men. Ball games, squash, and boxing pit him against foes in a male atmosphere. Football and basketball give him topics of talk. He converses only with men. Sometimes he works out with strange devices in a gym. He thinks by looking hard he'll mean business to his cohorts.

His hourly demands become your life's clock: You make sure to get the shirts from the cleaners before he comes home. You leave shopping with a friend in plenty of time to get dinner on. You show up when you are supposed to and where you were told. You fill up your days with chores he wants you to do even if you don't. You hide your children's misdeeds from his attention; you pick what you say *very* carefully.

His environment is a blank. He doesn't live singly very often or for very long; he's a marrier. A firmly attached female is part of his image, so he almost always has one. He weds young. He has to prove that like his old man, he can have a family. He reattaches to another woman quickly if a union ends, to prove his masculinity wasn't faulty.

He drives a manly car, never a flighty one. No Subaru for the Maximal Misogynist. He'll drive anything from an enormous Ford station wagon to a Lincoln Continental as long as it's heavy.

A good deal of money goes into his upkeep. *He's* the public person, you're the private one. *He* needs the office, tools, automobiles, and suits—you can do with less. That is, until party time. When you come to the office or go out to dinner, your presentation becomes important. He'll demand you get your show together. He wants money spent on the public part of the house, the part that can be seen. You decorate and dust the living room and dining room, but you hold the laundry machines in the basement together with hairpins and bubblegum. They don't matter.

Sometimes he wants his mate like a mannequin who does no work at all. But even if his woman labors hard, he promotes the image that she is just an expensive item he deigns to keep. If you throw that picture into doubt, with your work, money, or independent purchases, you cause major blowups.

Sex Signals

To help his owner-provider portrait of himself, he seeks women who are ill-prepared for survival on their own, who believe that they're weak. He likes conformist women; not those who march to their own music, but those who sass just a little before they back off. Frequently he selects women already burdened with young children and having trouble supporting them. He can spot a woman who has not fortified herself from a mile off. When a woman has no degrees, skills, investments, experience in life, or willingness to go solo, he knows it full well. If she hints at wanting to be possessed, he's ready to make the purchase.

He presents a very strong image to such women. He knows they are attracted to shows of masculine might. He makes decisions. He always drives the car. He announces he doesn't like a dress or hairdo to see if you do things his way.

And sex. Sex with him is lusty, not lovey. Maybe it's a little aggressive, as if he's spearing so much meat. He's not one for long and tender foreplay; he insists on a hard, driving rhythm. He always makes you take his approach. He likes the missionary position, the role of leader. No questions asked. A little rape is not unlikely, especially if you resist him or if he wants to reconcile after a battle. There's no question that as his property you are at his disposal. He doesn't like turn-downs. He comes back for more, three, four, or five times in a row. Lovemaking is through when *he's* through and you're thoroughly wiped out.

Money Markers

Money is a primary key to the relationship. If you take the monetary support, you take the licks: It's the Maximal Misogynist's idea of getting what he buys. He may provide a monthly paycheck; he may have you on a diet of diamonds; he may have you living on hope. You still end up as a two-bit target.

You see, all the money is *his* money. If you have personal income or funds, he commandeers them, and he keeps the checkbook. More than likely he won't let you work. If you do help support the family, he makes sure you never earn as much as he does. He insists you quit jobs, or he makes you lose them.

He wants everything you're wearing and using to be bought by him. He forbids gifts from your family. You may think you're a wife; to him you're a bought woman. He alone makes major purchases. He holds the titles to car and home. And he's tight. He may let money out, but he keeps tabs on every expense. He resents medical bills. You do not need to waste money, according to him, seeing doctors. He expects food budgets to be small, but he'll smash the dishes if dinner doesn't suit him.

Money is power to a Maximal Misogynist. Psychological dependence may rope you into the relationship, but the economic knots he ties keep you from getting out.

Family Aspects

Naturally he demands the role of head of the family. No guff allowed; he's an authoritarian father as well as husband. He usually wants children, though some cold and lonely ones do not. Generally children help support his masculine self-image and keep a wife in her place. He wants to make a perfect world for his kids, but he usually ends up hitting them too. Wife abuse and child abuse go hand in hand. Children make the most defenseless targets of all.

He relates to his mother, brothers, and sisters only as a dictator and authority. Relations often spot his wife-beating first and call him on it, but he has probably bullied them for years, so they no longer affect him. His father is another matter. A passion, probably negative, exists between father and son. The Maximal Misogynist forever tries to make his father treat him as the new head man.

In-laws represent a threat and interference. A Maximal Misogynist will attempt to sever your ties with your own family as early and as completely as possible.

He attempts equality with male friends. He *has* no female friends. It's a man's world, and he spends a lot of time there. Among men he builds a false camaraderie: men's talk, men's jokes, men's pursuits— all to the detriment of women. His alliances lack intimacy and are extremely status-conscious. He plays know-it-all and who's-doing-better in money, business, and sports. He flirts with cocktail waitresses. He cultivates the idea that other men are like him.

As far as the Maximal Misogynist's liabilities go, he doesn't have one—he *is* one, a walking, talking fatality. He's the wrong-way ramp on the freeway of life. It's not that he doesn't *like* women; he utterly disrespects them. You don't turn someone you love into a fall guy. Let's face it. There's no saving grace to a threat to your life.

What Is in Store for You?

Consider the Maximal Misogynist like a pack of cigarettes. No matter how slick the package, how long, short, mild, strong, filtered, or flavored the contents, he is hazardous to your health. There are many ways to play with fire. But only one rule—*Don't!* You could get killed.

Admittedly the Maximal Misogynist may be the man of some women's fantasies. But there's a big difference between reality and imagery. In your daydreams if a man passionately overpowers you, *you* control it; *you* arrange all the circumstances—who the man is, how far he goes, what things he does to you. But when the Maximal Misogynist is fact, not fancy, you're not in control. *He* is. He doesn't know your boundaries. He probably doesn't even know his own. Once he starts, he'll go as far as his frenzy carries him. It's best to keep brutes in the fantasy world. There they can make your heart beat and your lips moisten, but they can't break your nose.

With the Maximal Misogynist there are no stages, just rages. Once he hits, you can predict how the relationship will go—from bad to worse. The beatings can stay low level for years; maybe they suddenly accelerate. Or they can gain at a slow and steady rate from twisted thumbs to broken bones. If you think the first time was just an oddball circumstance, for heaven's sake you sure know when it happens again. He has no reason to quit if you don't stop him. Unfortunately the ways to stop him are ultimately only one: RUN.

As long as you don't hit the road or call the authorities, you're in for a condition of chronic battery. And a life of secrecy. His brutality gets regular, the intervals less lengthy. And his abuse spills over: the children, perhaps your sister, even an aged mother.

He may remain forever cool, always hit so it won't show. But it's possible that *some* blow, *some* day, will be too hard. Neighbors hear; some friend sees the black and blue. A doctor comes into the scene. In that event, your life can go from secrecy to total publicity. Outsiders and officious strangers will come into your days. And each is from some agency that you thought would never touch you. The police, the district attorney, social workers, probation officers, juvenile protection officials get to know your name. Or else your demise makes the headlines.

What Are the Telltale Signs of Trouble?

When a man interprets every offer of assistance as an accusation of his weakness, it bodes no good. If the subject of weak and strong concerns him a bit too much, I'd be wary. Some men just say "all a woman needs is a good screw"; some men act on it. If he follows through on the "good screw," the "good punch" theory might be coming, too. If he says women need to be put in their place, then gets angry when you step out of it, it's time to get wise.

Threats to hurt you before he really does it should bring you to a test. *Call* the threat. It's worth it to find out. Three ends can result, and you can decide accordingly. He'll either stop threatening, never, never repeat it, and never hit; fine. Or else he'll continue to threaten, but still not hit—you should take a walk in that case; he's keeping you in line with fear; it may not hurt your body, but it hurts your psyche. Or else he'll harm you; then, go immediately.

Find out if he has a childhood history of abuse and consider it a dangerous sign if he still admires the parent who punished him.

There are no mild alarms with a Maximal Misogynist, only grave omens. Any one means you should make a break.

What Are the Chances?

The likelihood of changing a Maximal Misogynist is almost nil. Certainly it's nil when you're his target. He needs professional help and he needs it badly. That requires time, money, and desire; he's unlikely to invest any of these. He's even less likely to confess. He can't take criticism. He's afraid of being thought insane, much less weak. He's terrified of the depth to which his anger might really go, and anyway he thinks other men are the same. He feels little or nothing unless he boils over and doesn't recognize when a blowup is coming or why, so he rarely admits he has a problem. He's *sure* it won't happen again. Your leaving, the police, and the threat of jail, assault charges, and court may bring him to seek change. But even with therapy, he's a risky gamble. And if you were in the "before" picture, you probably won't be in the "after." Often when he is caught, he just plays along until he's left alone again, anyway.

I advise flight at any cost. And as soon as possible. Even if you have been with a Maximal Misogynist for forty years, have suffered *many* beatings, have children, have no money: *GO!*

Go *naked* if you have to!

Call for help, go to the neighbor, lock yourself in a room, use the arm of the law. Before the next blow falls.

The next trick is—don't go back. That's the hard one. But, believe me, he's not going to stop any faster than a leopard changes its spots.

Many women are terrified of leaving for good. But remember, there's help out there; you don't have to swing it alone. A lot of people can help you. Battered-wife centers, hot lines, social workers, medical officials, and safe houses are available to women almost everywhere now. It not, try the police, district attorney, or any family counseling clinic. Spouse abuse is a national issue receiving congressional attention. Many states have programs for aid to get you back on your feet. Secret shelters exist. Jobs can be found. Use every contact and phone number you can get. When you decide to get out, it's not time to be shy.

If you do stay—out of fear or out of hope for a brighter day—or if you go back, at least attempt to change the conditions. Get counseling for yourself, even on the sly. Shore yourself up and sort out your situation. Many psychologists now not only offer ways to self-enlightenment, they also offer fight training, healthier ways to quarrel. If your Maximal Misogynist has *any* ray of hope, perhaps you can convince him to go with you.

See if you provoke the massacres; then see if you can waylay the effects before they've begun. Avoid explosive phrases, subtle flirtations, forgetfulness, or agitation that you know will set him off. *Then* begin quiet, firm stands for self-control. Slowly get stronger. Learn self-determination, an occupation, even a martial art! Leave him short a punching partner and don't slip back again.

Most probably these methods will still lead to the termination of your relationship anyway. But perhaps there will be more grounding for you when you finally close the door. If nothing else, they may help you skirt serious injury. He may resist your changes with further violence. Then, all I can say is—save yourself and the children. Above all else, don't *threaten* to eject or leave him. *Just do it!*

Where Do You Fit In?

Who ever heard the sound of one hand slapping nothing? The Maximal Misogynist is a two-way street. You hold an indispensable part.

If you're continually catching what a Maximal Misogynist is pitching, it's time to start thinking that possibly, for some reason, you're a willing victim. The key word is *willing*. If you are, masochism has a hold on you. When you more than believe the weaker-stronger theory of sex, you surrender; your whole pattern requires examination. Whoever told you submissive is natural and subjection is beautiful? Get that person's name and expunge the memory.

To get and keep a man, you don't have to give yourself over to him. Men don't own women. You are *not* property; you're a *person*.

Since women have been purchased and paid for for so long, it's easy to confuse the categories. But even dowries never included a pound of flesh, and bringing home the family paycheck never meant paying for a scapegoat—not even in the old days. You own *yourself*. And you should enter relationships out of free will. That means giving up the illusions that a man is to possess you, protect you, care for you, feed you, and decide for you. It doesn't make you more of a woman to have a man. Your womanhood is also something you own alone. When you don't care for your belongings—you and your womanhood—somebody else is liable to take them and knock them around. When you ask another person to cover for you it *costs* you; that's a basic business lesson. Unfortunately, women often learn life's economics a little late.

Once you accept that law, you can decipher not only what you want but *how* you intend to pay for it; you can determine if what you're getting is worth the price. You pay a hell of a lot when you play punching bag. No matter what you get for it, from Jello to jewels, you almost certainly overpay. It might be simpler just to go and make money yourself. Go from Snow White to Scarlett O'Hara. Dreams are hard to give up, true. But any illusions surrounding Prince Maximal Misogynist burst into extreme reality every time he hurts you.

Try to be whole *on your own*. Nothing is worth self-denigration and flagellation. Try assertiveness training, courses in confidence and self-assurance. Get job training. Find classes on insurance, mechanics, and child raising. Make friends with efficient, operative women and watch how they handle life. And imitate. It takes a lot to leave an abuser and to go out on your own. Sometimes a known evil looks better than what's unknown. But here's one reminder that should help shake you up and out: Whatever you let happen to you will be passed on. If your man hits you, later that's what your children will do, and they will lose what means the most to them—the most important people in their lives, those who love them. And that's a hideous legacy.

Notes and Particulars

18/ The Kid

Related Type: The "But I Really Like Women" Manipulator

Positivity Scale: + −

A time machine came along and froze the Kid just at the moment when he stood between youth and maturity. It transfixed him forever in that awkward age. Then, despite all efforts to prevent it (letters from his doctor, Coke-bottle eyeglasses, color blindness, and *selective* deafness), he was drafted into adulthood.

It was a mistake. He should have been 4F. But now that he's in the army of aging humanity, he's found one way to fit. He plays perpetual recruit. He locates a sergeant, a mess hall and barracks, and becomes Beetle Bailey. Under the charge of his superior officer he bungles most chores and errands. He never has to figure out what orders to give. He may end up with menial tasks and occasional K.P. duty, but he runs no risk of promotion. He's such a duck that most people let him alone, which is, of course, just what he wants.

The Kid will never grow up all the way. He's real nice; everybody likes him. He's good-humored and tells jokes, although they don't always work. But he certainly doesn't pull his weight in his daily duties. It's enough that he keeps a job. He usually manages that.

He is, however, a steadfast husband and daddy for the kids and often, he's one thing more—an almost genius who displays a streak of brilliance that becomes his saving grace. The world acclaims him and you get off on it. Perhaps he's one of the only people in the world who knows the formula and properties of Nucleicgastropotiasis-13. Or can run the LXMN-532 computer, translate Middle Minoan, or tune ZYT Typhoon racing cars. He read when he was two and did fractions at four. He took his mother's washing machine apart and put it back together again (with two more, experimental gears; it would never wash again) at five.

Everybody knows he's a former whiz kid. As he grew bigger, they let him turn his whiz into a sweet, passive knack for getting everyone else (especially women) to do everything for him, to care for him like a child and not get mad about it.

When it comes to ladies, he's negatively selective: He lets women pick him. That cuts his effort in half. Generally he leans to the shy and quiet, but resolute, woman. Her fortitude offers him a Linus blanket. She reveals ability and efficacy, plus tenacity: everything an admiral ought to have. To him that's paradise. He can bumble away in peace and tranquility and leave her to run his life.

Story

Sonia, whom I've known since elementary school, didn't really start out the Kid's sort of woman. She became that way by adapting. And that's just how she coupled up with Ollie.

Sonia was shy but too proud to let it show. So she set about making herself as undetectable, undelectable, and nondescript as possible. The old nobody-loves-me-guess-I'll-go-eat-worms complex. She got all the way through high school and beyond pretty successfully. She never appeared lonely, merely unnoticed. Then all of the sudden, she decided she didn't want the unattached act to continue.

Behind her screen she had always been a hard driver and a high achiever; when she wanted something, she got it. She had excellent grades and was a fine pianist. She worked on committees, helped put out the school newspapers, and could bake a better chocolate cake than anyone else. True, she had never known how to be or get what the so-called "popular" women could. But then she'd never tried to learn.

About that time she noticed Ollie. Not that Ollie was new. He tripped into the crowd somewhere along the line (nobody remembered when). In fact, except for when he was fussing with electrons, protons, and neutrons, he was virtually always underfoot. Nobody ever shooed him away, yet nobody ever took him seriously either. He was *tolerated* more than anything else. He fumbled everything he tried to do. But he was funny and canny. Ollie didn't appear aware of women at all. The only figures he cared about were symbolic; the only mass that mattered was relative. Yet he preferred female company and hung out with women more than men. Women rarely played basketball, at which he was hopeless. Women put up with him more resignedly. Once convinced of his faultless incapacity, they simply ceased to expect him to perform.

Sonia started thinking. While the others had jealousies, heartbreaks, and disasters, she saw something unique, albeit odd, right in her own backyard—Ollie. She didn't want to play the field, nor did she want to become a bench-sitter. In Ollie she saw a man who would be all hers, with permanence practically guaranteed. Her only competition was a cyclotron. To Sonia that was worth a lot of other prices: Kool-Aid spilled in her lap, broken dishes, pink laundry, and so on.

So she asked Ollie to dinner—candles and everything. Then she took him on a picnic, to the zoo, to a concert. Then she led him to bed. Neither one of them knew much about sex firsthand. But both had *read* a lot. They developed a simple style that suited them both. Besides, their sex life, if not elaborate, had a special quality: No one else had ever shared it. Eventually it led to the nuclear fusion of a family.

Maybe you could call their life repressive. To this day Sonia never lets anything, including friends, work, and outside interests, interfere with her purpose. She deals in daily activities while Ollie dwells in some microcosm. He's charming, aggravating, gentle, awkward, apologetic, and irredeemably forgetful. He looks twelve; Sonia looks older. He doesn't seem to know Sonia is around. You couldn't say she gets much attention. But if his mind isn't at home, it's only with some atom or other. He doesn't provide an explosive sex life—sex is no big deal for either of them. But infrequent as it is, it's enough to generate *some* energy.

What would happen if she ever needed more from him? That's the unbroached question. So far she's got the hatches battened down. But lately a crack has appeared. Sonia didn't really think Ollie would stay so irresponsible, nor did she foresee that her work would expand so rapidly while his participation remained so totally unchanged.

Not many women are like Sonia. Most want more emotion and attention. Sonia rarely "bothers" Ollie for anything. Not many like the tremendous work load and the isolation. And while Sonia gets to run her ship, she never makes waves that change her life.

The Kid is a matter of weights and balances. He's got his virtues but has plenty of drawbacks as well. At least he's easy to recognize. Just think of Harpo Marx, Lou Costello, Jerry Lewis, Stan Laurel, and Einstein—rolled into one likable klutz. What's hard to see is that he aims to stay that way.

How Can You Identify One?

You can't say he walks into your life. He stumbles. He doesn't exactly court you—he shows up hungry. He *still* scarfs a bowl of granola before he takes you out to dinner. And he'll always think hamburgers, hot dogs, Coke, and instant oatmeal are a gourmet's delight.

The Kid. Well, what can you say? He's so boyish, so *seemingly* without guile, so wide-eyed and charming . . . plunk, you're sunk. Even those who won't go out with him let him hang around. Each Kid provides a new meaning for incompetence. He's not outwardly lazy; indeed, he tackles everything. He just manages not to be able to *do* anything. And in the most amazing ways: He can't boil an egg, can't change a tire, can't write a check. And worst of all, he can't pick up a dropped towel or dropped jockey shorts: He never sees anything below his knees.

He even looks like an eternal adolescent. The parts of his body seem to belong to different people—some full grown, some not. His arms hang too low or too high, never at his hip line. His feet were meant for someone bigger. He hasn't quite filled out yet. His beard is still trying to thicken, or else he can't quite keep up with it and attacks it only randomly. He suffers from chronic colic and cowlick.

He either lacks hand–eye coordination, or else he merely absents his mind from his errand. If it's the particular job at which he's expert, however, suddenly he's dextrous and precise as can be. One of the few ways he connects his brain to his daily survival is his humor. He gets a lot of mileage out of his boyish grin and wit. He turns clumsy into comic. He creates a perfect evasionary tactic: He fails at little things so amusingly that few recognize the truant that dwells within.

Behind his bumbling façade, he's honest and true. He can't tell a lie; he has no way to hide one. When shirking work, he just keeps quiet and hopes no one will notice. If caught, he feigns surprise, immediately jumps in, and promptly knocks over the pot he's asked to stir.

Basically he's a happy person even though he lives almost exclusively in his own world. To him life is always like a day that

Mother Earth bakes cookies. He's as detached and delirious as a child in an enchanted forest. He's always tripping on what he's thinking. But like a dreamy child, he misses many things in his blissful wandering. He pays little heed to people's coming and going, so naturally he commits multiple faux pas. You never know when he'll embarrass you, like a boy who yells, "But I'm twelve," when you get him an eleven-and-under ticket, or even when he'll hurt your feelings. He'll hardly notice your crying, much less a new dress. One of his drawbacks is that he never learns. He makes the same mistake time and again. He wants to make amends, but he never can. A lot of Kids, either in urban centers where they didn't grow up or after a painful divorce, get so fearful of interference they turn into a combination of Kid and Instant Barricader.

Outer Signs

The Kid's clothes never fit right. Just how badly depends on who bought them. When he shops alone, he always gets the wrong size. What's more, he picks such unlikely colors and styles that people cross the street when they see him coming. The more you don't like his garments, the more he wears them. Soon people try to take over and give him proper outfits, thinking they are helping him. He puts their selections deep in his closet. Then one day, he goes on a safari through his belongings and puts together an outfit of gift items in a way no one else would be able to conceive of. As a result, he does have his own definite style; you could call it contemporary-historical conglomeration in the casual mode. Often he ends up in T-shirts and jeans on which he spilled acid. His tennis shoes lace to the shin bone. (He thinks he has weak ankles.) Whatever his shoe size, you're tempted to bronze them. No one else could mold footwear into such a formation.

His skin is a disaster, part of his continued adolescence. His fingernails are down to the quick and not necessarily clean. He doesn't like the sun in his face, so he collects baseball caps, which is a good thing with his cowlick. His features don't matter to him; he never looks at them.

The only way he could possibly make the whole thing work is to become the Kid.

Most often he owns a bus, a van, or a big old car or wagon. He needs room for lots of objects in his vehicle: old tires, greasy machines, microphones, amplifiers, all the neighborhood teenagers. Usually the Kid has an affection for his car as if it were his pal. He *wipes* it a lot instead of cleaning it. He might put on decals, but otherwise he won't decorate it. Or he might keep the outside exactly as it came but strip down the inside and add a mobile tool warehouse, small laboratory, or some other madness.

His living space is just as you would guess—like the wreck of the Hesperus. When you meet him, he lives in a room in someone's basement, often his parents'. Or perhaps he hibernates in a converted garage. Or he might share an old frame house with five other Kids, where nobody does the dishes. Disarray somehow makes him comfortable.

When it comes to decoration, he thinks of paint (he reaches the same conclusion when it comes to covering dirt). He has a facility of picking the most garish colors imaginable, like a combination of canary yellow, avocado, and electric blue. He might have a few posters; he never changes them. Soon, they look as if they were left by the former tenants—or the tenants before that. Or perhaps you can't see them behind the enormous T.V. antennae. If you're the decorator and you ask him to hang a picture, he'll require four helpers. He *thinks* he's the fix-it type. But it's not worth asking him; it just doubles the labor.

Of course, some Kids are *geniuses* at fixing. They repair everything. Even when repairs aren't needed. They like to take appliances and rip them apart. But when it comes to putting together, they're not always so good. You come home unexpectedly and find the dishwasher on the floor—in sixty-three pieces. Unfortunately, it *remains* there for three weeks to come.

The Kid always seems busy at something. In fact, he appears tireless. He keeps the world's oddest schedule and needs the least sleep. He works from two to six A.M., then sleeps from seven to eleven after two bowls of Cheerios. Then he's up at his employment, prowling garage sales, or looking at old books. Then he shows up at someone's home just in time for supper. He eats seven meals a day—anytime and anyplace. Or he eats no *formal* meal but snacks without stop.

Actually he treats himself quite well, just in an idiosyncratic manner. He certainly sees to it that he's left unbothered. He gets himself relieved of all petty time-consuming duties or thought-consuming decisions.

Sex Signals

He doesn't approach you romantically; he just places himself on your runway. Any other suitor who comes to your door has to pass your personal court jester. He's harder to shake off than a Siamese twin. He plays a waiting game. And he'll try and try again. Romance often comes to him later rather than sooner in life.

The Kid disguises any strong sexual motivation. When anything happens—a kiss or an embrace—it's unexpected, almost accidental, with no lead-up. He's affectionate but often so eager he leapfrogs to the heart of the matter and skips foreplay. He needs instruction and often never discovers what you want. He's energetic more than experimental. He sticks to simple basics and some of the milder variations. Then he falls asleep—*instantly*. He'd rather make love lots of times in one night than once every day. Once you're familiar with one another, his rate slows down and he needs reminding. Very sexually charged Kids aren't *longer* lovers—just more frequent. They are often premature ejaculators. Some young Kids, under their beguiling cover, go on streaks of seeking one-night stands. But, strangely, as they become older and older Kids, they find such sex harder and harder to get.

The Kid doesn't treat women as mothers, he just brings out the mothering in you. Few women can compensate for his incompetence any other way. He has a client-manager contract with you. It's hard to say if he loves you or grows increasingly fond of you.

Money Markers

He doesn't use much of *anybody's* money. He's not very liable to get the big bucks. If his genius brings monetary reward, that's fine, but he'd rather fiddle than work hard for money. He doesn't keep track of finances. You do.

Since he doesn't even know how much money you have together (he assumes *you* know), he's a moderate spender. He takes great delight in saving and using old, used things. He finds funny bargains and gleefully feels he tricked the merchant. He buys leftover paint cans, clocks that work except for one part, or wrapped mystery packages that were lost in the mail. Most of the time he ends up losing money. He often has no cunning about what he's doing, so he winds up with items that were no bargain at all. He does short-form taxes even when he shouldn't. He doesn't read the fine print in contracts and makes verbal agreements and gets sued. His needs aren't elaborate. You and he probably don't go out much either. At best you attend third-run movies or go to places where unknown bands try out.

Family Aspects

When it comes to fatherhood he says, "Sure, that'd be nice," as if that's all there is to it. He rarely thinks of what's involved, even later, when you're snowed under a mountain of diapers right before his very eyes. He thinks kids are playmates and, besides, *you're* there to feed them. He's totally unmindful of their schedule.

Yet in most ways, he's really a great father. Since he's just like his children, they think he's a pal, not a parent. And they're always sure of his love. Half the time he's with them you never know where they are, what they're doing, or when they'll show up again. But while you may not think they rest in safe hands, somehow they always come back whole.

The Kid's parents tend to shake their head a lot. There's nothing else they *can* do. They don't understand what *didn't* happen to him. But they really can't fault him, because he's nice and he's smart. He hardly hears what they're saying, but he smiles fondly at them. He loves them but thinks of them as misguided peers. You'll have to be the one who takes their calls, advice, and admonitions; he can never be found. They're grateful to you.

As for your family, he'll pull your fathers and brothers right back to puberty with him, leaving all the women cooking and cleaning in the kitchen, when he can. Your mother and sisters will disgustedly lose patience, but in his presence will remain totally disarmed.

The Kid collects a parcel of friends who all look like odds and ends. He makes pals of everyone as he goes along. Some are short-term, some long-term, some clear from junior high. He's not at all good at making enemies, which is too bad, because he tends to get cheated. Due to his indiscriminate nature, all too often he opens himself, you, and the children up for unnecessary blows from the world. But he's better off gullible than *completely* cut off.

Despite how friendly he is and how many buddies he has, he manages a funny separation from his pals. He always remains autonomous enough to do his own thing. Since much of his life is mental, nobody *can* enter it.

When people refer to him, they use the phrase "put up with." Or they ask, "How do you do it?" but don't expect an answer. Nobody shuns him; nobody screams at him. The worst he receives is a mild kicking after he's been around for *ages*. He rarely gets angry though he can certainly whine. He hardly ever changes. In fact, no one expects or encourages him to alter. That's his major drawback: He's gotten everyone to consider him his own justification. Whenever he breaks a lamp, falls down the stairs, or pours lemonade down a bodice, everyone says, "Oh, it's just him." As if just being the Kid explains— and excuses—everything.

What Is in Store for You?

One day he bumbles into your women's committee meeting one more time to ask where the screwdriver is. He just *has* to know what's happening, and any excuse will do. Then he addles the ladies so much that when he finally goes they start talking about men instead of grass-roots congressional bills. And you know you'll have to do all the campaigning yourself because the meeting accomplished nothing. That sort of day epitomizes life with the Kid to a T.

Rather than being a waif, he's more an enfant terrible. What he *doesn't* do is what's in store for you. And if you are blinded by his brilliant part and count on the rest to catch up, better count again. The Kid may look insignificant but he's the world's greatest scene stealer. He always finagles the center of attention. So no matter what you do, your future with him lies in the orchestra pit. Simplicity of character doesn't imply a lack of intellect. The Kid has his genius to attract attention. After all, he's good enough to manage a portrayal of someone on the brink of adolescence. Obviously he's realized that his freedom is invested in its maintenance. He's successfully learned what we'd all like to know: How *not* to do what you don't want to do.

You know how, when some people leave gaps in conversations, you feel compelled to fill them? And you find yourself chattering away out of compulsion or embarrassment? *Anything* to avoid a heavy, awkward silence. The Kid is one of those people—only with him it's actions, not words. The more he leaves, the more you do for him. And the more you do, the more he leaves for you. His appetite for irresponsibility is almost infinite. He not only silently encourages you to overdo, he somehow pushes you to do it.

Your role has a way of growing ever bigger and bigger. You become like the lady in the commercial who stands by the back door of her home, arms extended. Children, dogs, and husband heap dirty clothes on her as they exit. When the camera moves outside, you see that she lives in a box of laundry detergent.

Too much of your life can simply get entangled with him. You not only care for him, you defend him; you not only cater to him, you talk about him more than yourself. He becomes your motive and even your main pronoun. Constant duty tends to make people feel boxed in. Sometimes you may feel a straw that breaks the camel's back (yours). But more often something else happens: You alter yourself in such a way that no load becomes too heavy for you. You turn into a Valkyrie or perhaps a battleaxe. But you don't necessarily receive more adoration for increased ministrations. Though in some corner of his own he looks lovingly upon you, the Kid drifts off all the more into his own world. In fact, he practically *vaporizes*. Soon you cling to the *idea* that he loves you more than to the demonstration.

At least the Kid offers a steady road; the twists and curves are few. He's unlikely to leave you. He rarely has amorous adventures. He comes home to eat, but he may be unwilling to go out at night or take any holidays. His idea of a vacation is to be in a mobile home where you are still in the same situation you have at home. Only on wheels. Eating out means pizza. Chop suey ranks as fancy. When you insist on relaxation, he thinks in terms of playgrounds and campgrounds. He may not only forget birthdays, he won't even know it's Sunday.

But on the brighter side, you get one advantage from the Kid that few men provide. You take no guff from him. He doesn't care how things are done, banked, or bought. You're not always being appraised by your mate. Anything you do is O.K. He's a guaranteed opportunity to run your own country. You may have to provide the labor, but you're also the Oval Office.

In the end of a long, long run with the Kid, you two tend to grow into one of those couples who are so interdependent they need no one else. Sometimes they're sweet, sometimes they're grumpy.

What Are the Telltale Signs of Trouble?

In quite a different situation from the other Twenty-two Types of Men, the Kid turns out to be just *exactly* what he seems. He keeps on *not* getting any older or any more graceful. If a creature like one of Walt Disney's unwieldy dragons starts licking your fingers, consider the cost of his Purina—and if you're willing to pay it. His rapid heartbeat means he has to eat and eat—and eat. Just count how often he's caught in awkward situations.

It's a storm warning if he doesn't notice your moods and feelings, but it's worse if *you* don't. You can tell things are bad when you're angry, sad, elated, miserable, or about to crack into crumbcake, but keep on acting like a robot. If you exist simply to *operate,* you're heading for problems.

If your Kid is so oblivious and inattentive that he can't come through for you when the chips are down, heed this. You can't need someone who isn't there to need. In that case you'll have to send him away and hire help. If he returns nothing you should cut the leash and turn your attention to those who pay back—namely you.

And if he does come through for you, consider yourself vindicated. Despite the trials and tribulations, you were right to be there all along.

What Are the Chances?

What do you do about the Kid?

Of course, typical of life's problems, there's no one right answer. You could stay with him, leave him, stay and try to change him, or *leave* and try to change him. You could simply stay with him a while and then leave him. Or you could do *all* the above in any order you choose. But what's best? Well, here's the hint. Staying with him but attempting changes probably outweighs the other choices. Leaving him (or threatening to) in order to enact change, then going back to him, is highly common and ranks as second choice. But if you're fed up to the gills and think that changing him is an impossibility, your only choice is to head for the hills.

The Kid can change only in measured degrees. I wouldn't expect miracles. He's always going to be what he is. But after all, he doesn't carry a hard line of unalterable male superiority. He doesn't even play the game of "If you really loved me, you'd clean my tub for me." He just plays deaf and blind. And he's probably never heard an ultimatum or had his shades knocked off. You simply have to bring what you consider intolerable to his attention, but only do so if you really mean to change him. There's a common word for half-hearted notification. It's called "nagging." Any child knows that when you say, "If you don't straighten out . . ." that you don't really mean it. In fact, you're stating that you expect repetition. Watch those "If you don't"'s and stick to "I am [followed by action]" statements. Move things by insistent steps steadily to bring matters to a head. And remember he'll always need plenty of time to himself.

It may turn out that you simply misread your capacity, that you need more attention, more help, and much less work. He may never come up to the responsible companion of your desires. In this case, contemplate a friendly, loving leaving; you don't have to carry on. Backing out is one kind of winning: It offers the relief of one less person who requires your constant service. With the Kid it's better to go with sad resignation than with anger. He's such a resilient and entrenched character that if you can't take him, leave him and don't waste time on blame.

On the other hand, he may be your cup of tea even if he never budges an inch and you have to make all the crumpets. So if you elect to stay with him, try to accept the situation, don't fault him, and—avoid becoming claustrophobic. Deep down you may prefer to read Agatha Christie rather than handle the push and pull of a more attentive relationship. There's nothing wrong with that. A lot can be said for having someone around not to talk to. As for the work and responsibility, just consider that you're getting executive training. Not everyone gets to be both labor and management. Maybe you can use your experience later. You can open a hangout for wayward juveniles. Or you may want to think of yourself as a single parent. Read all you can about unitary parenthood. Your stress, your fatigue, your

problems will be very sin.ilar. When the buck stops with you all the
time, it's never easy. But at least your big Kid returns to your bunk in
a way that little ones don't.

Where Do You Fit In?

You may need distance but avoid recognizing the fact. You may
want intimacy but so divert it into mothering that you defeat yourself.
Two very diverse propositions, it's true. But either one can lead to a
stint with the Kid. For that matter, you might have both tendencies—
mixed up. You might seek removal, so when you do draw close you
can only do so behind a maternal shield. An adult-to-adult love affaii
can be just *too* close. In either case, the Kid well suits you. As long as
you can stay relatively apart from him while providing care and
upkeep, it's all right with him.

If you have a fatal weakness for the Kid but you feel some strange
lack of satisfaction, the time is nigh to determine how much distance
really means to you and, for that matter, how much you unconsciously
equate nurturing with loving. Women often have trouble admitting
fear of intimacy. After all, according to popular credo, you're
supposed to want a man and even be love crazy. It's hard for any
woman to own up to contrary tendencies. People will ask, "What's
wrong with you?" But women, too, need autonomy and authority. If
you want a lasting union or think you *should* want one yet prefer to
remain aloof, you have a problem.

There's nothing wrong with wanting to be president of your own
company or even with finding comfort in misanthropic removal, unless
the joy you take in solitude and in having command is secret, or if you
think something is wrong with you. Or if you use devious devices such
as mothering and overloading instead of forthright acceptance. If you
like self-determination, those cases, you might want to check out the
Oldie But Goodie, the Loving Polymorph, or the Limited Partner as
better alternatives. But if both you and the Kid are happy with your
relative removal, recognizing your preference honestly makes life
easier.

Perhaps you fell into these traps quite unwittingly. All women are
taught to nurse and nurture to some degree. One can easily confuse
romantic concern with mothering. It could be that you learned no

other version of love—care came to mean "taking care of." But this is a limited view of a huge emotional potential, and it can often involve self-suffocation and self-denial.

Adult love tends to have a far wider range of passion than parental feeling. You should really sample some of the varieties while the sun shines. Why get trapped in a colorless love by treating a man as a child, or a nothing existence by being too tired to feel, when you can experience more? Certainly, feelings can be frightening. But look at it this way—starting to explore them doesn't mean you can't retreat. Learn to operate a swinging door. You can let in company, intimacy, and sensation when you want them and put up a Closed for Business sign when you need solitude. Chances are you can build such a swinging door better as an adult than as a mother.

Notes and Particulars

19/ The Gay Man Type Two— You Won't Meet One Anyway . . .

Related Type: The Gay Man Type One—Intimacy Except For . . .

Positivity Scale: ?

You won't find a relationship here and you shouldn't. Not in any sense even close to intimate. Not even if he was married once and changed in later life. This man simply excludes women from his world.

You can't scale a sheer cliff or swim a whole ocean.

You're excused.

Notes and Particulars

20/ The Picasso

Related Types: The Minimal Misogynist
The Idle Lord
The Man Who Would Be Mogul
The Gender Ascender

Positivity Scale: + − −

Don't be fooled by appearances. Just because a man looks like an ordinary biped doesn't mean he is one. He might be a Picasso.

The Picasso doesn't necessarily splash walls with zigzag lines and cubes, cover everything with a coat of rose or blue and make little visual jokes on chrome, ceramic, and plastic, although many Picassos are also artists. He may make underground films, proclaim a revolution, or spread the word on how to save a soul or where to get your latest human potential—as a guru, never as a follower. He may shine as a leading light of surgery or transform the court with his facile mastery.

Indeed, the Picasso's occupation can be almost anything. For it's not what he does, it's how he struts it. Whatever his endeavor and however he feigns humility, he's as grand as a Mufti can be, forever a cut above regular. Heaven forbid he should be just any Joe who trucks along and does his job whether he's gifted or not. You see, the Picasso is convinced that some higher-up in the supernatural department boinged him with a magic wand and made him a prodigy. He's got something that belongs to a very few. He's got bippety-boppety-boo. He believes he has special talent, vision, wisdom, saintliness, or genius. The trouble is, whether or not he has any of these things, he simply *assumes* he does. He doesn't necessarily prove it, but he claims the right to be unruly. And there's the rub. When a man finds it hard to accept commonness, even mortality, life with him hardly verges on paradise. It's more like tyranny.

If he's gold, his lady must be silver. The Picasso picks sterling women. He likes beauty not in the form of a flashy bauble but in the shape of a tea tray—he wants you noticeable but serviceable, admirable but tractable. Nice to demonstrate, easy to put in place. And it helps if you lack polish.

Story

One woman I interviewed unfolded a perfect Picasso tale. Her Picasso was even an artist.

Patsy met Leo when she was an art student; so was Leo. But Leo was different, destined to make waves and change styles. Or so he said—mainly by criticizing others. Leo loved to hang about the huge school studio with his cronies—all male. With jeans hanging low, sockless sneakers, splotched shirt, he would sip on a can of beer and crush it between his thumb and fingers. No dent, no macho. He would lean on a sculpture and disparage education. ("Art is not for teaching. People have 'it' or they don't.") He acted like a Doe Stalker around young craftswomen. But basically Leo was a settler, not a hustler. He needed a number-one follower, and Patsy looked like the prizewinner.

Patsy worked in ceramics where she had incipient, yet-to-blossom talent. She wasn't at all unable; she was simply unsure. She needed time. All the better for Leo. In every one of Patsy's departments, Leo was quite superior. Patsy liked her art, but she wanted other things as well: love, work, creativeness, happiness, even a family. Not so for Leo. As far as he was concerned, there was only one nirvana and he was there already. He was a rarity, a truly great painter. All he needed was fame, money, and world recognition.

Leo impressed Patsy with his knowledge by making her feel she had none of her own. Every simple statement she offered he reduced with ridicule. He addled her with sarcasm, twisted her with teasing, heckled her into speechless adoration, and badgered her into bed. That was the beginning and the end of their courtship. After that, he latched onto her like glue and told her that she couldn't do better.

Leo's idea of sex was to have Patsy in, on, and out of bed and, in fact, all over the place—a lot. But Patsy found that sex with Leo was like a volcanic eruption (his) to which she was merely audience. She wanted to tell him so, but the cat had her tongue. Besides, he convinced her that he was a perfect lover and she a mere novice. She decided to distrust her own feelings, or lack of them, and abide by him for some big happening later on. He told her it was coming, if she'd just relax and let it.

She also stayed for another reason—Leo's portrait of glory. He was big time, she was little. Only with him and if she turned her art to domesticity "at least for the time being" could she see Paris, parties, and bejeweled high society. Meanwhile, living penniless in a garret would be "romantic." It all sounded pretty attractive to Patsy.

Soon Leo won a grant, Patsy got pregnant, and they were off to Italy. They lived in Florence in a miserable four-storey walk-up. They stretched pennies with pasta. In four years they hatched three babies. While Patsy's belly occasionally deflated, Leo's ego didn't—it swelled and swelled. He grew even more despotic and grandiose, while Patsy got haggard. He refused to help her in any way or even show common courtesy. The domicile was her job, unworthy of His Eminence. He was certainly too dandy for the diapers. He came and went as he pleased. He drank a lot.

In response to Patsy's first few mild complaints, he broke dishes and smashed windowpanes. He trounced off day or night to his huge studio despite illness and infancy in the homestead. Patsy and the babies had two rooms and no running water. Though she rarely saw him, she never asked for help. She thought his genius gave him such allowances and that every artist's struggling years were like this. Still, she figured that if she really needed him he'd be there for her.

Then one week Patsy and all the children fell sick. Soiled clothes lay everywhere and not a single grocery sat in the larder. Patsy hit bottom; she finally asked for aid. Leo flew into a rage. How, he shouted, could she expect him to lower himself to household chores? He stomped off for two days. That was the end of Patsy's illusion.

Patsy wired home for money, packed and left. But it wasn't over yet. No sooner did she arrive home than Leo came begging for forgiveness. But Patsy demanded promises first. She wanted decent habitation, equal freedom, space, and help. She got his agreement forthwith. But the instant she returned to Leo, he reneged on all the terms. He got a house, but he wouldn't let her have a room. He tore down walls to suit his fancy and never repaired them. He got a job, but he wouldn't give her enough to manage on. He overloaded her with chores and had fits if she failed to perform them. Soon she was worse off than when she started.

She left again. He followed. She went back. That happened *three* more times. Each time he reassumed his usual outrageousness. How could she expect to decorate their abode when *he* was the artist? How could she demand space when he required sanctuary? How could she ask for company when he was busy *creating?*

He also started having affairs. Or rather he started having them more obviously. That was the last straw; finally Patsy saw that Leo so feared being ordinary and meeting normal expectations that she would always be the victim of his self-importance. And she simply couldn't afford it. So with regrets she kept the little children and divorced her big one. It was rough. Leo refused to pay support; he stormed her home and tried to win over the children. But she held tight. She raised her family a while before she could return to art, but now she's doing fabulously. And Leo is teaching at the old art college.

Some of the most glorious trees overshadow other plants, so they remain forever shrubbery. The Picasso can be magnificent—he's thrilling and dazzling. He can offer an unconventional life and alluring romance. But he can also obliterate sunshine. It's best to learn to identify him. Then if you decide to sit in his shade, you can figure out whether you can still survive in the light that's left.

How Can You Identify One?

When you ask a Picasso what he does, he answers with his name. If you inquire who he is, he tells you what he does. The implication, of course, is that he's a one and only.

He's not unlike a Coke. He's got strong flavor, a lot of character, and is quite effervescent. And after he recites his commercial at you often enough, you're inclined to believe that he's not just any old cola—he's the Real Thing. If there were only some way to put him to the Pepsi challenge, perhaps he would be easier to spot. But to see that he's just one of many and not unique, you would need at least two Picassos, a blindfold, and an outside observer. And that's nigh impossible. In the first place, Picassos avoid each other like the plague, so it's hard to get two together. And second, they're too jealous to let you taste them both at once. Besides, the outside observer would ruin all your fun!

The Picasso is surprisingly hard to recognize. Not because he hides his iron-fisted ego, not because he changes his style from before to after, but because he's so *convincing*. After a short blast of his charisma, you no longer see the spots that reveal him. He turns you into a true believer. And once you acknowledge that he's extraordinary, you make your first mistake: You agree that regular rules don't apply to him. You're in for trouble.

The Picasso tingles; everything about him vibrates with intensity even when he's quiet and soulful. If you don't think he's wired, just look at his hair—it almost stands up by itself. Sometimes it's kinky. And whatever the color, it's vivid, even when, as often, it's prematurely grey.

He's somewhere between the age of one and six. He doesn't know where his edges are, has no sense of boundary. He's afraid of his mortality. He believes in magic. And he thinks he can get away with anything. He fears that if he loses control, he just might collapse into a black void, so he demands to get his way in all matters, even the trivial—even if he has to throw a tantrum to get it. Then, to avoid the horror of nothingness, which uniformity, monotony, and regularity evoke for him, he's forever doing *something*. He's never inactive. If he's not doing his thing, he's thinking it, living it, or saying he *is* it. Any time you "bother" him, you're interfering with his *genius*. And he requires extra special attention.

Outer Signs

The Picasso creates himself down to the very last detail. Even in casual disarray, his image bears a constructed precision. Though he may claim clothes are mere social drapery and disavow concern with them, he dresses for effect. He can range from sockless rebel leader to spotless head surgeon, but in any case he practically *paints* his look. In a T-shirt or starched collar, he's in costume. He always knows exactly how in and how out his shirttail is.

His automobile (it's never a "car") is either spotlessly chromed and polished, humming along in awesome magnificence, or else it's disheveled just enough to throw a pie in society's eye. He prefers classic Jaguars and original Ramblers.

As far as his living quarters go, if anyone can find a hovel with cachet, he can. It's either tiny, always with the impeccably right atmosphere for his purposes, located in the midst of just the right amount of ghetto. Or else it's in an old fire station complete with brass pole, or a converted cable-car rotunda: It's cavernous, loft-like, with faultless northern exposure. It brings to mind poverty, elegance, and madness. Every rug and tatter is precisely Picasso. You always know you're in *his* place—even when you live there.

Often he has an office or studio as well. It always includes some sleeping arrangement. It might be an attic or garage, an old storefront, or it might have acres and acres of glass and ceiling. But never fear— he has a garret even if he claims your whole house for it.

Wherever he wanders, he pulls either a leader or anti-leader pose. Both bring followers, which he *loves;* awestruck attendants confirm his uniqueness. He ambles to a corner, where he leans one shoulder on the wall. He picks his toes while he sits cross-legged or glares across his tripod, but somehow he always draws notice. Sometimes he discovers how to be intensely silent and use stillness like an electromagnet to scoop up the curious; other times he's extraordinarily talkative and does a monologue to proselytize his opinions.

He allows himself a full range of emotions; since he won't be bound by convention, he becomes a constant potential explosion. Picassos will do things in public and private that no one else would *dare*. He intimidates by embarrassment. He boils, fumes, or booms out his moments of anger and ecstasy. He might even go so far as to become destructive. While most people get tired of saying no and give in on some issues, not Picasso. His refusals continue endlessly.

He treats himself pretty well. The extent to which he'll go to get his way is nothing short of amazing. But there's something about his self-adoration that constantly taxes him and becomes his tragic flaw: He so desperately wants immortality, he can never let himself relax. He lives as if the minute he lets his guard down, he'll keel over, that no one will notice quickly enough that he's a genius or an angel and save him. He brings upon himself false goals and shallow rewards: Once he jumps the gun on history, not to mention the Almighty, and proclaims himself special during his own lifetime, nothing ever comes out good enough again. Some Picassos get so stuck in this syndrome they can't produce a thing; most are never satisfied with what they are.

Sex Signals

His lady certainly can't be perfect in his eyes. He wants you beautiful, talented, or notable, but only as a counterpoint to enrich him. He conjures the caretaker from your depths; he can take any Wonder Woman and turn her into Diana Prince—out of the sequins and back to the glasses. Every now and then he wants you to take a spin and show you off to the crowd, but not for long. He only shares the spotlight for a second, and then it's back to the wings.

He's quick to move in on you, slow to give commitment. When it comes to steady, he always says, "Well, *maybe*." He expects bed immediately. He tests you for intimidation.

Sex with a Picasso has several twists. He's sure he's superb, but he still wants proof from you. He wants to *make* you come; the way you want to doesn't count. If you don't do what he desires, he accuses you of being hung up. He expects some sort of surrender, yet he's never sure he got enough of a surrender from you and always wants more. Ultimately he pays more attention to his own pleasure—forgoing your climax if he feels like it. He wants you excited and willing whenever he's hot but doesn't return such spontaneity. He also gets up first and leaves you lingering.

He considers himself, and is, a very sexual man. Sex is the first and foremost spice to his life. But he's never quite . . . intimate.

Money Markers

Money is on his mind a great deal of the time. Either he broods about his own or he cries that somebody else has cash and he doesn't. The Picasso usually works for his money, but only at the work he wants to do. He's not the Idle Lord: He doesn't demand that others provide his lucre for nothing in return. But he can go through quite a bit of the stuff and rarely makes as much as he thinks fitting.

He *can* be honorable about your money, but more often if he decides he needs your finances, he'll use them. He always uses more of your mutual funds than you do. Sometimes he hoards the treasury and won't let you have access, or he might allow you provisions but not luxury. Since money is an outward proof of his ability, he prefers you not to work or to work only for subsistence, certainly to have less prestigious employment than his.

Family Aspects

The Picasso doesn't think about children except negatively. Children threaten him, and he'd rather avoid them; he simply can't stand the competition. He knows that in comparison to *real* kids he will suffer. It's less likely someone will say, "Aren't you acting like a child?" when none is present. But since the Picasso tends to have long-term affairs, frequently women have children with him by accident or design.

He seldom helps with childcare or lets the little tykes interfere with him. He might grow closer when they are older, but he still won't wash their laundry or keep them for a whole day and night. He ignores infants; and he treats their mother very badly, particularly during pregnancy and early infancy.

He has a great capacity for making his parents and yours feel out of place and uncomfortable; he gives them no grace. He won every battle growing up; instead of letting go with age, he *still* has them squirming. He's abrasive with all elders and most relatives. He more or less ignores his brothers and sisters, who are often very angry with him, with long memories of everything he got away with.

That the Picasso ends up with pals at all seems a contradiction. After all, he's not good at sharing attention. He avoids other men and carries on an odd combativeness with them. Yet, after the initial sparring, he establishes a clique of equally powerful honchos. He rarely has friendships with women that aren't in some sense sexual. The pals you have together tend to be all his selections. He doesn't like your friends and slowly rids you of them.

The friendships he and you maintain aren't the usual, supportive, passionless sort. The Picasso's affairs, as well as yours, tend to happen within your circle of acquaintances. The Picasso often acts as if he could gain strength by claiming his rivals' possessions, so it's frequently his semi-friend's or quasi-competitor's lady that he beds. Sometimes an old group of Picassos have been together and at each other so long they have virtually practiced sexual round-robin, moving around to each other's partners. You may end up living with your ex-Picasso's buddy!

*   *   *

The Picasso doesn't admit to his own fears, yet he does his best to terrify others. Since it's terribly important to him to surpass all other people and to make anyone and anything else dull, you lose the joy of just being average with him. You get a dynamic dash in not living in a run-of-the-mill style—if you can handle his mania.

What Is in Store for You?

Whether your Picasso is a microsculptor, a macrobiotic dieter, a drummer, engineer, or contractor, you should inspect life with anarchy before you join the party.

Picassos tend to be a ten-year disaster. Once devotion sets in, it takes longer than you think to come to an awakening—and then longer *again* to make up your mind which direction to move in. The Picasso isn't so much "In for a dime, in for a dollar." He's "In for a day, in for a decade."

He has a credo that goes, "You have to take me exactly as I am all the time and not interfere with me in any way because *I am so special!*" From that axiom he derives a lot of postulates for you to live with; combined, they make your happiness pretty hypothetical: 1) He imposes a "take me or leave me" condition. 2) He gets to make the rules but he doesn't have to follow them—you do. Rules, you see, are for *un*special people to follow, for the unique to break. 3) He gets all the attention.

What looks like life in a glamorous bell jar all too often turns into a dust bowl. Obviously a lot depends on how he expresses his mania, how far you can stretch your stamina, and how much you think your union is worth. In his unawareness of limits, Picasso goes as far as he can; he seems unable to stop himself or call upon his kindness. Once you settle down, you become the last person who can contain him— you're the one he's pushing farther. He likes to think you're more hooked on him than he on you. The more he pretends he's detached, the more he sows in you the seeds of apprehension. In reaction, you agree to less-than-satisfactory conditions, which get even worse.

While thumbing his nose at society is one thing, venting his spleen at you is another. It's hard to remain unaffected by his sharp tongue, pointed wit, temper tantrums, and refusal to help. When you take a stand against him, he gets better for a while, but when you shy away again, his gestures return. As time goes on, he expands his caustic vocabulary. While in the first stages of a union with him, he seems just a difficult man whose habits you must learn, later it appears more as if he creates new turbulence to test your adjustment. Life with the Picasso proceeds like a croquet game in Wonderland: He changes the rules from post to post, it's always his turn, and he insists the wickets move to fit his whimsy; meanwhile, your own mallet grows as ineffectual as the neck of a flamingo.

You do what he says. If he decides to work at night, you can expect sex only by day. If he needs the dining room for a study, you'll have to take the table elsewhere. If he suddenly seeks rest and peace, you'll sleep upstairs with all the kids. If he decides on a new place to live, you up and pack the boxes within forty-eight hours. He picks where you go and what decorations go on the walls. You wash clothes by hand because machines disrupt him. He claims the bath for a darkroom, so you use the kitchen sink. He deserts you with a day-old infant to take up residence in his office because he "can't stand crying." You hang about the streets for twelve hours because he can't work in your proximity. You can't wear loud clothes because it disturbs his followers. Pretty soon you wonder about yourself, "Just who *is* this Alice with no possessions or character?" Possibly he wonders, too. It's not out of the question for the Picasso to get possessed by someone else's arms.

Not all his disturbancs are *simple* irritations. Picasso involvements have a built-in time limit. When he seeks homage, your applause can only gratify him for so long. Then he begins to feel dragged down. He seeks praise elsewhere—without giving you up. It's he who says, "My wife just doesn't understand me." He doesn't admit he's no longer happy with you or himself. And he's the kind who wants to try a trial separation or vacation but doesn't want a divorce.

If dwindling tribute doesn't cause him to panic, age certainly does. When the years grow upon the Picasso, he worsens acutely. After all, age brings life's termination ever closer. Expect to find him using strange as well as predictable ways to cling to youth as time goes on. The Picasso is prone to a big mid-life crisis. He finds everything that reminds him of his age (that is, his whole life—plus you) very threatening.

Life with him makes *you* prone to a good crisis, too. About the time of the seven-year itch, disappointment in his affection, his glory, his wanderings, and his tyranny can clash mightily with your needs. You slam into a big brick wall. While his crisis becomes perpetual, however, yours only lasts five years. If you haven't rocked the boat before, you start to do it now. You have an affair with his pal or someone else, or maybe you toss him out. Perhaps you wander out one day and forget to take the babies with you. It's *your* turn for art and *his* for Pine Sol.

Usually with the Picasso you part and reunite a number of times. You alternate who wants and who doesn't want the union. Meanwhile you cross-inflict affairs and injure one another. Occasionally Picasso couples pull through this stage to reach agreement and satisfaction once again. More often those who remain intact do so less than ecstatically and bear many scars. Many simply do not make it.

When a relationship with a Picasso ends, it's surprising how much you *don't* end up with. Easy divorces and good settlements from him are rare. Prepare for rancor, bellowing, and custody threats. Once it's totally over, he might disappear and never make payments.

What Are the Telltale Signs of Trouble?

With the Picasso (as with all of the Twenty-two Types of Men), you need a bit of scepticism. You *should* believe in your man, but you should also consider his conditions.

Consider his baiting of you an omen. A bad one. It's first in jest, next in sobriety. He introduces you to his crowd, but is critical of yours. He takes you around as if either you're on a leash or you have ring around the collar. When a man shows you off as *his* accomplishment or his hanger-on, you're destined to become old hat. Even in his first moves, the Picasso overshadows you and makes you feel like an undeveloped nation. All you're expected to do is adhere to his prowess, praise his honor, purchase his products, do the work that's beneath him, and never ask for autonomy. Right at this point you should consider action. Remember it takes ten years for the storm to turn critical unless you force the issue.

The dots and dashes bleep disaster when he demands total determination over your circumstances because *he's* the sensitive one. That indicates you're not a citizen. Anytime, in any relationship, when a man implies you don't quite deserve him, you've got a real problem to face. For whatever reason you originally latched on, once he treats you like a peasant, there's an uprising coming. Sooner or later you'll take up your scythe and march on the monarchy.

Stay mindful of the fact that when a person uses both outrage and rage to win, he'll use them anytime he chooses. You'll spend your life walking on needles and pins, never knowing what will cross him. When that begins to happen, it's time to consider getting another bed to lie on—this time not on nails.

If, despite all warnings, you decide to try a Picasso, do yourself a favor: Get a notebook and keep a record. On the chance that everything great occurs that he says will happen, you can sell his biography. And in case no kudos come to him, perhaps you can write a novel. At least that could make you *some* money if all else fails.

What Are the Chances?

My advice is to avoid the Picasso. He's much like a cantankerous weed; he stays tenaciously rooted in his home ground even when he sends out runners into other gardens. Even after an apparently total extraction, he tends to pop up again. So while he's in some senses dependable, you never know where he'll resurge or what thorns he'll sprout. The Picasso saps the energy from all but the hardiest women with the most vital inner strength. He's a long termer but that doesn't mean he *ever* turns into a Peace rose; some men aren't even *late* bloomers. Picasso doesn't change; he's too freaked out by age and dying. The only women I think benefit from Picasso are those hardy souls who get a kick out of irritating specimens like poison oak and won't get a rash in direct contact with them. Ladies with that immunity are rare.

If continuous uproar doesn't upset your equanimity and saying "now, now" to Eric the Red is within your ability, Picasso does satisfy a curious need for safety and perversity. Security exists in that you can probably remain in a Picasso involvement permanently. Notice I say "involvement," not *union.* The perversity is in how much you're willing to put up with and still stay on. Some of your years with a Picasso might be fulfilling but some might be close to a sickness or suspended animation.

Women who get involved with him generally get wiped out. Ten years with a Picasso can leave deleterious effects that take a good deal of recovery. But if you decide to tag along with a Picasso anyway, try to approach him like a Girl Scout on the trail: Be prepared. If you expect his cycles and crises, you won't feel cheated. You can keep an eye on yours as you fluctuate with his; you might have an intriguing life. I also suggest something else: Cleaving to Caesar doesn't make you Cleopatra unless you make one of yourself. Try to stay in the style of a high-class courtesan or else present yourself as an *equal* Picasso; don't slide into a handmaiden role. That way you win more lasting respect from the Picasso, plus some attention of your own. But don't expect a simple life. Perhaps you should refuse to marry and you should keep your *own* studio. And don't forget, you'll have to stay purposely pretentious right to the Grande Dame age. I also counsel that you consider not having children in a Picasso relationship.

If your present relationship with a Picasso is already well into deterioration—you haven't the desire to play extraordinary and you just want to live—then it's time to pull up stakes. Prepare for two or three go-rounds, then untwine—for good. Despite temptations, you should try to limit repeats and starting over with this man. After one or two chances and it still hasn't improved, don't get yourself talked back into the hothouse.

For the Picasso to give up his hold on special treatment means he has to face life, with all the drawbacks and benefits of transience; he has to make a very deep and personal change. If he does so, you'll find he's redefined himself so drastically he's hardly recognizable; he'll certainly no longer be a Picasso.

Where Do You Fit In?

Usually it's not only the Picasso who has a strict self-evaluation; so does his lady. All too often the woman who does the Picasso believes she's *adequate*, but not as adequate as he is. Such self-depreciation may show in such phrases as "I hardly deserve him" or "He could always toss me over for another" or "Women like me are a dime a dozen or maybe a nickel for three." The Picasso, in his mania, feeds upon such trepidation in his partner.

Feeling not as wise or worthwhile as the man you love is bad enough, but with the Picasso this tendency usually has another detrimental aspect. To live with him and take his tyranny, you almost have to be (consciously or unconsciously) a hassle avoider. Somewhere, somehow, you learned to live in fear. Perhaps your parents' tempers were so severe or their discipline so costly in guilt or other ways, you began carefully to tiptoe around them. You discovered that submission was easier or cheaper. Or you simply grew afraid of what they could or might do. Perhaps you learned these traits not from your family but from the Picasso himself—but *something* taught you intimidation. With the Picasso, apprehension lives in your back pocket.

Of course, with a number of the Twenty-two Types of Men, a woman sometimes wants a union not only for love but because she feels that stardom isn't available to her alone, that, due to her own mediocrity or lack of opportunities, she won't make it to the top of the hill. She sees a mate as offering advancement and glamor. And the Picasso is one of those fellows who seem to bear promise. He may obtain fame and the society to go with it; he may offer avenues to fabulous events and exotic places. But with the Picasso, since he declares himself the one and only in importance, there's no way you can ever be as good as he is in his eyes. To accomplish equality you have to be fearlessly obstinate; if you have the least little vacillation, he gains ascendency. The Picasso can make anyone hesitate and back off.

Watch for any cowardly or demurring traits in yourself. Don't let yourself get put down or pushed around, in public, private, by yourself or any other. Stand up for your own authority over your life. You have a right to equivalence in your relationship even if what you do is less prestigious in society's eyes. And if you need help to conquer alarm and intimidation, *get it!*

Nothing is worth the price of living in timidity. Whatever you fear—desertion, pain, loneliness, or disregard—you'll find that if you evade it by shutting up and submitting despite opposing feelings, the price is just too high. Fear makes a bad self-image go into an ever-worsening tailspin. Fear is what makes you unable to end a deteriorating union, what makes you set a man up to desert *you* when you ought to leave *him*. Only you can paint your own life and feel satisfied about it. Since the best associations come from two free and independent people, why do anything that makes you feel chicken?

When the next big bully turns on you, don't be a shrinking violet. Stand up tall and come up roses.

Notes and Particulars

21/ The Amoral Passion Monger

Related Types: The Intensely Intimate (But
                   Crazy)
                   The Disaster Broker

Positivity Scale: − − −

Remember the man who threw acid in the face of a woman he claimed
to love? Or the one who sealed up a summer girlfriend in his basement
and kept her there? How about the suitor who burned down a club full
of people because the woman he desired went there with another man?

THE AMORAL PASSION MONGER IS DANGEROUS. He
believes he can do anything in the name of love. He does what he feels
is necessary to keep you for himself because *he* loves *you;* it doesn't
matter how you feel.

To say he overvalues his own passion is too mild. He thinks by
securing his love object, he can secure his own reality. He goes beyond
buying or begging. He leaves the realm of rules and reason.

You usually aren't a singular victim. Amoral Passion Mongers
pursue one woman after another, even several at once. Many marry
and still continue, wedding one woman after another without divorc-
ing the others.

Recognize the very early warning signals and avoid this man at *all*
costs. Notice a threateningly heavy pursuit after only one or two
meetings. Pay heed to demands from a man that you give up your
freedom, remain true to him, wed him or come live with him long
before you would normally conceive of committing yourself. Watch
out for inordinate jealousy from a man who follows you, calls
incessantly, shows up at your home or work. Beware of a man who
sends uncalled-for gifts, especially if they reveal knowledge of your
personal habits he could only gain by watching your every move.

When a man threatens you with harm if you don't become his, believe him and guard yourself.

Some men do wacko, wonderful things when they're in love. They send a thousand roses or singing telegrams, or paint your name on a bridge. But what they do never threatens you physically. Their loony, extraordinary gestures are *for* you, not *to* you.

Use your feelers. They should tell you something is wrong. The passion is too extreme. The timing is off. The movements, the words, the gestures, and the demands are not ordinary. Whatever you do, if it happens to you, don't flirt with fire. Use any legal and any other means to end it totally. Don't contact or communicate with the man. After a certain point you might have to leave town on the midnight Greyhound carrying only a pair of pants and a new name. If necessary, do so. You can't be blamed for his fixation, but you can for not heeding your knowledge that such excessive ardor is uncalled for and crazy. So before he hurts you . . . get help. Have him removed. Just plain *go* if you have to. But do something.

Notes and Particulars

22/ Intimate Type Three— The Limited Partner

Related Types: Intimate Type One—The Loving Polymorph
Intimate Type Two—The Oldie But Goodie

Positivity Scale: + + +

He's a cream-of-the-crop lover. He's willing to be your one and only partner. But there's a condition. You've got some competition, competition that will always come in first.

The Loving Polymorph is a potpourri of everything he can be. The Oldie But Goodie brings home the bacon to his lady in the castle. The Limited Partner follows a compulsion that takes up the lion's share of his devotion, but after that he's a *primo* pal and confidant.

Like the other Intimate Type Men, the Limited Partner prefers involvement and closeness, but it's his vocation, hobby, or belief that is vital to him. His private passion is the most important thing in his life, and he's simply unwilling to subordinate it to anyone or anything.

Usually the matter that transcends all else is his work. His labor doesn't *completely* consume him: He's not hell bent, like The Man Who Would be Mogul, for power, position, or duty to the point of spending every hour with five phones, ten pens, and a drawing board in hand. He does want camaraderie and commitment from a special someone. He loves; he *enjoys* things. He takes pleasure in you. He wants a relationship. But his relationship ranks second in priority. If forced to choose, he would part with the woman who hinders his primary resolve.

288

What suits him best is a match. If you have some major interest that competes with your love life . . . if you have a career or a calling that means more to you than anything . . . or if you simply thrive on your own autonomy and prefer plenty of time to yourself . . . and yet you still desire an intimate sidekick—get a Limited Partner man.

The lady who displays such individualism is just the Limited Partner's cup of tea. When he picks his consort he proceeds with particular caution. Usually he errs once or twice until he clearly and painfully discovers that his enterprise comes before his alliance. Once he discovers this, he seeks a woman who also requires a certain detachment. He likes self-reliant women who know their minds; a combination of composure and drive carries him away. If you state your stance and keep your equilibrium, if you relish both romance and something other, you could make some Limited Partner as happy as a clam, and he you.

Story

Probably the most go-getting, persevering, self-confident person I have ever met is Nadine. She was determined to become a doctor—and not just a pediatrician. She wanted a hemostat in hand and a green surgical mask on her face. She threw her class and professors into total turmoil when she told them she aimed to cut brains.

But Nadine was no ice maiden. Nor was she a bulldozer; no one could dismiss her as "masculine." She preferred Chanel to PhisoHex any day. She had just never had a doubt about her destined profession since the day she was four, a fateful birthday when, despite grandparental disapproval, she insisted on a doctor's kit and refused a nurse's. Nadine had no desire to forfeit a love life. She needed hugs as much as anyone, but early on she knew that she would relegate a stressful passion right into the wastebasket if it interfered with her wielding a scalpel.

One long involvement with a classmate nearly unstrung her. After that she kept her alliances short-lived the rest of the way through medical school. She had little energy for personal drama even as an intern; nonetheless, casual attachments left her feeling as if something was missing. Many of her more devoted suitors seemed dependent persons who soon leaned on her one way or another. She knew that a relationship without the strain of too little or too much emotion existed somewhere, but she didn't know where or how to arrange it.

Then she met Colin. In most ways he seemed totally different from her—divorced parents, himself divorced, devoted to the arts. But one similarity stood out: Nothing but nothing was as important to Colin as one particular thing; for him it was architecture. The main thing he wanted was an empty space, a pencil sharpener, and no telephone. The second thing he sought was somebody to love who was present only *some* of the time. He found strangers and occasional bedfellows ultimately unsatisfactory. He desired a special, quite emancipated permanent partner with whom to live.

Rather than having a romantic love, Colin and Nadine developed a heavy case of "like," although eroticism certainly played a part and they got ever lustier the more they grew committed. They rely on one another although they are no-nonsense negotiators about who does what. They are publicly linked to one another although they don't go everywhere together. When they do go to some event, they often come at different times and in separate cars. They delight in the soirées they give. They call each other without fail when apart, late, or unable to appear. It's hard to say if they miss one another. Rather, they figure that consideration and civility allow them to maintain respect while they do as they please. They love to spend hours together saying nothing while reading in their king-size bed. They steadfastly refuse to acquire any knowledge whatsoever about the other's profession. But they find all kinds of common interests. Their main controversy remains the division of labor; they've almost split up over the issue several times. Now they hire help even when funds are short, and they keep to a rigid assignment of who oversees what work.

Frequently they discuss, objectively, whether they will remain together. If conditions change and Nadine goes to Pago Pago, Colin will not follow, although he'll fly in occasionally. When Colin gets obsessed and irascible, Nadine withdraws to her office. They intend to stay together if at all possible. But their deal reads that if autonomy leads them astray, they will arrange a part-time affiliation or part completely with a fond good-bye.

They discuss the issue of children about once every five years. They continue to decide against them. They agree that with so few moments together they would rather greedily hoard them to themselves. They love restaurants, travel, and other delights in which children present an obstacle, and since they still turn each other on, they have the time to add wine and candles.

The Limited Partner takes more talk and in some ways more commitment than either of the other Intimate Type Men. One of his difficulties is that he prefers to avoid heavy discussions, and the bottom line is always that you have to rely on yourself. It takes determination and, at the same time, flexibility to overcome matters that would knock many others apart—solitude, separation, self-direction. But the rewards can be tremendous. More Limited Partner males than females used to exist; now there are nearly equal numbers of such men and women. Both recognize the fact that life with controlled intimacy is a levelheaded possibility.

How Can You Identify One?

The storms of total entanglement? He'd rather not weather them. All-encompassing intensity? He says no, thank you. He doesn't want to come out and play Polymorph. And provider is not his favorite role. He's a singular person who finds satisfaction and solace on his own. And yet he wants life's best sensations and richest experiences. So although he knows love could bring a rocky road, he risks the possible bad breakup for the potential good sharing.

Considering the Limited Partner's composition and counterpoint, you could call him a really good composer of fugues. He goes about life as if it were a well-tempered clavier. He plunks down time and attention in measured sequences throughout his daily schedule. He takes simple themes and adds variations.

Outer Signs

In personal habits, he's clean, clipped, and cool. A statement in efficiency. His hair just licks the tops of his ears. And his beard never, never looks like whiskers.

The Limited Partner's clothes and trappings resemble a walking résumé. He states himself briefly and swiftly: not too full and not too narrow, no complications. Sometimes he goes with the dictates of fashion, sometimes not. But he never wears patches, tatters, or patterns. (Strangely enough, he prefers his food complicated and highly flavored.)

His speech bears a certain reticence: He pauses before vocalizing; his smile only goes halfway. Instead of laughing, he shows pleasure by crinkling up his crow's-feet. He's not so much a *happy* man as one who has dealt with *unhappiness* and learned the joy of contentment.

His aura of control seeps into his environment: He keeps his papers straight and clipped, or he lives in a marvelous mess you could call "perfected chaos," in which he knows where everything is. He listens to Haydn, Bach, and Mozart because the themes repeat beautifully, or else he switches to Coltrane.

He sees things holistically: Just a snap and a focus and he's got the picture. He's inclined to generalize and reluctant to spell out details. He may not know how he reaches his conclusions. Often Limited Partners claim introspection is a waste. Sometimes his quick conclusions make him seem insensitive to others. He isn't. He just doesn't know how to solve problems for anyone but himself.

He prefers his tools to be an extension of himself, not an obstruction. He selects a smooth car, if not automatic then something that fits him like part of his body. A Porsche is not unlikely, or an Alfa Romeo or Corvette. He takes care of his car; usually the Limited Partner keeps it well oiled, well tuned, and well polished. It may be his only baby. He doesn't like to lend it to anyone, not even his mate.

Rather than just having a place to flop, he cares to provide himself with a *home*. Even prior to partnering, he makes his apartment homelike or else buys his own house. He becomes attached to his nest, which is surprising considering his other detachments. He tends to opt for massiveness and expanse although he doesn't choose size for the impression it makes, like the Man Who Would Be Mogul. He likes lots of room for a sense of *quiet*. He always picks someplace private. He often creates a Spartan atmosphere. When he does fill up the walls, it's with books or some special collection. The idea of *use* always concerns the Limited Partner—even in parapets and mantels. So as well as having art, his collections consist of objects that work or once worked, such as old cameras, utensils, or tools. When his vocation is such that he can work alone, his residence becomes an office as well as a domicile. His bedroom functions as his work room and his bed doubles as his desk.

After pairing up, he requires privacy as much as ever. Although he has a place of business elsewhere, he establishes a household nook for himself that no other living soul gets to dust—a den, a study, a space in the basement or garage. He encourages you to keep a place of *your* own and to have a separate desk. When he's at work or in his hideaway, he may cut himself off for hours. He puts the phone in the refrigerator, pulls the shades, and puts the unopened mail under the kitty litter.

When he comes out of his compulsion and into the warmth of communication, he does it fast. He heads for the kitchen, which may well be part of his turf—the cooking is often his household job. Limited Partners very frequently take a fancy to food preparation: They go for haute cuisine such as French or Chinese and disdain Kansas Provincial.

Sex Signals

When he meets a woman, he takes the time to peruse; he's very selective. He seeks an affectionate sexual co-conspirator. But he also wishes to avoid a champion or keeper. He's definitely not the Kid. Sometimes it seems as if he doesn't even really need a friend. Indeed, as the relationship develops, he has little to say that wasn't all said in the first few months.

Love is important to him. He wants permanence and commitment to have a reason. And he likes the tie to be both mental and physical. When he's with you, he's with you all the way. Your conversations more often center on things (such as crock pots, rose bushes, and exhibits at the museum) than on feelings. Still, he's the kind of companion you don't *have* to talk to. His silences are eloquent.

Certainly he converses sexually. And usually loudly and clearly. He likes sex to be private, very special, erotic as opposed to giddy, a touch traditional. He gets quite artful; he makes love as if he were Rembrandt painting a masterpiece. He studies your lines, your contours and corners. He builds you up layer after layer, until you burst into color. He has an air of control. He may like to make love often for a while—and then have long quiet spells. But even the quick morning sketches he sometimes performs are *very* deftly stroked! Despite his reserve, he's quite a sexual man. Once you're paired, that sexuality envelops you both.

The Limited Partner commits himself to his partner. Once mated, no matter how much he moves about on his own, he never carries on as if he's single. He doesn't pretend he's unattached in order to maneuver better, like The Man Who Would Be Mogul. The Limited Partner values his affiliation and his honesty. His attachment is real and has no secrecy to it.

Money Markers

The Limited Partner usually likes money matters as separately managed as lives; he gets almost too square about financial arrangements. The subject of money always makes him tense and touchy, touchy enough to make him unhappy if all his money is combined with someone else's. He doesn't like supporting you or you him. Most likely he has his account and he likes you to keep yours. And just the way you don't switch cars, you don't use each other's checks.

You do have a mutual fund that goes for expenses you run up in common. Generally you summon up equal amounts; sometimes you go 60/40 or 70/30, according to salary. But you always keep records, rebalance, or write out actual loans. The drawback in this arrangement is all the decisions: Do electricity, Nyquil, and olive oil go down as mutual expenditures? And if so, are driving gloves, high heels, and secretarial services separate?

You may become formal business partners in various ventures. He may invest with you and for you; he prefers real estate. The Limited Partner is cautious with money. He likes it to grow slowly and carefully. But whether or not he turns out a wealthy man, he rarely lets either you or himself flounder into ruin.

Family Aspects

Most Limited Partners look askance on children. They hesitate over or simply decline the notion. It's not the *responsibility* of children that deters them, it's the interference. After all, the Limited Partner is a self-interested man, and he well recognizes his inclinations. He prefers to spend his limited leisure and money on grown-up pleasures. He knows that a child could threaten and encumber his highly prized work. Occasionally, as he gets somewhat older and his career, money, and relationships are more solid, or if his mate expresses a strong desire, he becomes inclined to try fatherhood. But even then he tends to limit the number. He allows for one well-cared-for child.

He not only backs off from descendants, he backs off from ascendants and collaterals as well, namely parents, siblings, and cousins. He may well be an only child or the child of divorced parents, who learned to love his solitude early. The Limited Partner keeps his ties to his family as trimmed, formal, and symbolic as possible. He notes Christmas, Mother's Day, and other days with cards, calls, and perhaps a gift. He may pay the necessary two-day visit. Because of the distance he feels from them, he worries about how he will handle the future care of his parents. He views your family as yours. He rarely makes any but the most formal tie with them.

The Limited Partner usually maintains longstanding friendships with one or two men from his same field of endeavor. He sees them in the office, at home, for lunch and sports—in other words, often. He might jog with his pal. Despite how bookish or isolated he seems, the Limited Partner is surprisingly athletic. Sometimes he and his two friends go bowling or play squash. But mostly they visit and chat; their conversations are so continuous they never seem to start or terminate. He and his pals seem commonly to fear aging. They figure they'll all go together if they stay tightly knit.

More than likely the Limited Partner has one or two good women friends, too. Probably they had an affair and managed to become platonic chums. Usually they are from the same profession. Rather than lose one another, they shift into friendly consultants.

Beyond his regular circle, however, the Limited Partner says no. He easily turns down invitations. Mostly he prefers the one person he doesn't have to chat with—you. You two make up a closed community of just each other.

He's not good at changing. He resists experiments. The way he makes independent decisions without consulting you can be irksome, and sometimes he acts businesslike about emotions. But he's a great partner and an intimate lover. He's rich in wonderful qualities. His own determination makes him a constant source of interest. His energy never dwindles. He's loving and sharing, honest and trustworthy. And you don't have to take care of him. He can take care of himself.

What Is in Store for You?

Here's a whole new recipe for cooking up a twosome. The ingredients are the same—combine one man and one woman—only you don't completely blend them. Sometimes this methods makes for a successful concoction. Sometimes the attempt fails and the sauce simply curdles. But if you follow the instructions carefully, one thing is for certain. Nobody gets diluted, stewed, or creamed.

No, *The Joy of Cooking* is not the reference book for the Limited Partner repast. The book you need is a text of basic law. The term "Limited Partner" comes straight from legal practice. It concerns contractual agreements between business partners. While among the Twenty-two Types of Men some relationships are connubial, this particular alliance in many ways parallels commercial association.

You can enter a legal deal in one of two ways. You can go for a general "one for all and all for one" union or you can name your terms. Naturally these two methods differ in significant respects—how much the parties have to lose or gain and how much say-so they get. In a general partnership you share all obligations, expenses, debts and profits, no matter who makes them; ostensibly *no* separate decisions exist. In a limited partnership you are obligated only for the amount of money, work, and bother that you agree to; that's also all you can lose. But you can also only gain according to the share you put in, and you are responsible only for those conditions that you concede, so that's as far as your say-so goes. You get no vote in matters beyond your stated participation. *You* make your decisions, lose your losses, and gather your profits alone; your partner doesn't share them. You have no gamble in your associate's failures, but you get no automatic chunk of any successes either. In short, you take fewer risks for a narrower range of benefits. And while you get less control over your partner, you get more over yourself.

Among conjugally united Limited Partners, particular agreements differ vastly. But the idea of restricted cooperation remains the same. A contract can be narrow—including only time and sex—or it may extend to money, work, space, fidelity, care, property, objects, pastimes, passports, and patents. The Limited Partner hears your tribulations as a listener and sounding board, but he never absolves you of your problems. You consider his requests, but you don't have to meet them. You can tell him your desires. But you seek fulfillment yourself.

On the good side of the coin, the relationship involves a tremendous, adult acceptance of whatever the other does, which is the best of love. On the bad side of the coin, you live in a constant balance of dependence/independence and duality/autonomy. It's a very, very tricky equilibrium. In some respects you have to become dependent in order to stay together (as any couple does), so you bow to compromise. But in other ways you have to stay independent *in order to* remain together. If you don't follow your own life, you break your basic promise. That means that on a daily basis you have to know just what, how, and when to either show your stuff or keep your distance. And since any person's dependency needs ebb and flow, from start to end you have to watch your cycles the way a weatherman watches the clouds.

Other aspects of the Limited Partner twosome also prove problematic unless you stay stable and detached. While the Limited Partner is honest, as are all the Intimate Men, he has trouble telling you everything he feels. He gives you blanket statements such as "I love you," but he can't describe just how and why. You have to accept what he says as enough. He even deals with himself in terms of broad opinions. He talks about his limitations; you have to live with them. He knows very well what he does and doesn't like, can and can't take, will and won't handle, perhaps a little too much so. Often he gets stuck in his own self-definition and over-restricts himself. All the things he won't do you have to do alone.

Without some well-guarded release valves, things can definitely boil over. He or you might have trouble dealing with inactivity for any long period. He or you might only be able to leave that central obsession alone for *so* long. Your life is never entirely flexible or easygoing. And yet you have a powerful potion. When you're on a par financially and emotionally, when you're interested in one another, have many common pleasures, and both independence and affection, you develop a kind of love beyond the romantic. It's often called fraternal. But it's sororal as well!

What Are the Telltale Signs of Trouble?

The Limited Partner believes in the Rational Man. He thinks he *is* one, that logic, plans, and outlines can solve anything. And he's just humorless enough regarding himself to tell you so.

When a man grades you as excellent but not at the top of his list, you have an immediate decision to make. If you find you really want to win an A and be teacher's only pet, you should change to another class posthaste. But if a B+ is O.K. and, in fact, the grade you *want*, you've got a subject that could well be your major for life.

The Limited Partner has three cover terms that indicate trouble: money, time, and work. The more frequently he brings up one or more of these topics, the more he signals internal disturbance, anger, resentment, disappointment, or frustration. Sometimes he simply feels his independence threatened, and he starts to distance himself. The funny thing is, of course, the same set of signals operates for you. When you feel he intrudes on your cash, concerns, or time clock, doubtless you retreat. You can emerge from these troubles in one of three ways: Heed the readings, get to the bottom, and work out the problem; find another outlet where you can 'fess up to your emotions without changing course; or pop up and declare that the Limited Partner setup isn't working out for you.

Occasionally a resentful or jealous Limited Partner turns into a Minimal Misogynist. He finds himself embroiled in difficult feelings and he cites you as the cause. He attacks you as the object instead of revamping himself; he grows cold. Sometimes he rationalizes everything so thoroughly he eliminates all closeness. It's depressing when someone claims people have sex only because they "need" it. In any of these cases you may have to consider dissolving your relationship.

What Are the Chances?

The point of commitment is to go the distance. The Limited Partner has every intention of doing so.

Limited Partner couples come in several variations. Most commonly the partners have diverse preoccupations, say, tinker and tailor. Sometimes both members have the same profession but go separately: two doctors, two lawyers. Sometimes a loving pair are partners in some establishment—a store, office, or shop. Occasionally the career of one mate involves the occupation of the other: he sings, she manages his singing; she dances, he promotes her. In all cases, Limited Partnerships succeed only when the parties coordinate their individual ambitions and labor with their personal relations. I am loath to wave the finger of prophecy. But it seems the more entangled business and bed, the more difficult the balance. When partners mix it up by night and day, in work and play, the more cause for adversity and more iffy the chances.

With the Limited Partner the trying is good in any case. All kinds of Limited Partner pairs make fine long hauls of varying lengths up to and through old age. Some intend to go for broke right from the start. Some never try to second-guess the fates and make it just the same.

In order to thrive along with constant divergences in taste, opinion, scheduling, will, and location, you need particular fortitude. You can make it or break it, depending upon your ability to keep your equanimity. Since it's such a tightrope act to balance him and balance you, juggle your work and love life, weigh your togetherness and solitude, I suggest you keep your burdens limited. If you have a mind to add any other problems, such as children or extra commitments, judge carefully: Your two lives may add up to enough without added extras. You may or may not stipulate sexual fidelity. It seems most Limited Partnerships are either monogamous or very discreet. Jealousy is anybody's Pandora's box. You may demand certain times off. You might perhaps prefer to live on separate coasts. But you'd better get subjects like sex and socializing out of the closet.

Limited Partners have more weapons available to hurt one another than do many other couples. They can use distance, lack of response, competition, autonomy, rule-breaking as means of humiliation. Just because you diverge from your mate doesn't mean you should get two-faced. Be careful not to turn your delicate balance into a sparring match.

You have so little time for intimacy, remember to fight for it. The key to the treasure chest means keeping the love alive. If you like the idea of the Limited Partner and you like your man, I advise not only caring for the companion, but caring for the companionship. You *can* avoid touchy subjects and stick to common interests—until you have nothing left but hollow company. Your joys and sorrows are what keep the life blood flowing.

Because of all these complexities, breakups do occur, and despite all the preparations, dissolutions are often more painful than you would expect. Sometimes your careers take you separate ways. I suggest that you fight for your union, but if all else fails, part as friends and don't look back. What you learn from one Limited Partner you can apply to another. The Limited Partner alliance is worth trying again.

Where Do You Fit In?

Some women prefer enclosed spaces and well-known ground; although they go out a certain amount, they really like to be at home. Others love to be out thrashing about the world; home is where they are least, although they want at least some semblance of a nesting place.

The main trick to the Limited Partner relationship is simply recognizing who you are. If indeed you don't want your autonomy tampered with, prefer a certain amount of distance, back off from over-abundant intimacy, and have an ambition decidedly removed from a romantic relationship, your nature is bound to become apparent.

The problem is when you don't recognize your penchant but still act it out: Your career goes right, but your love life goes kerthunk. You think you want a permanent alliance but enter unions you know are bound for the same fate as the *Andrea Doria*. You talk about the right man, but somehow he never comes along. You keep picking losers and then ask why. You start to explore a number of good unions but find reasons why they won't work out, and you run. You find a nice situation and get so impossible you push your lover out. You say good unions no longer exist, and you sit in your living room and watch the days pass. You Instant Barricade ("I'm not ready yet") or Romper Room ("One-night stands are so free of constraint").

The point is, there's nothing *wrong* with wanting solitude or self-determination. When a man hangs around too long in the morning, and you say, "A diller, a dollar, a ten o'clock scholar," and send him on his way, you haven't committed a sin. If he thinks you have, he *is* the wrong man. There's nothing wrong with not wanting a male or a mate at all.

It's only after you establish in what ways you do and don't want an in-depth consortium that you can decide if you want at least a partial one. Only when you no longer envision attachment as imprisonment can you determine how you want to link up. Then alone does controlled intimacy become a levelheaded possibility.

Once you discover that you do want a mate and maybe a long-term mating, but only under certain conditions, you've got work to do. Rather than acting out, you need awareness of your wants. Rather than making assumptions, you have to *express* yourself. And be ethical about your own rules. If you want autonomy, ask for a pact in which you maintain *yourself*. When it comes to the Limited Partner, better think your statements through before you make them. It's up to you to keep them.

Notes and Particulars

Aids and Indices

Positivity Scale

1/The Instant Barricader	+ −
2/Intimate Type One—The Loving Polymorph	+ + +
3/The Minimal Misogynist	+ − −
4/The "But I Really Like Women" Manipulator	+ + −
5/The Doe Stalker	+ − −
6/The Gay Man Type One—Intimacy Except For . . .	+ + − −
7/The Intensely Intimate (But Crazy)	+ + − −
8/The Gender Ascender	− −
9/The Courtier	+ + −
10/Intimate Type Two—The Oldie but Goodie	+ + +
11/The Idle Lord	+ − −
12/The Romper Roomer	+ − −
13/The Man Who Would Be Mogul	+ − −
14/The Father Knows Best	+ −
15/The Disaster Broker	+ + − −
16/The Sugar Pie Honey	+ −
17/The Maximal Misogynist	− − −
18/The Kid	+ −

CHECKLIST OF TRAITS

Detail specific traits for the men you know.
* Enter name, initials, or code.

TRAITS OF:	Primary Motivations	Dress	Auto	Surroundings	Residence	Decor and Objects	Mannerisms	How He Treats Himself
EXAMPLE "Jeffrey"	No Strings Sex	Very Casual No Socks	Dented M. G.	Near water	Swinging Singles Apt.	Couch & Beds No pots and pans	Likes con- venience No attach- ments Cheap beer	Jogs a lot Drinks a lo
Man # 1								
Man # 2								
Man # 3								
Man # 4								
Man # 5								
Man # 6								
Man # 7								
Man # 8								
Man # 9								
Man # 10								

Patterns of Approach	Sex	How He Treats You—Before, During, After	Money His Yours	Children	Family	Friends	Assets	Liabilities
Fast and Inquisitive	The Olympics	Slapdash and no after	Spends on self No "dates" & no "din-din"	No way	?	Fellow rompers	Light entertainment	Plenty

COMPILATION OF COMBINATIONS

Example   Louie is a
Combination of:
1. <u>Gay man type 1</u>
2. <u>The Courtier</u>
3. <u>The Kid</u>

Man # 1 is a
Combination of:
1. _____
2. _____
3. _____

Man # 2 is a
Combination of:
1. _____
2. _____
3. _____

Man # 3 is a
Combination of:
1. _____
2. _____
3. _____

Man # 4 is a
Combination of:
1. _____
2. _____
3. _____

Man # 5 is a
Combination of:
1. _____
2. _____
3. _____

Man # 6 is a
Combination of:
1. _____
2. _____
3. _____

Man # 7 is a
Combination of:
1. _____
2. _____
3. _____

Man # 8 is a
Combination of:
1. _____
2. _____
3. _____

Man # 9 is a
Combination of:
1. _____
2. _____
3. _____

Man # 10 is a
Combination of:
1. _____
2. _____
3. _____

Man # 11 is a
Combination of:
1. _____
2. _____
3. _____

Man # 12 is a
Combination of:
1. _____
2. _____
3. _____

Man # 13 is a
Combination of:
1. _____
2. _____
3. _____

Man # 14 is a
Combination of:
1. _____
2. _____
3. _____

Man # 15 is a
Combination of:
1. _____
2. _____
3. _____

Man # 16 is a
Combination of:
1. _____
2. _____
3. _____

Man # 17 is a
Combination of:
1. _____
2. _____
3. _____

Man # 18 is a
Combination of:
1. _____
2. _____
3. _____

Man # 19 is a
Combination of:
1. _____
2. _____
3. _____

Man # 20 is a
Combination of:
1. _____
2. _____
3. _____

CHART OF POTENTIAL PROGRESSIONS

Type	No change / Change Unlikely but Possible	Possible Change for the Worse	Possible Change for the Better
The Instant Barricader			intimate Type 3-The Limited Partner
Intimate Type 1-The Loving Polymorph		The "But-I-Really-Like-Women" Manipulator* / the Sugar Pie Honey** / The Idle Lord + / The Instant Barricader*	
The Minimal Misogynist		The Man Who Would Be Mogul*	
The "But-I-Really-Like-Women" Manipulator		The Gender Ascender † *	Intimate Type 1-The Loving Polymorph
The Doe Stalker			
Gay Men Type 1— Intimacy Except For...			
The Intensely Intimate (But Crazy)		? ?	Intimate Type 1-The Loving Polymorph*** / Intimate Type 3-The Limited Partner***
The Gender Ascender		The Maximal Misogynist*	
The Courtier		The Kid / The Idle Lord*	
Intimate Type 2— The Oldie But Goodie		The Father Knows Best + / The Gender Ascender + + / The Man Who Would Be Mogul* Picasso*	
The Idle Lord			
The Romper Roomer		The Doe Stalker* + *	
The Man Who Would Be Mogul			
The Father Knows Best			Intimate Type 2—The Oldie but Goodie

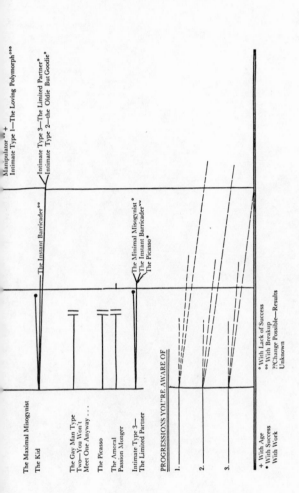

The Maximal Misogynist

The Kid

The Gay Man Type
Two—You Won't
Meet One Anyway . . .

The Picasso

The Amoral
Passion Monger

Intimate Type 3—
The Limited Partner

PROGRESSIONS YOU'RE AWARE OF

1.

2.

3.

+ With Age
• With Success
With Work

° With Lack of Success
°° With Breakup
?Change Possible—Results
Unknown

Manipulator °° +
Intimate Type 1—The Loving Polymorph °°°

Intimate Type 3—The Limited Partner °
Intimate Type 2—the Oldie But Goodie °

The Instant Barricader °°

The Minimal Misogynist °
The Instant Barricader °°
The Picasso °